Hire Purchase Under Shirkah al-Milk (HPSM) in Islamic Banking and Finance

M. Kabir Hassan ·
Muhammad Mostofa Hossain ·
Aishath Muneeza

Hire Purchase Under Shirkah al-Milk (HPSM) in Islamic Banking and Finance

A Shari'ah Analysis

palgrave
macmillan

M. Kabir Hassan
University of New Orleans
New Orleans, LA, USA

Muhammad Mostofa Hossain
University of Malaya
Kuala Lumpur, Malaysia

Aishath Muneeza
International Centre for Education
in Islamic Finance (INCEIF
University)
Kuala Lumpur, Malaysia

ISBN 978-3-031-50104-3 ISBN 978-3-031-50105-0 (eBook)
https://doi.org/10.1007/978-3-031-50105-0

This Palgrave Macmillan imprint is published by the registered company Springer Nature Switzerland AG
The registered company address is: Gewerbestrasse 11, 6330 Cham, Switzerland

Paper in this product is recyclable.

Preface I

In the rapidly evolving landscape of Islamic banking and finance, the concept of Hire Purchase under *Shirkah al-Milk* (HPSM) has emerged as a significant and promising mode of financing. This book delves deep into the historical development, Shari'ah permissibility, essential contracts, practical application, and Shari'ah issues related to the application of HPSM. It provides a comprehensive understanding of this dynamic and evolving field.

- Chapter 1 delves into the historical development of HPSM in the Islamic banking and finance industry. It explores the origins and evolution of this mode of financing, tracing its roots to the principles and teachings of Shari'ah. By understanding its historical context, readers will gain valuable insights into the evolution of HPSM and its relevance in the modern Islamic financial system.
- Chapter 2 focuses on *shirkah*, the first essential contract in HPSM. *Shirkah* is the cornerstone of HPSM, and this chapter unravels its principles, concepts, and legal implications. Readers will gain a profound understanding of the nature and significance of *shirkah* as a cooperative partnership and its role in facilitating HPSM transactions.
- Moving forward, Chapter 3 explores *ijarah*, the second essential contract in HPSM. *Ijarah*, or leasing, plays a crucial role in HPSM by enabling the transfer of the right to use an asset for a specified period. This chapter elucidates the fundamental principles of *ijarah*

and its application within the framework of HPSM, providing readers with a comprehensive understanding of this important contractual arrangement.

- Chapter 4 brings attention to the final essential contract in HPSM, which is sale. Sale is the culmination of the HPSM process, where the ownership of the asset is transferred from the bank to the customer. Through an in-depth analysis of the sale contract and its various forms, this chapter sheds light on the intricacies of this crucial transaction and its compliance with Shari'ah principles.
- Practical application of HPSM is focused in chapter 5. In this chapter, readers will explore the implementation and operational aspects of HPSM. The chapter discusses the practical considerations, challenges, and strategies involved in structuring and executing HPSM transactions, providing valuable insights for practitioners, researchers, and policymakers alike.
- In chapter 6, readers will find a comprehensive examination of how Islamic and conventional hire-purchase transactions are treated from accounting entries. This in-depth analysis equips readers with a hands-on understanding of both HPSM variants, and ultimately enriches the study's overall value.
- Chapter 7 is dedicated to exploring the Shari'ah issues related to the application of HPSM. It addresses the various challenges, controversies, and arguments surrounding HPSM from a Shari'ah perspective. By delving into the intricate details and exploring multiple viewpoints, this chapter equips readers with a deeper understanding of the Shari'ah implications and considerations associated with HPSM.
- Chapter 8 showcases additional *ijarah* and *shirkah* contracts within the contemporary Islamic financial contexts. This chapter delves into the concepts of MMP (*Musharakah Mutanaqisa Partnership*), BBA (*Bay bi thaman Ajil*), and IMD (*Ijarah Mawsufah fi al-Dhimmah*). It also delves into the realms of *ijarah* and *musharakah sukuk*, contributing to a comprehensive exploration.
- Chapter 9 is included to provide an introduction to hybrid contracts. Within this chapter, the focus lies on elucidating the hybrid contract's definition, its alignment with Shari'ah obligations, and concessions permitted by Shari'ah for hybrid contracts, as well as delving into other pertinent aspects to this unique contractual arrangement.

- Finally, Chapter 10 provides a comprehensive conclusion, summarising the key findings, insights, and implications discussed throughout the book. It serves as a valuable reflection on the knowledge gained and encourages further research and exploration in the field of HPSM.

This book is a testament to the growing importance and relevance of HPSM in the Islamic banking and finance industry. It serves as an indispensable resource for academics, researchers, students, practitioners, and anyone seeking a comprehensive understanding of the historical, conceptual, practical, and Shari'ah aspects of HPSM. The insightful analysis, practical insights, and nuanced discussions presented in this book make it an essential addition to the library of anyone interested in the dynamic world of Islamic finance.

New Orleans, USA — M. Kabir Hassan
Kuala Lumpur, Malaysia — Muhammad Mostofa Hossain
Kuala Lumpur, Malaysia — Aishath Muneeza

Preface II

Islamic finance has gained prominence since the 1970s, becoming a significant presence in the global financial landscape. Although its principles and philosophies are not new, as they were outlined in the Holy Qur'an and the Sunnah of the Prophet Muhammad (pbuh) over 1400 years ago. However, modern Islamic finance has garnered attention and recognition in recent years. This emergence is often associated with the revitalisation of Islam and the desire of Muslims to align all aspects of their lives with Islamic teachings. Today, Islamic finance has made significant strides and achieved remarkable milestones in the financial industry. It has expanded globally, transcending borders and attracting attention beyond Muslim-majority countries. Operating on ethical principles, Islamic finance has introduced responsible and transparent financial practices, fostering fairness and risk-sharing. The industry has showcased innovation by diversifying its product offerings to meet the evolving needs of customers. Furthermore, Islamic finance has played a crucial role in infrastructure development, promoted financial inclusion, and contributed to financial stability through its risk-sharing mechanisms. These achievements have elevated the recognition and acceptance of Islamic finance as an ethical and sustainable alternative in the global financial landscape.

Following its inception, Islamic Banking and Finance (IBF) has introduced various modes of financial contracts in the global financial landscape. These contracts are developed in accordance with Islamic Shari'ah principles to attract customers and compete with conventional counterparts. In modern times, IBF has demonstrated innovation by creating multi-variant contracts that have been modified from their classical structures to meet the evolving needs of stakeholders. One such example is the Hire Purchase under *Shirkah al-Milk* (HPSM), also known as *al-ijarah muntahiyyah bi al-tamlik*, which is implemented by several Islamic financial institutions worldwide, including Islami Bank Bangladesh Limited (IBBL). Hybrid contracts, like HPSM, are a combination of different contractual elements, making banking products more versatile and adaptable. In the case of HPSM, it is an advanced version of a traditional hire-purchase contract, comprising three contracts: *ijarah* (lease), *shirkah* (partnership), and sale. The *shirkah* contract in HPSM has a short-term duration. HPSM is a contemporary method of purchasing practised globally, offering deferred payment schemes or instalments as a hybrid banking product.

In HPSM, the ownership of the asset is jointly held by the bank and the client. The client makes regular instalment payments, while the remaining balance is treated as a mortgage owned by the bank. During this period, the client is authorised to possess and use the goods as long as they fulfil the specified conditions. Upon completion of all instalments, the asset becomes the sole property of the client. However, there are ongoing debates regarding the permissibility of HPSM. These disputes stem from various factors, including differences in determining the fundamental nature of the transaction (whether it is initially considered permissible or prohibited) and potential contradictions with hadiths that discourage certain types of combined contracts. Hadiths prohibit transactions involving the combination of sale and purchase contracts, and merging two contracts into one. These concerns raise questions about the positioning of HPSM products within contemporary Islamic financial institutions, emphasising the need for clarification and investigation.

Customers of a bank, especially when dealing with Islamic banking products, should have access to adequate knowledge and transparent information regarding the specifications, compliance with Shari'ah principles, and overall strategy of the products they engage with. However, there is a notable absence of a comprehensive book solely dedicated to HPSM from a Shari'ah perspective, with only limited scholarly articles available. This lack of comprehensive guidance on HPSM can lead to uncertainty and confusion among stakeholders regarding the product's compliance with Shari'ah principles, which poses a significant concern.

Therefore, there is a need to publish a comprehensive book that focuses on the theoretical and practical application of HPSM from a Shari'ah standpoint. This book aims to provide insights into the general concept of HPSM, including the policies, rules, and sub-contracts involved in its practical implementation by Islamic financial institutions. Additionally, it will comprehensively cover the documentation process and address the Shari'ah issues that may arise in the application of HPSM.

This book is expected to benefit students, policymakers, and practitioners by providing a comprehensive understanding of the application of HPSM in the Islamic finance industry. It aims to equip readers with the knowledge and insights necessary to address and overcome Shari'ah-related challenges associated with HPSM. By delving into the theoretical and practical aspects of HPSM, the book will enable readers to enhance their understanding of this Islamic banking product and explore ways to improve its implementation while ensuring compliance with Shari'ah principles.

New Orleans, USA — M. Kabir Hassan
Kuala Lumpur, Malaysia — Muhammad Mostofa Hossain
Kuala Lumpur, Malaysia — Aishath Muneeza

Contents

Abbreviations

AAOIFI	Accounting and Auditing Organization for Islamic Financial Institutions
A/C	Account
B/L	Bad/Loss
BBA	*Bay' bithaman 'ajil*
BDT	Bangladeshi Taka
BNM	Bank Negara Malaysia (Central Bank of Malaysia)
CIB	Credit Information Bureau
Cr	Credit
Dr	Debit
ERR	Expected Rate of Return
FTV	Finance to Value
HP	Hire Purchase
HPSM	Hire Purchase under *Shirkah al-Milk*
IBBL	Islami Bank Bangladesh Limited
IBF	Islamic Banking and Finance
IBFI	Islamic Banking and Financial Institutions
IFI	Islamic Financial Institution
IIFA	International Islamic Fiqh Academy
IIFA-OIC	International Islamic Fiqh Academy of Organisation of Islamic Cooperation
IMD	*Ijarah Mawsufah fi a- Dimmah*
IsDB	Islamic Development Bank
LC	Letter of Credit
MMP	*Musharakah Mutanaqisah* Partnership
MYR	Malaysian Ringgit

OIC	Organisation of Islamic Cooperation
PLS	Profit-Loss Sharing
RAA	Radia Allahu ‘Anha
SAW	Sallahu Alaihi wa Sallam
SPV	Special Purpose Vehicle
SWT	Subhanahu wa Ta’ala
USD	US Dollar

List of Figures

CHAPTER 1

Historical Development and Permissibility of HPSM

Abstract The Hire Purchase under *Shirkah al-Milk* (HPSM) in the Islamic banking and finance industry plays a significant role in facilitating financing arrangements. HPSM, which is widely practised by both conventional and Islamic banks, has found particular prominence in several jurisdictions. Despite some procedural and conditional variations, the overall practice of HPSM in both types of institutions demonstrates noteworthy similarities. This financing arrangement is structured as a combination of three distinct contracts: *shirkah, ijarah*, and sale. Under the HPSM framework, the bank finance or supplies the required types of equipment or goods on a rental basis. Crucially, the ownership of the leased property or equipment is jointly held by the bank and the client. The transfer of ownership takes place at the final stage of the contract, adhering to the customary practices aligned with Shari'ah principles. This chapter aims to delve into the historical evolution of HPSM, sheds light on its Shari'ah permissibility, and provides insights into the practical implementation of this financing arrangement in the IBF industry.

Keywords Hire purchase · *Shirkah al-Milk* · HPSM · *Musharakah* · *Ijarah* · Sale

M. K. Hassan et al., *Hire Purchase Under Shirkah al-Milk (HPSM) in Islamic Banking and Finance*,
https://doi.org/10.1007/978-3-031-50105-0_1

Preview
Hire Purchase under ***Shirkah al-Milk*** (HPSM) plays a significant role within the Islamic banking and finance sector, facilitating essential financing arrangements. Both conventional and Islamic banks widely adopt HPSM, and its influence is particularly evident in multiple jurisdictions. Despite some procedural and conditional differences, the fundamental practice of HPSM exhibits largely similarities between these two types of institutions. This financing model encompasses a unique blend of three key contracts: ***shirkah***, ijarah, and sale.

In the context of HPSM, financial assistance or essential equipment and goods are extended by the bank on a rental basis. An essential aspect of this arrangement is the shared ownership of the leased assets between the bank and the client. The conclusive transfer of ownership occurs at the contract's final stage, adhering meticulously to established Shari'ah principles and customary practices. The purpose of this chapter is to delve into the historical progression of HPSM, shed light on its adherence to Shari'ah principles, and provide comprehensive insights into the practical execution of this financing structure within the Islamic banking and finance industry.

1.1 Development History of the HPSM Contract

The term HPSM is also known as "leasing ending with ownership" or in Arabic called *"ijarah muntahiyyah bi al-tamlik"*. The application of hire purchase was introduced in England in the nineteenth century, where it was commonly referred to as lease purchase (*al-bay' al-ijarah* or *al-ijar al-tamlikiyyah*) or lease ending with ownership (*ijarah muntahiyyah bi al-tamlik*) (Al-Zuhayli, 2003). The origin of this contract dates back to a British musical instruments vendor who sought to facilitate the sale of his musical products to customers by introducing the hire-purchase agreement. Following the introduction of the hire-purchase concept, the demand for the contract has seemed to increase rapidly, and the same has been offered around the world by many companies to sell their various types of products. For instance, "SINGER", one of the biggest home appliances and electronic products companies, started hire purchase-based sales to attract consumers to their several products (Dusuqi, 1994). Later on, in 1952, in the United States of America, this mode of transaction has widely been accepted with a new term, "leasing", introduced by a company called "United States Leasing Corporation". Numerous companies have since adopted the hire-purchase model, leading to its widespread implementation across various regions in Europe; one of the leading companies among them is the "Mercantile Credit Company". However, the first European leasing company was established in France in 1962 called "Locafance". The hire-purchase concept then was quickly acknowledged and gained recognition thereafter and started getting applied in many other parts of the world (Al-Dusri, 2001).

Further, the hire-purchase mode of financing has become widely attractive among those customers who want to own a property but are incapable of paying the full cash price upfront. Abdullah (2005), hence, explains that by opting for a hire-purchase plan, individuals can acquire their desired property by making an initial payment and committing to regular payment or instalment terms over a mutually agreed-upon duration. Essentially, the consumer is given possession of the property in exchange for a promise to pay for it gradually over time. Throughout the payment tenure, the customer is entitled to full ownership and use of the property, devoid of assuming any ownership risks until all instalments are completed. As a result, this form of hire purchase has gained widespread recognition among customers seeking to obtain ownership of assets, especially consumer items.

In contrast, the theory of hire purchase being a combination of multiple contracts in separate sequences was considered uncommon among traditional Muslim scholars since no reliable sources indicated such a contract. Muslim jurists, instead, tended to address hire and purchase as separate concepts and discuss them under distinct titles such as "The Book of Sale" (*Kitab al-Buyu'*) and "The Book of Letting" (*al-ijarah*). Notably, in various Islamic jurisprudence (*fiqh*) texts, these two headings were presented sequentially, despite being discussed separately. However, contracts such as hire and purchase are often considered essential in Islamic commercial activities, perhaps due to their close relationship with each other. When categorising different forms of contracts within Islamic financial realms, "the basic contract in many cases and situations are contracts of exchange and contract of the utilisation of usufruct. The former is a contract of sale or *bay'*, which implies the transfer of ownership of a property from one party to another, while the latter is a leasing contract (*ijarah*) which affects the transfer of usufruct of a property from one to another. Both contracts of sale and hire constitute the main commercial activities because all residual contracts are mostly dependent on these two contracts" (Abdullah, 2005).

Hire purchase was introduced by IFI in the 1980s. Currently, this is considered one of the most frequently applied contracts in the IBFIs domain. HP was known by different names around the world, such as, *al-ijarah al-muntahiyyah bi al-tamlik*, *al-ijarah bi al-shart al-tamlik*, and *al-ijar al-muntaha bi al-tamlik* (Zakariyyah, 2004), *al-ijarah ma 'a al-iqtina '* (Abu Ghuddah, 1998), *al-ijar alladhi yantahi bi al-tamlik* (Usmani, 1998), *al-ta'jir al-muntaha bi al-tamlik* (Abdullah, 1988), *al-ta'jir al-muntaha bi al-tamalluk*, al-ta'jir ma 'a al-mawa 'idah bi al-tamalluk (Kuwait Finance House, 2016), *al-iijar al-satir li al-bay'* and *al-iijar al-muqtaran bi al-wa 'd* (Al-Sanhuri, n.d), hire purchase under *Shirkah al-meelk* (IBBL, 2022). HP has been a potential contract of Islamic banking and finance and has rapidly been recognised in its next decades of application. Abdullah (2005), therefore, brings works of literature where the comprehensive discussion of HP is exhibited; some of those works of literature, for example, are "Component of Islamic Banking by Sadeque in 1982", "Money and Banking in Islam by Ziauddin Ahmed in 1983", "Islamic Banking and Finance by Hassan in 1985", "Leasing: An Islamic Financial Instrument by Alawi in 1986", "The Experience of Islamic Banks in the Middle East by Al-Tatnimi in 1986", "Principles of Islamic Banking, *Masraf* Faysal *Al-Islami*, Islamic Banking Contract by Shirazi in 1988", and so forth. These writings played considerable roles in promoting the concept of HP in the financial spectrum, especially in the Islamic banking and finance industry, as it has been one of the best fits for the customer to avail their long expected asset, i.e. houses, personal vehicles, etc., based on the Shari'ah rulings. Along with the above works of literature, the HP has been promoted by well-established Islamic financial institutions during that time, including al-Barakah Investment and Development Company, Jedda, Faysal Islamic Bank of Bahrain, Bank Islam Malaysia Berhad, Dar al-Mal al Islami Trust, Geneva, Al Rajihi Banking and Investment Corporation, etc. (Lewis & Algaoud, 2001), and Islami Bank Bangladesh Ltd, Bangladesh.

Malaysia introduced a separate act on hire purchase to regulate the form and contents of hire purchase agreements, the rights and duties of parties to such agreements, and to make provisions for other matters connected therewith and incidental thereto whose number is [act no.24 of 1967] which further revised in 1978 (Act 212 w.e.f 15 November 1978) and amended by the Act A1384 which came into operation on 15 June 2011.

1.2 Legality of HPSM

Hire purchase under *shirkah al-milk* (HPSM), like other contracts of IBF, requires attaining all necessary conditions that validate the contract from the Shari'ah perspective. For example, the mutual agreement among the contracting parties in the contract, obtaining the principles and attributed obligations during the contract period, a clear declaration of the contract period, and the rental amount in the agreement. Since hire purchase under *shirkah al-milk* encompasses the fundamental regulations of *musharakah*, ijarah, and sale, hence, the necessary conditions, i.e. contracting parties, offer and acceptance, the subject matter of the contract, and the necessary considerations of these three contracts, would be discussed in upcoming chapters.

According to Resolution No. 110 (4/12) of International Islamic Fiqh Academy (IIFA), the hire purchase under *shirkah al-milk* (*ijarah muntahiyyah bi al-tamlik*) is analogous to an ordinary *ijarah* in terms of its rules, except its association with a promise by the lessor to the lessee to transfer the possession once the *ijarah* term is completed (IIFA, 2021). However, IIFA (2021) develops criteria of permissibility and prohibition and the permissible and prohibition forms for an *ijarah* contract that ends with ownership as follows:

a. Prohibition criteria dictate that if a transaction involves the simultaneous conclusion of two separate contracts for the same commodity and duration, the contract then rather should be deliberately prohibited.

For a permissible contract, the following should be followed:

a. These contracts can be categorised as two distinct and independent agreements that are concluded at different times. In this arrangement, the sale contract would come after the lease contract, or there would be a promise permitting the lessee to obtain ownership by the end of the contract period. Both the option and the promise hold equal significance under the Shari'ah rulings.
b. There must be a genuine intention from both parties to enter into a lease agreement rather than using it merely as a cover for the sale contract. In other words, it is important to ensure that both parties

have a real desire to engage in a lease agreement and that the lease agreement is not simply a way to disguise a sale contract.

c. In a lease agreement, the responsibility of providing a guarantee falls upon the property owner instead of the lessee. Therefore, any damage that occurs, not resulting from the lessee's misuse or negligence, will be the responsibility of the owner, and the lessee will not be held accountable, even if the damage makes the property completely unusable.
d. In cases where the lease agreement includes insurance for the leased property, it is imperative that the provided cooperative insurance adheres to Shari'ah principles and is non-commercial. Furthermore, it is the responsibility of the owner to assume liability for procuring this insurance.
e. During the lease period, the lease agreement must strictly comply with the Shari'ah regulations pertaining to *ijarah*. However, upon the transfer of ownership to the lessee, the agreement must also adhere to the Shari'ah principles related to the property owner.
f. During the entire lease period, the lessor is responsible for the cost of maintenance, except for operational expenses, rather than the lessee bearing these costs.

IIFA (2021) further elaborates on some permissible forms of ownership transfer in a hire-purchase contract, which are:

a. Under a lease agreement, the lessee is granted permission to utilise the property for a predetermined duration in exchange for a specified rental fee. Additionally, there exists a separate contract wherein the property is gifted to the lessee at the end of the lease period on the condition that all rental payments have been made. Alternatively, as per the Academy Resolution No. 13 (1/3) on *hibah* (gifts), it is considered acceptable for the property owner to promise a gift of the property to the lessee upon the completion of the lease period and the full payment of rent.
b. Academy Resolution No. 44 (6/5) of its fourth session stipulates that a lease agreement may contain a clause permitting the lessee to purchase the property at the current market price following the end of the lease term and full payment of all rental obligations.
c. In a lease agreement, it is permissible to include a provision that the lessee can be granted to utilise the leased property for a

predetermined duration by paying a specified rental amount. Furthermore, the lessor may commit to selling the property to the lessee at a mutually agreed-upon price following the lessee's full payment of the rental amount.

d. Under a lease agreement, the lessee is permitted to utilise the leased property for a specific duration and pay a predetermined rent amount. Meanwhile, the owner provides the lessee with the option to purchase the property at any point in time if the lessee chooses to do so. Subsequently, if the lessee decides to exercise the option to purchase the property, the sale will be conducted under a new contract at the prevailing market price at that time, based on the Academy Resolution No. 44 (6/5). Alternatively, the sale may be made at a different price, which will be mutually agreed upon when the sale contract is concluded.

IIFA (2021) likewise elaborates on some prohibited forms of ownership transfer in a hire-purchase contract, which are:

a. An ownership transfer contract at the end of a rental agreement, which permits the lessee to become the owner of the leased property based on the total rental payments made during the lease period, without requiring a separate sale contract. This type of agreement facilitates a smooth transition from a lease to a sale without the need for any supplementary contracts.
b. A provision can be included in a lease contract that grants the lessee to use the property for a specified duration by paying a predetermined rent amount, additionally includes a sale contract simultaneously in the same agreement, which is stipulated to take place once the lessee has paid the full amount of rental obligation that was pre-agreed or at any predetermined future date.
c. An appropriate lease contract can include an option for the owner to sell the property to the lessee at the end of the leasing period.

Scholars, such as al-Zuhayli and others, state the Shari'ah conformity of hire purchase as follows:

a. The background of an Islamic hire-purchase contract typically involves separate *ijarah* and sale contracts, each with its own specified time sessions. However, combining the two contracts into one can render the entire operation invalid since it may be perceived as violating the principle of having two distinct contracts. Therefore, it is generally recommended to maintain the separation of the *ijarah* and sale contracts in Islamic hire-purchase arrangements. The two contracts function independently and are executed sequentially rather than simultaneously. Hence, in this regard, HPSM is a Shari'ah-compliant product as all three contracts in HPSM take place in separate time sessions instead of being occurred together at the same time, which confirms its legality (Al-Zuhayli, 2002).

b. Based on the Shari'ah ruling, there is a well-accepted Shari'ah maxim which affirms that everything is permissible principally *(mubah* to use, consume, or transact) unless there is an explicit Shari'ah text that prohibits it. So, there is no reason that causes the hire purchase to be prohibited (Abdullah, 2005). The principle of the maxim "what is not prohibited is permissible" in Islamic finance allows individuals for universal accreditation to engage in contractual dealings that do not violate the principles of Shari'ah law. In order to comply with these principles, the contracts used in Islamic finance must not contain any elements of *riba* (interest) or *gharar* (uncertainty). Furthermore, the contracts must not violate the fundamental principles of combining contracts. Therefore, as long as contractual dealing does not violate these principles, a contract like HPSM is deemed to be permissible under Islamic finance. A contract would only be prohibited when *riba*, gharar, or speculation is proven either as a means of the contract execution or as its objective; otherwise, the contract would render be a valid one. Thus, since the Islamic hire-purchase contract is liberated from such prohibited elements, then the contract should not be prohibited but rather be permissible in line with Shari'ah.

c. An Islamic hire-purchase contract involves an initial agreement between two parties to engage in an *ijarah* contract, wherein the lessee will use and pay rent fo the leased property during a predetermined duration. Following the completion of the *ijarah* tenure, as stipulated in the contract, either party of the two will acquire legal ownership or title to the leased asset. This agreement is reached through mutual consent between the parties involved in the contract.

d. According to the Maliki school of thought, it is permissible to combine *ijarah* and sale contracts in a single agreement. One example of such an agreement is when a buyer buys a fabric at a set price with the stipulation that the seller or tailor should produce a garment for him. Essentially, the buyer in this agreement is hiring the tailor to produce the garment for him before finalising the purchase agreement, which is acceptable to the Maliki school of thought.

In contrast, the authenticity of the Islamic hire-purchase agreement was issued by a specific legal ruling (*fatawa*) of the International Islamic Fiqh Academy (IIFA) in its meeting held on 10–16 Rabi 'al-Awwal 1406/28 December 1985, along with its conditions mentioned earlier in this current discussion. The academy has approved the application of a combined contract that includes *ijarah* and a sale agreement if both contracts are made for the same subject matter. However, if the contract generates two or more subject matters, the contract is deemed to be invalid. Hence, if an individual rents a car with five seats for a designated time frame and subsequently decides to buy a fifteen-seat van from the same owner for a different purpose under the same contract, the agreement would not qualify as a valid Islamic hire-purchase contract. This is because the subject matter or purpose of the original contract has been diverged according to the agreement, which is not permissible in Islamic finance. In Islamic hire-purchase contracts, the subject matter and purpose of the contract must remain consistent throughout the duration of the agreement in order to be considered valid.

Jordan Islamic Bank, in addition, issued a legal ruling on hire purchase. According to the bank's argument, an Islamic hire-purchase contract does not engross the combination of *ijarah* and sale within a single agreement. Rather, in this type of contract, the lessee retains the choice to buy the leased asset once the lease period concludes. In other words, the contract is not structured as a single or combined contract but rather as two separate contracts: an *ijarah* contract and a sale contract. The lessee is granted the privilege to acquire the asset upon the completion of the lease period, and this option does not constitute an obligatory element of the original contract. According to the ruling, an option can be added to the *ijarah* contract as a form of exchange, such as a sale (*bay'*), but it must ensure that the exchange of usufruct for the asset is accompanied by consideration in the form of rent. To understand differently, incorporating a choice to buy the property after the lease term ends should not contravene the essential tenets of the *ijarah* contract, which mandates that the lessee provides rent in return for utilising the asset. The option to purchase should be viewed as a separate contract of exchange, subject to the same conditions as a sale contract. However, it is important to specify the period during which the option can be exercised. If the lessee does not exercise this right, the *ijarah* contract will persist as an active lease until the designated tenure reaches its final stage. Almost all jurists of every school of thought, excluding the Shafi'is, permit an option in the *ijarah* contract (Abu Sulayman, 1992). Abu Hanifah (Al-Musili, n.d.; Samarqandi, 1984) approves the employing an option within three days, while; other Muslim jurists (Ibn Juzi, n.d.) extend the period from one hour up to one month based on the circumstances and the types of the product. Ibn Qudamah (1994) accordingly brings the statement of Ahmad, Abu Yusuf, Muhammad ibn al-Kaslan, Ibn al-Mundhir, Ibn Abi Layali, and Ishaq, where they state that the duration for exercising the option is contingent upon mutual agreement between the contracting parties. The duration of the option can vary, and it may be either concise or protracted, yet, it is essential that the specific agreed-upon period is clearly defined and understood by all parties involved. As a result, if the lessee opts to exercise the purchase option within the stipulated period, the ownership of the leased asset transfers to the lessee, and the *ijarah* contract is considered concluded at that juncture (Abdullah, 2005).

The International Islamic Fiqh Academy (IIFA) approved a resolution endorsing the Islamic hire-purchase contract four years after the issuance of the *fatwa* (legal ruling) by Jordan Islamic Bank. The resolution, which was passed during the 44th meeting held in Kuwait from 10 to 15 December 1988, allowed the hire purchase to be offered to the customer in two ways: either as an instalment sale with adequate security from the lessee or as an *ijarah* contract with an option provided to the lessee, which can be exercised after completing the *ijarah* instalments. After completion of the *ijarah* tenure, the lessee has three alternatives to decide, he may persist with the *ijarah* agreement, or he is allowed to halt the *ijarah* agreement and handover the rented assets to its actual owner, or he may obtain the property by paying the existing market value.

Furthermore, a *fatwa* was issued by the International Association of Muslim Scholars in its meeting held in Kuwait on 7–11 March 1988, highlighting that an Islamic hire-purchase contract can be valid if it comprises two separate contracts, namely *ijarah* and gift (*hibah*). Certain conditions must be met to ensure the validity of the contract. Firstly, the specific duration of the *ijarah* period must be agreed upon and known to both parties, and the rules of *ijarah* must be followed throughout the entire tenure. Secondly, each instalment amount must be fixed and determined in advance. Finally, ownership of the asset is transferred to the lessee through the gift (*hibah*) contract after the completion of the *ijarah* tenure (De Lorenzo, 2000).

Consequently, Irawani Abdullah (2005), as evidence of a hire-purchase transaction, elucidates a legal ruling of the Kuwait Finance House. Over the course of the following years, the Kuwait Finance House made two significant decisions while considering the approval of an Islamic hire-purchase contract.

1. The lessee in a legitimate hire-purchase contract may not be obligated to commit or promise to buy the leased property at a specific time during the infancy stage of the *ijarah* contract. The reason behind this is that the contract will ultimately conclude as a sale contract, which is distinct from the *ijarah* contract and does not solely rely on a promise.
2. The exercise of a speculative price in a sale does not accurately reflect the true market value of an asset. Therefore, in an *ijarah* contract that ultimately results in a sale contract, it is acceptable for the price to be determined either by the current market value or by a symbolic amount as per the mutual agreement between the lessor and lessee.

As per Utsmani's (1998) interpretation, the asset will continue to be solely owned by the lessor even after the *ijarah* contract has been completed. The lessor, in this matter, may retain the right to reclaim the property or sell it to the lessee or a third party at their discretion. "The original position in *Shari'ah* is that the asset shall be the sole property of the lessor, and after the expiry of the lease period, the lessor shall be at liberty to take the asset back or to renew the lease or to lease it out to another party, or sell it to the lessee or another person. The lessee cannot force him to sell it to him at a nominal price, nor can such a condition be imposed on the lessor in the lease agreement. But after the lease period expires, and the lessor wants to give the asset to the lessee as a gift or to sell it to him, he can do so by his free will".

1.3 Stages of HPSM

The HPSM contract follows a three-stage process that involves addressing specific issues at each stage. The first stage involves the joint purchase of the property or asset, followed by the transition from *shirkah* status to *ijarah*, and finally, the transfer of the asset's legal ownership to the lessee.

1.3.1 *Purchasing Property Under Shirkah al-Milk*

"*Shirkah* means partnership. *Shirkah al-milk* means to share in ownership. When two or more person supply equity, purchase an asset, own the same jointly, share the benefit as per agreement and bear the loss in proportion to their respective equity, the contract is called a *shirkah al-milk* contract" (IBBL, n.d.). *Shirkah* is the initial contract of HPSM, and the purchase of required property is carried out at this stage through a *shirkah* contract.

1.3.2 *Transformation into Ijarah Contract and Underlying Issues*

A comprehensive description of the *ijarah* contract will be provided in chapter three. Therefore, in this discourse, certain significant aspects of the *ijarah* contract will be emphasised during its implementation as it transitions from *shirkah al-milk* to *ijarah*. Under the *ijarah* contract, the lessor has the right to sell the leased asset to a third party without seeking prior approval from the existing lessee. This is because the leased asset is still under the ownership of the lessor, who has the privilege to utilise the property within the confines of his possession. However, at the same time, the lessee's entitlement in usufruct must be duly realised while ensuring the proper implementation of the contract—Resolution No. (11) of the Shari'ah Board of Al-Rajihi Banking and Investment Corporation states that once the buyer is empowered to obtain ownership, the seller must be released from any liability regarding the property and the lessee's rights.

According to the AAOIFI Shari'ah Standard No. (9), in the event of total destruction of the leased property leading to the termination of the *ijarah* contract, the rental payments made by the lessee will be deemed as compensation for the benefit derived from the property. If the property is subsequently destroyed, the lessee will not be obliged to pay any further rent to the lessor. Moreover, The Shari'ah Board of the Kuwait Finance House and the Unified Shari'ah Board of al-Barakah, in their respective *fatawa* No. 233, 253, and 9/9, have established that terminating a lease contract due to unforeseeable circumstances of force majeure is permissible only if there is a compelling necessity to do so. The reason for allowing termination of the contract in such circumstances is to prevent a situation where a person with a legitimate excuse is forced to suffer losses that were not caused by the contract had it remained binding.

AAOIFI Shari'ah Standard No. (9) further affirms that an *ijarah* contract may be terminated if the lessee fails to pay the rent. This termination usually is considered valid and enforceable, as the payment of rent is a fundamental condition of the *ijarah* contract, necessary for the contract's validity and feasibility from the lessor's perspective that keeps the contract tenable, legitimate, and practical. Hence, in the case of otherwise, the *ijarah* contract becomes null and void in light of the Prophet's (SAW) statement, as the condition cannot be fulfilled:

المسلمون على شروطهم إلا شرطا أحل حراما أو حرم حلالا

> Muslims are bound by the condition they made, except a condition that legalises impermissible act or invalidates permissible act. (Ibn Majah, 1957)

In contrast, based on the AAOIFI Shari'ah Standard No. (9), the *ijarah* contract will not be affected by the death of either party, i.e. the lessor or the lessee, as the leased property and the usufruct remain unaffected. Thus, if the lessee passes away, the contract will continue until its agreed-upon term, and termination will only be accepted if the lessee's heirs can provide sufficient evidence that they are financially incapable of continuing the rental payments. In case of the lessor's death, his/her heirs are not allowed to terminate the *ijarah* contract if the leased property is protected and undamaged. This is because the heirs can still receive the rental payments from the lessee for the remaining duration of the contract.

1.3.3 Transfer the Legal Title Through Ijarah Muntahiyyah bi al-Tamlik

During the final phase of the HPSM agreement, which is the transfer of ownership of the leased property, the lessor makes an earlier undertake to the lessee that the property will be sold to the lessee after the *ijarah* period is completed as a means of effecting the transfer of ownership.

The International Islamic Fiqh Academy (IIFA), in its Resolution no: 13, alludes that "the lessor's promise to sell and the methods of transfer of ownership be separated from the *ijarah* is to ensure that the obligations and liabilities are not linked to each other". However, the lessee's promise to lease the property acquired by the bank or institution signifies that the lessee is obligated to enter into a lease agreement for the said property. The reason behind the lessee's obligation to enter into a lease agreement is that the bank acquired the property based on the lessee's promise to lease it. Hence, the commitment to lease the asset is a legally binding obligation that safeguards the rights of the lessor or the bank as per AAOIFI: Shari'ah Standard No. (9).

Additionally, in an *ijarah muntahiyyah bi al-tamlik* contract, it is allowed to lease the property back to the seller, provided that both parties agree to observe the terms of the contract for a specified period, to avoid the contract being considered as an *'inah* transaction—a transaction is a sale of an asset on a deferred basis, followed by the purchase of the same asset at a lower cash price, or vice versa, which meets the specific requirements of *bay*' 'inah (BNM, 2013)—because any change in the property or the value of the property during that observation period can cause different economic characteristics of the same property. IIFA, in its resolution no. 13, states that the fundamental obligation of this contract is that all regulations of a typical *ijarah* are retained in *ijarah muntahiyyah bi al-tamlik,* unlike the commitment of transferring the possession to avert the association between *ijarah* and sale agreements. Eventually, in the event that the transfer of ownership becomes intricate due to unforeseen circumstance that is not related to the lessee, then the lessee will only be required to pay rent according to the prevailing market rate. This is due to safeguarding the lessee from any financial disparity, as he has already made payments as rental instalments which are higher than the existing rental value of the market to obtain an officially recognised ownership of the leased asset. If the market rental value exceeds the paid rate, the rental payments must be adjusted accordingly based on AAOIFI Shari'ah Standard No. (9) (AAOIFI, 2017). Figure 1.1 highlights the process of an HPSM contract IN IBFI.

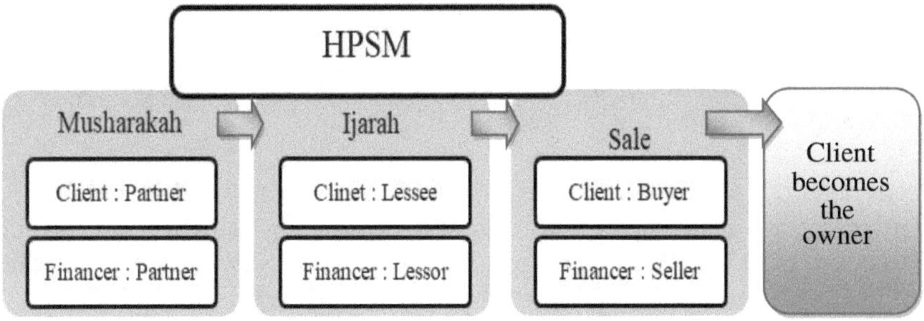

Fig. 1.1 Process of an HPSM contract (*Source* Author's own)

1.4 Shari'ah Requirements, Essential Elements, and Conditions of HPSM

The Shari'ah requirements must be observed as a priority in any Shari'ah-compliant contract to prevent any prohibited (*haram*) element. The genuine meeting of Shari'ah requirements in a contract enhances transparency, satisfaction, and confidence among the contracting parties in dealing with each other. A contract, in most cases deemed to be invalid if it fails to meet its necessary elements (*rukn*) upon which the existence of the contract relies. On the other hand, there are conditions for both contracting parties in the HPSM contract that are also obligatory to validate the contract, like many other contracts in financial activities. Hence, the deficiency of specific terms and clauses in a contract can potentially cause harm to the parties involved in the future. Typically, property and product owners, as well as their clients, seek to safeguard their respective rights during their dealings with each other in which they do not sufficiently and solely rely on documentation and certification to override the need for proper adherence to Shari'ah screening. So, in order to protect the rights of all contracting parties, the "terms and clauses" ensure their rights in that transaction (Abdullah, 2014). Thus, Shari'ah requirements, necessary elements and conditions are inevitable to make the contract Shari'ah-compliant.

As per Shari'ah requirements, the following measures in a contract must be eliminated in any contract, and they are:

1. *Riba* (*usury*), i.e. receiving benefits against a loan.
2. *Maysir* (Gambling), i.e. occurring a contract through speculations.

3. *Gharar* (uncertainty), i.e. uncertain period, rental amount, etc.
4. *Ghash* (cheating), i.e. hiding the truth.
5. *Fuduli* (valueless), i.e. exchanging any product which has no value and purpose of use.

Generally, if the above Shari'ah prohibitions are exercised in an HPSM contract during its implementation, the contract would become invalid based on the Qur'anic verses and the prophetic (SAW) statements that are frequently traced in the Qur'an and books of hadiths.

As discussed earlier, the HPSM contract attains three separate contracts that occur at intervals, namely *shirkah*, ijarah, and sale. Each of these contracts requires specific elements and conditions. However, these elements and conditions are largely similar for all three contracts, as they involve the same contracting parties at different stages, which will be discussed in the upcoming chapters.

1.5 Differences Between Islamic and Conventional Hire Purchase

Hire purchase is a contractual agreement that incorporates the Shari'ah principles of *ijarah* and sale contracts. It necessitates that the parties involved actively participate in the transaction while fulfilling the necessary conditions. Despite the hire purchase representing a promising and feasible opportunity in the banking and finance sector, however, certain Shari'ah principles forbid the application of this type of contract which have been highlighted by many Islamic finance experts and scholars. Realising its potential, Islamic economists have been aware of the hire-purchase contract and, thus, have taken proper footsteps to develop a framework that addresses the complex challenges and provides appropriate policies concerning the applicability of hire purchase in line with Shari'ah principles. Once the framework was established, Islamic hire purchase diverged from conventional hire purchase to a certain extent. Although there are still some similarities between the two, however, these similarities do not conflict with Shari'ah compliance. This has resulted in a distinctive Islamic hire-purchase model. In the practical states, Islamic hire-purchase and conventional hire-purchase contracts often appear similar in most cases. For example, both types of transactions involve all types of goods, including consumer goods and transportation, such as motor vehicles (transportation). Both transactions are applicable to the same range of customers, regardless of whether they are individuals, sole proprietors, partnerships, corporate entities, clubs, association societies, or trade unions. In the case of a company, both private and public limited companies are eligible to be involved in the contract upon they meet the necessary requirements (Ramli & Onn, 2007).

Despite the significant similarities between the two types of hire-purchase (Islamic and conventional) transactions, there are also notable differences between them too. In an *ijarah* contract, the lessor (bank) is typically responsible for paying the maintenance costs. However, there may be different approaches to this issue, such as an agreement that obligates the lessee to bear certain costs. In contrast, the prevailing practice in conventional banks for hire purchase is for the lessee to bear all maintenance costs (Ramli & Onn, 2007). In conventional practice, hire purchase is typically considered a regular type of loan, while in Islamic hire purchase, it is valued as a mode of finance. Under a conventional hire-purchase arrangement, the lessee obtains legal ownership of the asset after fulfilling the agreed-upon payment obligations and completing the specified tenure, all of which are covered by a single agreement. In contrast, Islamic hire purchase involves two separate agreements: the first phase covers the *ijarah* contract, while the second stage covers the sale contract. Practically, HPSM is implemented through three distinct contracts, namely *shirkah*, ijarah, and sale.

In order to execute the Islamic hire purchase under *shirkah al-milk* (HPSM), it is mandatory to follow the Shari'ah principles of *shirkah*, ijarah, and sale in all phases, and the asset ought to be permissible (*halal*) in line with Shari'ah to utilise. Islamic hire purchase must not permit the practice of any prohibited (*haram)* element by Shari'ah in the contract, such as gambling, selling alcoholic beverages, or establishing a club or bar where drinking wine is permissible, and prostitution is allowed. In contrast, conventional hire purchase does not engross any Shari'ah-related considerations or prohibitions during contract execution. Additionally, Islamic hire purchase (HPSM) involves transferring ownership through three distinct contracts, while ownership is typically transferred in conventional hire purchase once the final rental payment has been settled. The late payment fees for monthly instalments in Islamic hire purchases are viewed as compensation, and the amount charged is usually lower than in conventional hire purchases, where such fees are considered interest in conventional banks and are charged at a higher rate. For example, an Islamic hire purchase habitually offers a compensation rate of 1% per annum, whereas a conventional hire purchase may charge around 8% per annum as late payment interest. The funds for Islamic hire purchases are sourced from the Islamic pool of funds, while conventional hire purchases may be funded from any source, regardless of its compliance with Shari'ah principles (Ramli & Onn, 2007). Table 1.1 represents the common dissimilarities between Islamic and conventional HPSM.

Table 1.1 Differences between conventional and Islamic hire purchase

Item	*Conventional*	*Islamic*
Terms	• Loan • Interest Rate • Late Payment Interest • Hiring Charges	• Financing • Profit Rate • Mark Up • Late Payment Charges
Goods	Limited to consumer goods and motor vehicles, mostly	All types of goods are permissible by Shari'ah and non-perishable
Contract	All *'aqd* in one contract	All are separate contracts
Profit Margin	Cost Price × Interest rate Year	Cost Price + Profit Instalments
Responsibility	The lessee bears all costs of maintenance	The owner bears basic and structural maintenance costs by the lessee
Payment obligations	Commences from the date of execution of the contract for Funding	Commences only upon the delivery of the property to the lessee
Delayed payment	– The lessee will be charged a penalty – Normal interest based on days overdue	– Prohibits the levy of penalty – Addressed by various means, such as the inclusion of a donation clause or by the cancellation of the Contract (In Malaysia) – Serving alert notice and legal action if there is no positive response in IBBL
Termination	If the hirer defaults to two successive payments, the asset shall be repossessed by the owner	Termination can only be done by mutual consent unless there is misuse by the lessee
Transfer of legal title	The term of the transfer can be specified in the same contract as the hire-purchase contract	Gradual sale or Gift or Token Consideration or Specific Amount

Source Ramli and Onn (2007); Author's own (partial)

1.6 Problem-Based Question with Solution

Ahmed is interested in purchasing a car through hire purchase but wants to ensure that his financial transactions align with Shari'ah principles. He has conducted research and learned about the differences between Islamic and conventional hire purchases. However, he is still unsure about which option would be more suitable for him. What factors should Ahmed consider when deciding between Islamic and conventional hire purchase, and how can he ensure Shari'ah compliance in his financial transaction?

Solution

Ahmed's decision between Islamic and conventional hire purchase depends on several factors that he should consider:

- Shari'ah Compliance: Ahmed must ensure that the hire-purchase option he chooses adheres to Shari'ah principles. Islamic hire purchase follows specific contracts and principles that are in line with Shari'ah, while conventional hire purchase does not have the same considerations. Ahmed should prioritise Shari'ah compliance in his financial transactions.
- Ownership Transfer: Ahmed should understand how ownership transfer occurs in each option. Islamic hire purchase involves multiple contracts, with ownership transferring at the end of the agreement. In conventional hire purchase, ownership is typically transferred after the specified tenure under a single agreement. Ahmed should evaluate which ownership transfer mechanism aligns better with his preferences and financial goals.
- Maintenance Costs: Ahmed should consider who bears the responsibility for maintenance costs. Islamic hire purchase often includes provisions for the lessor (bank) to cover maintenance costs, while conventional hire purchase typically requires the lessee to bear these expenses. Ahmed should assess the financial implications of maintenance costs and determine which option is more advantageous for him.
- Late Payment Charges: Ahmed should compare the late payment charges associated with both Islamic and conventional hire purchases. Islamic hire purchase considers late payments as compensation, generally resulting in lower charges compared to the interest

rates applied in conventional hire purchase. Ahmed should evaluate the potential impact of late payment charges on his finances.

- Funding Sources: Ahmed should be aware of the funding sources for each hire-purchase option. Islamic hire purchase is financed through Islamic pools of funds, ensuring Shari'ah compliance. Conventional hire purchase can be funded from any source, regardless of Shari'ah compliance. Ahmed should evaluate the importance of funding sources and ensure that the chosen option aligns with his ethical and religious beliefs.

To ensure Shari'ah compliance in his financial transaction, Ahmed should consult with an Islamic finance advisor or approach an Islamic bank. They can guide the specific terms and conditions of an Islamic hire-purchase agreement, ensuring that Ahmed's financial dealings are in accordance with Shari'ah principles. By considering these factors and seeking expert advice, Ahmed can make an informed decision between Islamic and conventional hire purchase, ensuring that his financial transaction aligns with his faith and personal preferences.

Chapter Review Questions

1. What is another term for HPSM?
   a. Lease purchase
   b. Lease ending with ownership
   c. *Ijarah muntahiyyah bi al-tamlik*
   d. All of the above
2. Where did the practice of hire purchase originate?
   a. Saudi Arabia
   b. England
   c. United States of America
   d. France
3. Who introduced the concept of hire purchase?
   a. A British musical instrument seller
   b. United States Leasing Corporation
   c. Mercantile Credit Company
   d. Locafance
4. When was the concept of leasing introduced in the United States of America?
   a. Nineteenth century
   b. 1952

   c. 1962
   d. 2001
5. Which was the first European leasing company?
   a. United States Leasing Corporation
   b. Mercantile Credit Company
   c. Locafance
   d. SINGER
6. What is the third stage of the HPSM contract?
   a. Purchasing the property under *shirkah al-milk*
   b. Changing to the *ijarah* contract and underlying issues
   c. Transfer the legal title through *ijarah* muntahiyyah bi al-tamlik
   d. None of the above
7. During the *ijarah* contract, the lessor is permitted to sell the leased property to any other third party without permission from the lessee. Why?
   a. The lessor owns the property and can act within the limit of their ownership
   b. The lessee has no rights during the *ijarah* contract
   c. The lessee's rights are automatically transferred to the new buyer
   d. None of the above
8. According to the AAOIFI Shari'ah Standard No. (9) under what conditions can an *ijarah* contract be terminated?
   a. Complete damage to the leased property
   b. Non-payment of the rental by the lessee
   c. Death of any one of the contracting parties
   d. All of the above
9. In an *ijarah muntahiyyah bi al-tamlik* contract, what is the purpose of separating the lessor's promise to sell and the methods of transfer of ownership from the *ijarah*?
   a. To protect the lessor or bank from liabilities
   b. To ensure the lessee's rights are protected
   c. To prevent the contract from involving 'inah
   d. None of the above
10. How many separate contracts are involved in executing HPSM?
   a. One
   b. Two
   c. Three
   d. Four

Answers

1. d
2. b
3. a
4. b
5. c
6. c
7. a
8. d
9. a
10. c

References

AAOIFI (2017). *Shari'ah Standard*. Accounting and Auditing Organisation for Islamic Financial Institutions.

Abdullah, A. M. (2014). Leasing Ending with Ownership: Its Permissible Forms. In *Leasing Ending with Ownership and Leasing Bond (Ijarah al-Muntahiyah bi al-Tamlik wa Sukuk al-Ijarah) Its Ruling and Contemporary Application* (pp. 3–19). Islamic Banking and Financial Institute Malaysia (IBFIM).

Abdullah M. A. (1988). Al-ta'jir al-muntaha bi al-tamlik wa al-Suwar al-Mashru'iyyah fih. *Majallah Majma' al-Fiqh al-Islami, 4*(5).

Abdullah, N. I. (2005). *Islamic Hire-Purchase in Malaysian Financial Institutions: A Comparative Analytical Book*. Loughborough University..

Abu Ghuddah, Abd al-Sattar. (1998). *Ijarah*. al-Barakah Banking Group.

Abu Sulayman, Abd al-Wahab. I. (1992). *Aqd al-Ijarah, Masdar min Masadir al-Tamwil al-Islamiyyah: Dirasah Fiqhiyyah Muqaranah*. Al-Bank al-Islami li al-Tanmiyyah.

Al-Dusri, Ahmad Abd al-Latif. (2001). Al-bu'd al-tanmayi li al-ijarah. Paper presented at *Mu'tamar al-Mu'assasat al-Maliyyah al-Islamiyyah*, 5–6 May, Sheraton Hotel, Kuwait.

Al-Musili, A. (n.d). *Al-'Ikhtiyar* (Vol. 2). Dar al-Arqam.

Al-Sanhuri, A. Abd al-Rajjaq. (n.d). *Al-Wasit fi al-Sharh al–Maudu'i* (Vol. 4). Dar al-Nahdah al-Arabiyyah.

Al-Zuhayli, W. (2002). *Al-Mumalat al-Maliyyah al- Muasarah: Buhuth wa Fatawa wa Hulul*. Dar al-Fikr.

Al-Zuhayli, W. (2003). *Financial Transactions in Islamic Jurisprudence* (M. A. El-Gamal, Trans.). Dar al-Fikr al-Mu'asir.

BNM. (2013). *Bai''Inah (Shariah Requirements and Optional Practices) Exposure Draft BNM/RH/CP 028-2*. Bank Negara Malaysia.

De Lorenzo, Y. T. (2000). *A Compendium of Legal Opinions on the Operation of Islamic Banks: Ijarah, Sarf, and Riba*. Institute of Islamic Banking and Insurance.

Dusuqi, I. Abu al-Layil. (1994). *Al-Bay' bi al-Taqsit wa al-Buyu' al-Itimaniyah 'Ukhra*. Kuwait University Press.

IBBL. (2022). *IBBL at a Glance*. http://www.islamibankbd.com/abtIBBL/abtIBBLAtaGlance.php. Accessed 19 December 2022.

IBBL. (n.d.). Islami Bank Bangladesh Limited: Manual of Investment Under Hire Purchase Under shirkah al-milk in *Procedure for Investment Under Hire Purchase Under Shirkah al-Milk (Ijarah Muntahiyyah bi al-Tamlik) Mode of Investment*, Part 1. Islami Bank Bangladesh Limited. Dhaka.

Ibn Juzi, M. (n.d). *Al-Qawanin al-Fiqhiyyah*. Dar al-Qalam.

Ibn Majah. (1957). *Sunan Ibn MAjah* (Vol. 2). Mustafa al-Babi al-Halabi.

Ibn Qudamah, Muwaffaq al-Din. (1994). *Al-Mughi* (Vol. 4). Dar al-Fikr. Beirut.

IIFA. (2021). *Resolutions and Recommendations of the International Islamic Fiqh Academy of Organization of Islamic Cooperation*. International Islamic Fiqh Academy.

Kuwait Finance House. (2016). *Al-ta'jir ma'a al-mawa'idah bi al-tamalluk*. http://www.kfh.com/commercial/cars/Lease/index.asp. Accessed 27 June 2016.

Lewis, M. K., & Algaoud, L. M. (2001). *Islamic Banking*. Edward Elgar.

Ramli, R., & Onn, H. (2007). *Islamic Hire-Purchase (Ijarah Thumma al-Bay'-AITAB): The Handbook* (1st ed.). Islamic Banking and Finance Institute Malaysia (IBFIM).

Samarqandi, M. (1984). *Tohfah al-Fuqaha* (2nd ed., Vol. 1). Dar al-Kutub al-'Ilmiyyah.

Usmani, M. T. (1998). *An Introduction to Islamic Finance*. https://tinyurl.com/9zfmsbcv. Accessed 28 December 2022.

Utsmani, S.M. (1998). *Al-Mu'amalat al-Maliyyah al-Mu'asarah fi al-Fiqh al-Islami* (2nd ed.). Dar al-Nafa'is.

Zakariyyah, H. (2004). *Aqd al-Ijarah al-Muntahiyah bi al-Tamlik: Dirasah Muqaranah fa al-Fiq al-Islami wa al-Qanun al-Maiizi*. International Islamic University Malaysia.

CHAPTER 2

Shirkah: The First Contract in HPSM

Abstract *Shirkah* as the first essential contract in the HPSM arrangement sets the foundation for the subsequent contracts of hire and sale. It explores the principles of mutual participation, shared profits and losses. This chapter delves into the specifics of *shirkah* implementation within the context of financing the acquisition of goods or assets. It analyses the different types of *shirkah* contracts employed in HPSM and highlights the importance of defining the scopes of the partnership, the allocation of profits and losses, and the roles and responsibilities of the parties involved. In addressing the Shari'ah implications, the chapter examines the compatibility of *shirkah* contracts in HPSM with the Shari'ah principles. It explores the views of scholars and jurists regarding the permissibility of such contracts and compliance with Shari'ah requirements. The discussion also delves into the potential pitfalls and challenges that may arise in the execution of *shirkah* contracts within the HPSM framework, offering insights into how these can be mitigated. It deepens the understanding of the conceptual framework of *shirkah*, its practical implementation within HPSM, and its compliance with Shari'ah principles, significances, mechanisms, and Shari'ah implications, shedding light on its role as a fundamental element of this hybrid financing contract.

Keywords *Shirkah al-milk* · *Shirkah al-ʿaqd* · *Shirkah al-amwal* · *Shirkah al-amal* · *Shirkah al-wajuh*

M. K. Hassan et al., *Hire Purchase Under Shirkah al-Milk (HPSM) in Islamic Banking and Finance*,
https://doi.org/10.1007/978-3-031-50105-0_2

Preview

Shirkah, serving as the pivotal and foundational contract within the HPSM arrangement, establishes the bedrock upon which subsequent hire and sale contracts are constructed. It intricately explores the principles of collaborative participation, shared gains, and losses. This chapter is dedicated to an in-depth exploration of *shirkah's* implementation within the context of financing asset or goods acquisition. It undertakes a comprehensive analysis of the various *shirkah* contract types integrated into HPSM, emphasising the pivotal significance of clearly defining partnership boundaries, the equitable apportionment of profits and losses, and the delineation of roles and responsibilities for all parties involved.

Within the realm of Shari'ah implications, this chapter meticulously examines the *shirkah* contracts within HPSM context. It delves into the perspectives of scholars and jurists concerning the permissibility of such contracts and their adherence to Shari'ah requisites. Furthermore, this discussion ventures into the potential challenges and pitfalls that may arise during the execution of *shirkah* contracts within the HPSM framework, providing valuable insights into strategies for their mitigation.

By delving deeper into the conceptual underpinnings of *shirkah*, its pragmatic integration within the HPSM framework, and its harmonisation with Shari'ah principles, this chapter also offers a nuanced understanding of its significance, mechanisms, and Shari'ah implications. It sheds illuminating light on *shirkah's* pivotal role as an essential cornerstone within this hybrid financing contract, enriching the reader's comprehension of this intricate arrangement.

2.1 Characteristics of *Shirkah* or *Musharakah* Agreement

In a *musharakah* contract, the parties involved are known as the "*musharakah* partners". One party, known as the "*rab al-mal*", provides the majority of the capital and manages the business, while the other party, known as the "silent partner", contributes the remaining capital and does not participate in the management of the business. However, all parties in a *musharakah* contract may also be engaged in business management activities. The profit generated by the business venture is divided among the partners in proportion to their respective capital contributions. In the event of a loss, the partners will bear the loss in proportion to their capital contributions as well. This means that the partners share both the risks and rewards of the venture. One of the key features of *musharakah* is that it is based on a partnership agreement, which allows for greater flexibility in the management and operation of the business venture. Additionally, it allows the partners to work together to achieve a common goal and to share the risks and rewards of the venture. *Musharakah* is used in a variety of contexts, including the financing of real estate and commercial property, the funding of small and medium-sized enterprises, and the financing of infrastructure and development projects. It is also increasingly being used as a form of Islamic finance for the purchase of consumer goods such as cars and home appliances. It is important to note that *musharakah* is a form of Islamic finance, and it is based on the principles of the Islamic Shari'ah law, which strictly prohibits interest-based transactions. Kenton (2020) alike, states that:

> *musharakah* is a joint enterprise or partnership structure in Islamic finance in which partners share in the profits and losses of an enterprise. Since Islamic law (Shari'ah) does not permit profiting from an interest in lending, *musharakah* allows for the financier of a project or company to achieve a return in the form of a portion of the actual profits according to a predetermined ratio. However, unlike a traditional creditor, the financier also will share in any losses should they occur, also on a pro-rata basis.

2.2 What Is *Shairkah* or *Musharakah*

HPSM consists of three contracts in the following sequence, namely *musharakah* or *shirkah*, ijarah, and sale. In order to comprehend the HPSM, it is necessary to understand all these three contracts, and the focus of this chapter is on the first essential contract to structure HPSM, which is *musharakah*.

Musharakah or *shirkah* is an Arabic word which literally means sharing. In the domain of Islamic finance, the term "*musharakah*" refers to a contract entered into by two or more parties. However, compared to the term "*shirkah*", its meaning is more limited. Essentially, *musharakah* involves parties jointly owning equity or property and holding shares according to their agreed-upon percentage or negotiation. This is in contrast to *shirkah*, which has a broader connotation.

The Shafi'i school of thought identifies *musharakah* as a recognition of the shared ownership and rights of multiple individuals over a shared asset or property (al-Sharbini, 1994). The Hanafi school considers *musharakah* to be a partnership agreement between participants involving both capital and profit, whereas the Maliki scholars see it as a transaction where each partner allows the other to use the shared property while maintaining their own right to do so. On the other hand, the Hanbali scholars define it as a joint venture in ownership and control (Ibn Qudamah, 1994).

Scholars like Shafi'i and Hanbali use "*musharakah*" in a broad sense that covers both partnerships in ownership (*shirkah al-milk*) and contractual partnership (*shirkah al-ʿaqd*). However, Hanafi and Maliki scholars tend to use it mainly to refer to the latter type of *musharakah*, which is a contractual partnership (*shirkah al-ʿaqd*).

Tamer (2005) defines *musharakah* as a nature of a contract between an Islamic bank and one or more partners or clients, wherein the agreement can be terminated either at the end of a specified period or under certain agreed-upon conditions. This contract involves a joint venture in which one partner may contribute a larger share of the total capital than the others, and the partner responsible for managing the *musharakah* is allowed to make business decisions in a way that complies with Islamic law and that will result in profitability.

The AAOIFI Shari'ah Standard No. (12) introduced the *musharakah* as "an agreement where parties (two or more) gather their assets, labour or liabilities intending to create profits".

Musharakah, according to the BNM (2010), Shari'ah resolution

> is a contract of partnership between two parties or more to finance a particular business joint venture whereby all parties contribute the capital either in the form of cash or others. Any profits incurred from the partnership will be shared amongst them based on an agreed ratio, whereas any losses incurred will be borne by them according to their ratio of respective capital contribution. Currently, the *musyarakah* concept is applied in investment and financing activities. Financing based on *musyarakah* covers working capital financing, trade financing and asset financing.

The *musharakah* is a significant contract that plays a vital role in funding commercial endeavours according to Islamic principles. For instance, in a *musharakah* contract, party A, who has limited funds to start a business, can agree with party B, who has surplus funds, to finance the venture. The two parties collaborate and agree on the terms of the partnership, sharing both profits and losses. This type of financing negates the requirement for party A to secure a loan from party B. *Musharakah* is a commonly used contract for various financing purposes such as credit requisition, investment projects, real estate purchases, and financing other significant acquisitions. In real estate transactions, the partners seek a bank's evaluation of the property's value using the imputed rent method. The profits are divided between the partners based on a predetermined ratio and their respective stakes. Each partner who contributes capital also has a say in property management (Kenton, 2020).

2.3 Authenticity of *Musharakah* or *Shirkah*

Musharakah is treated as a valid transaction as it has its roots in the Qur'an, Sunnah, the consensus of scholars, and reasoning through both direct and indirect texts, and even predating the Prophet's (SAW) time. Allah (SWT) says in Surah Sad, verse no. 24:

ۗوَإِنَّ كَثِيرًا مِّنَ الْخُلَطَاءِ لَيَبْغِي بَعْضُهُمْ عَلَىٰ بَعْضٍ إِلَّا الَّذِينَ آمَنُوا وَعَمِلُوا الصَّالِحَاتِ وَقَلِيلٌ مَّا هُمْ

> Verily many partners (in all walks of life including business) are unjust to one another, but not so those who believe and do good deeds, and they are few.

The word "الخلطاء" in the verse refers to "partnership". *Musharakah* has mainly been in practice since the period of Prophet Dawud (SAW) and has never been prohibited by Prophet Muhammad (saw).

Allah (SWT) in another place in the Qur'an (Surah al-Nisa, verse no. 12) utters:

فَإِن كَانُوا أَكْثَرَ مِن ذَٰلِكَ فَهُمْ شُرَكَاءُ فِي الثُّلُثِ

> But if they are more than two, they share in third.

This verse as well legitimates the partnership contract, while a person dies without leaving any ascendants or descendants as hierarchy, but he leaves his siblings who are more than two in number, then they will share one-third of the property of inheritance. Hence, based on the two verses, it can convincingly be affirmed that the *musharakah* contract is a permitted financial contract of Islamic banking and finance if that runs in line with the Shari'ah principles as BNM (2010) stipulates that *musharakah* shall be practised in a just manner and as per the Shari'ah principles.

The indication of the legitimacy of the *musharakah* contract in Sunnah is also traced in several places. And this contract had been practised among the Arab people before Prophet (SWA) was nominated as the messenger of Allah (SWT). Prophet (SWA) says:

> يد الله على الشريكين ما لم يخن أحدهما صاحبه فإذا خان أحدهما صاحبه رفعها عنهما
>
> The aid of Allah (SWT) will always be upon two persons who are in a partnership as long as any one of them does not betray his partner. If one of them betrays the other, then Allah uplifts His aid from both of them. (Daruqutni, 2004)

The story of Sa'ib ibn Abu Sa'ib, who was the business partner of the Prophet (SWA) during the earlier days of Islam in Makkah, on the day of conquering the Makkah, He (SWA) said to *Sa'ib* upon meeting Him: welcome my brother and partner. And *Sa'ib*, however, did not dispute the approach of the Prophet (SWA) (AAOIFI (SS No. 12), 2017).

The indications of the permissibility of *musharakah* among the companions of the Prophet (SWA) are also trailed, such as:

> الربح على ما شرطا والوضيعة على قدر مالين
>
> The profit is based on what has been conditioned, and the loss is based on the amount of the capital (contributed by partners).

In another statement, it is said that:

> الوضيعة على المال والربح على ما اصطلحوا عليه
>
> The loss is based on the amount of the capital, and the profit is based on what has been stipulated. (San'ani, 1983)

Shari'ah scholars concur that the *musharakah* contract is a permissible business model since there is no explicit prohibition against it in Shari'ah. However, a few scholars oppose its permissibility, citing its suspicious aspects. They argue that the transaction resembles an interest-based contract since the primary objective is to lend money to clients, intending to generate additional funds from the same loan amount (Arshad & Ismail, 2010). Ibn Mundhir (2003) asserts, "All jurists agree on the validity of the *musharakah* contract since each partner contributes the same as his other partners, such as ***dinar*** or ***dirham***. And both contributions will ensure the formation of a single property". Abu Yahya (2003) elucidates the statement of Muhammad that all scholars of four schools of thought agreed that *musharakah* is a permissible contract for any common dealing.

The permissibility of *musharakah* can be established through the application of reasoning (*qiyas*) based on its widespread usage as a fundamental transaction in various jurisdictions since the inception of Islam. Jurists have expounded on the regulations pertaining to classical partnership transactions and have drawn connections to contemporary corporations. Consequently, the contemporary regulations governing multiple partnership transactions in Shari'ah will be adapted to suit the configuration of "modern corporations". This is because partnerships can be broadly categorised into two types: traditional *fiqh*-nominated partnerships and modern corporations as per AAOIFI Shari'ah Standard No. (12) (AAOIFI, 2017).

2.4 Types of *Shirkah*

Musharakah or *Shirkah* means to share something and terminology of Islamic financial transactions in modern IBFIs. The *Musharakah* contract is mainly divided into two:

1. ***Shirkah al-milk***: *Shirkah al-milk* is a legal concept in Islamic finance that refers to a form of partnership in which two or more parties jointly own an asset or property. There are two different methods of implementing this contract, which can be found in its existing form. This type of contract can be deliberately chosen by the parties involved, as it allows them to share the risks and rewards associated with owning the asset or property. In some cases, the *shirkah* contract may be the intentional choice among the parties to jointly own the asset or property. An example of *shirkah al-milk* can be perceived when two or more individuals decide to purchase a property together and jointly own it. In this scenario, the relationship among the parties is established through the *shirkah* contract. The parties themselves intentionally chose to enter into this type of contract to acquire the property. As a result, the risks and rewards associated with owning the property

are shared between the parties in accordance with the terms of the contract. On the other hand, there are situations where the *shirkah al-milk* contract comes into existence as a result of an occurrence or incident rather than being intentionally chosen by the parties. For example, after the death of a person, their property is inherited by their heirs, who then jointly own it. In this case, the *shirkah* contract is formed spontaneously as a consequence of the death of the person and not as a result of any deliberate action by the heirs. Despite the absence of intentional choice, the heirs still share the risks and rewards associated with owning the inherited property in accordance with the principles of *shirkah al-milk* (Arshad & Ismail, 2010; Usmani, 2008).

2. ***Shirkah al-ʿaqd***: *Shirkah al-ʿaqd* is the second category of the *shirkah* contract, which pertains to business partnerships formed by mutual consent of all parties involved in the contract. This type of contract is often referred to as a joint commercial enterprise and is further categorised into three sub-types of contracts (Arshad & Ismail, 2010; Usmani, 2008). These include:
   (a) ***Shirkah al-amwal***: *Shirkah al-amwal* refers to a type of *shirkah* contract where each party invests capital into a commercial enterprise. This type of contract is also known as a partnership of capital or a financial partnership. In this type of partnership, the capital contributed by each partner is used to start or expand a business venture. The profits and losses are then shared between the partners based on the terms of the contract.
   (b) ***Shirkah al-amal:*** This type of *shirkah* contract is also known as *shirkah al-taqabbul*, also known as *shirkah al-sana'i* or *shirkah al-abdan*. This contract takes place when all partners agree to jointly hire a third party to provide services to their customers. The fee charged from the customers is then distributed between the two parties (the *shirkah* and the hired third party) in accordance with their agreement. This *shirkah* contract is often used in service-oriented businesses where expertise or specialised skills are required. Each partner in the *shirkah* contract contributes their share of capital along with their own labour and expertise towards that particular partnership. The profits and losses are shared between the partners based on the terms of the contract, which may include the ratio of their

respective investments, the amount of labour contributed, or other factors.

(c) ***Shirkah al-wajuh***: *Shirkah al-wajuh* is a type of *shirkah* contract where all parties jointly own commodities without any prior investment. The commodities are purchased at a deferred price and then immediately sold at a spot price higher than the purchase price, resulting in a profit. The profit earned is distributed among the parties in proportion to their agreement or mutual understanding (Usmani, 2008). This contract is also known as a joint purchase and sale contract, where all parties share in the ownership and sale of the commodities. *Shirkah al-wajuh* is also known as a partnership in goodwill or creditworthiness, which is a type of partnership of liability. In this bilateral agreement, two or more parties enter into a partnership to purchase assets on credit based on their reputation or creditworthiness, with the goal of making a profit. The parties undertake to fulfil their obligations according to the percentages determined by the parties, and any profits earned are distributed accordingly. This type of contract is often used when parties want to jointly purchase assets but do not have sufficient capital to do so individually. By pooling their creditworthiness and reputation, they are able to secure financing for the purchase of assets and share in the profits that result.

It is important to note that in Islamic *fiqh*, the partnership contracts discussed earlier are commonly referred to as "*shirkah*" instead of "*musharakah*". The term "*shirkah*" is preferred because it is considered to have a more accurate and sensible meaning compared to "*musharakah*", which is a term that has been recently introduced by contemporary scholars focusing on Islamic modes of financing. In classical *fiqh* texts, the term "*musharakah*" is not frequently used, and it is primarily limited to a specific type of *shirkah*, known as *shirkah al-amwal*. This type of *shirkah* involves each party investing capital into a commercial enterprise (Usmani, 2008). It should also be noted that the term "*musharakah*" may also include "*shirkah al-amwal*", where partnerships are formed in

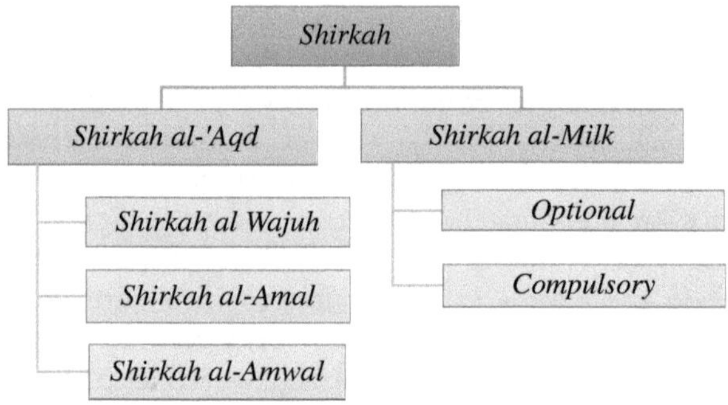

Fig. 2.1 Types of *Shirkah* (*Source* Author's own)

service-oriented businesses. Figure 2.1 exhibits the types of *shirkah* as follows:

2.5 Modern Classifications of *Musharakah* or *Shirkah* Contract

Tamer (2005) classified the *musharakah* into the following three different classifications, they are:

a. **Commercial *Musharakah*:** The scope of this *musharakah* contract is limited to a specific purpose, such as the buying and selling of machinery and commodities. In this type of contract, the bank and partner both contribute capital, but the partner is primarily responsible for managing the venture, including marketing and accounting, while the bank provides additional services such as progress monitoring and banking services during the contract period.
b. **Decreasing Participation *Musharakah*** (***Musharakah Mutanaqisah* or Diminishing Partnership**): Under this *musharakah* contract, the bank helps the partner gradually become the owner of the asset or venture. The partner's eventual goal in this *musharakah* contract is to obtain legal ownership of the asset as quickly as possible (Saeed, 1996), with the understanding that the bank will receive a portion of the profits from its financed portion according to the terms of the agreement. The concept of *musharakah mutanaqisah* involves a diminishing partnership contract that comprises two distinct agreements. Initially, the client enters into a joint ownership contract

(*shirkah al-milk*) with a bank or other financial institution. At this point of the agreement, the customer pays an initial share, typically around 20% of the asset's price, to become a co-owner of the asset. The remaining 80% of the funds are then provided by the institution/bank. As per the agreement, the client will make regular payments to gradually buy back the financier's 80% share of the asset until the ownership is fully transferred to the client. Meanwhile, the IBFI will lease their 80% share of the asset to the client under *ijarah*, and the client is obligated to pay rent to the IBFI for using its share. The rental payments are divided between the client and the IBFI based on their respective shares, which change as the client redeems the financier's share over time. With each rental payment, the client's share ratio increases, eventually leading to full ownership of the asset (Saad & Razak, 2013). A comprehensive discussion on the *musharakah* contract will be carried out in seven chapters too.

c. **Permanent Participation *Musharakah*:** In this contract, the bank becomes a shareholder and invests in a specific venture. The bank jointly manages and supervises the venture with its partner, using a profit-loss sharing (PLS) mode. The term "permanent" does not imply an endless partnership but rather refers to a partnership that lasts until the venture is completed or until the specific duration of participation has ended (Tamer, 2005). Figure 2.2 represents the modern classifications of *musharakah*.

AAOIFI Shari'ah Standard No. (12) adopted some contemporary classifications of *musharakah* contracts endorsing the previous classifications of Uthmani and named them "modern corporations". They are as follows:

a. ***Musharakah* Based on a Stock Company:** Where the total capital is divided into equal shares of commercial shares, and the liability of each partner (shareholders) is limited to their share of the capital.

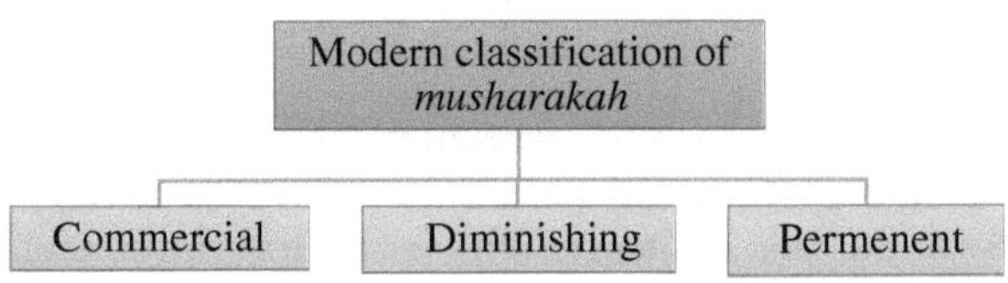

Fig. 2.2 Modern classification of *Musharakah* (*Source* Author's own)

b. ***Musharakah* Based on Joint Liability Company:** A joint liability company is a specific type of partnership where individuals agree to form a business and publicly register it as a company with a unique trademark. In this form of partnership, each partner assumes personal responsibility for any obligations and liabilities of the company that cannot be met by its existing assets. This means that if the company faces any financial difficulties, each partner is personally liable to cover any outstanding debts or obligations, regardless of the amount of their initial investment. This arrangement is different from limited liability partnerships, where partners are only liable for the amount of capital they have invested in the company.
c. ***Musharakah* Based on Financing Partnerships:** *Musharakah* financing partnerships involve operating partners who are treated differently in terms of ownership determination, with ownership calculated based on disproportionate lots of shares rather than equal shares. In this type of partnership, the financing partner is a sleeping partner and is not involved in the management of the company. As such, the managing partners bear personal responsibility for any obligations or liabilities of the company based on joint liability. However, the liability of the sleeping partners is limited to their shares of the investment and does not extend to their personal assets.
d. ***Musharakah* Based on Company Limited by Share**: *Musharakah* based on a company limited by shares is a type of personal partnership where all partners hold an equal number of shares in the company. The obligations and liabilities for both managing and sleeping partners are similar to those in a financing partnership. In this type of partnership, the financing partner is a sleeping partner and does not participate in the management of the company but the liabilities. Figure 2.3 represents the classifications of ***musharakah*** that have been proposed by AAOIF.

2.6 Significant Shari'ah Standards of the *Shirkah* Agreement

Each partner involved in the agreement must provide capital, and the bank, Islamic financial institution, or financier may impose certain conditions on the contract. The ratio for profit sharing will be agreed upon, while the allocation of losses will be based on the ratio

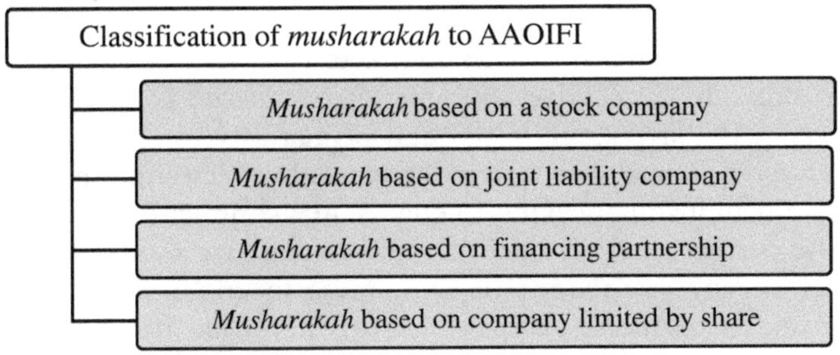

Fig. 2.3 Classification of Musharakah to AAOIFI (*Source* Author's own)

of capital contributions. Additionally, the profit-sharing ratio can be adjusted through mutual agreement among all partners. Capital will not be subject to any guarantee but may be used to recover losses in the event of negligence or violation of the terms of the contract. In cases where a partner wishes to purchase another partner's share, the price of the share must be determined either by the current market value or through mutual agreement between them. Nominal price cannot be used as a basis for determining the share price (BNM, 2010). As per AAOIFI (2017), Shari'ah Standard No. (12) Islamic institutions and banks are allowed to enter into partnerships with non-Muslims or conventional banks as long as the capital contributed by them is sourced in accordance with Shari'ah principles and the operational terms of the contract adhere to Shari'ah rules.

2.7 Mandatory Requirements of a *Shirkah* Contract

Shirkah is a concept that denotes the joint ownership of property. It is essentially a partnership between two or more individuals or institutions who collectively own property. The partnership itself is a fundamental aspect of the *shirkah* contract. However, in order for the contract to be valid, the partners must fulfil certain necessary conditions. These conditions include (Fatma, n.d.):

1. One of the necessary conditions for partners in a *shirkah* contract is that they must be of sound mind and capable of assuming

responsibility. Therefore, individuals who are deemed mentally unfit cannot enter into such contracts as partners.
2. In order to be eligible to enter into a *shirkah* contract, the partners must have attained the age of maturity (*rushd*) and puberty (*bulugh*). These two factors are considered essential prerequisites for any individual seeking to engage in a contractual agreement.
3. The parties entering into the *shirkah* contract should not be subject to any restrictions or limitations in conducting business or acting as partners, except in cases where one has been declared bankrupt.
4. Force contract is forbidden in Shari'ah. If either or both partners are forced to enter the contract, the contract would be invalid. Hence, both partners in the contract must be liberated from any kind of force.

The "contract" between the parties itself is the second component of the *shirkah*, and it must fulfil certain necessary conditions to prevent any uncertainty. These conditions include:

1. The investment and profits earned must be distributed among the partners in proportion to the terms outlined in their written or mutual agreement.
2. In order to avoid any confusion or uncertainty, the *shirkah* contract should clearly and specifically mention the precise percentage of investment and profits that each partner is entitled to receive.
3. In order to ensure the validity of a *shirkah* contract, all parties involved must be willing to provide capital. The capital can be in the form of cash or non-monetary assets, such as tangible or intangible properties. Furthermore, the contributed capital must be easily accessible for investment purposes (Arshad & Ismail, 2010).

During the duration of the *shirkah* contract, the third vital component is the asset, and it is crucial to adhere to the following essential conditions (Lahore, 2009):

1. One of the necessary conditions concerning the asset in the *shirkah* contract is that the asset should be present at the time of the contract's formation. It should be deliverable immediately and identifiable by its address or other specific details.

2. The asset must be in a permissible form that can yield a pure and lawful substance.
3. The asset must have a clear, identifiable owner that is known to all parties involved in the contract.

Another element of the *shirkah* contract is the benefit of the asset where necessary conditions are (Fatma, n.d):

1. In order to be considered of equal value, an asset must possess the same quality and appearance as the corresponding amount of money.
2. According to AAOIFI Shari'ah Standard No. (9) along with Fatma (n.d), an asset should only be used for purposes that are permissible under Shari'ah purview. This means that the asset cannot be used for activities that are prohibited by Shari'ah, such as selling pork in a shop or producing alcohol or wine in a factory.
3. All partners must know and be able to identify the asset.

2.8 Major Applications of *Musharakh* in the Modern IBF Industry

With the general principles in mind, in this discussion, we will highlight how *musharakah* can be applied in various areas of financing.

2.8.1 Project Financing

In project financing, traditional structures of *musharakah* can generally be employed. If the financier provides full financing for the whole project, the *mudarabah* structure is utilised. Conversely, if both parties invest, then the *musharakah* structure may be employed. In cases where one party is exclusively responsible for managing the project, and both parties invest, a combination of *musharakah* and *mudarabah* may be utilised (Usmani, 2008). Since *musharakah* or *mudarabah* was established from the beginning of the project, there are no issues to be realised with the capital valuation or profit distribution based on normal accounting standards. If the financier wishes to exit the *musharakah* arrangement, the remaining party may purchase their share at an agreed-upon price. This enables the financier to recover their investment and any potential profits. In contrast, the business owner has the option to continue the project independently or sell their share to another party, while financial institutions can sell their shares to other project partners. If the sale of the share cannot happen all at once due to a lack of liquidity, it can be divided into smaller units and sold over time until the financier fully exits from the project (Usmani, 2008).

2.8.2 *Securitisation of* Musharakah

Securitisation of *musharakah* refers to the process of converting financial assets (such as *musharakah* investment) into securities that can be sold to investors as to be *musharakah sukuk*. This process enables financial institutions to raise funds by pooling their *musharakah* investment and issuing securities backed by the underlying assets. By securitising their *musharakah* investment, financial institutions can attract a larger pool of investors and access new sources of funding. However, the process of securitisation must conform to Islamic financial principles, such as the prohibition of *riba* (interest) and the requirement for fairness and transparency in financial transactions. Accordingly, Usmani (2008) utters that securitisation is the process of transforming illiquid assets into securities that can be bought and sold on a secondary market, making it easier to access large amounts of financing. This process can be applied to *musharakah*, especially for big projects where a large sum of money is needed and can not be provided by a small group of individuals. Each subscriber of the *musharakah* is given a certificate that represents their share of ownership in the assets. These certificates can be traded as negotiable instruments once the project starts acquiring substantial non-liquid assets, but trading is not allowed when all the assets of the *musharakah* are still in a liquid form, such as cash, receivables, or advances due from others.

A *musharakah* certificate represents a share in the ownership of the assets and profits of the business venture. The certificate holder is entitled to a portion of the profits and is also responsible for a portion of the losses. It is different from a loan, as the certificate holder has a direct stake in the business and its success or failure. However, the difference between a bond and a *musharakah* certificate must be noted. The bond represents a loan that must be repaid, usually with interest, to the holder. The *musharakah* certificate, on the other hand, is a representation of the holder's direct proportional ownership of the assets of the project. If the assets are in liquid form, the certificate represents a certain proportion of money owned by the project. For example, if 100 certificates worth Rs.—Pakistan currency—1 million each is issued, it means the total value of the project is Rs. 100 million. If nothing has been purchased with this money, each certificate represents Rs. 1 million. In this case, the certificate can only be sold at par value in the market, as selling for more than its worth is not allowed in *Shari'ah* law and would be considered *riba* (Usmani, 2008). Chapter seven will highlight some other issues of *musharakah sukuk*.

2.8.3 Single Transaction Financing

Musharakah can also be employed in financing individual transactions, such as import and export activities, and meeting the requirements of small traders. In such cases, importers can collaborate with financiers on a single import transaction based on the *musharakah* arrangement. Financial institutions like banks can also utilise these instruments to finance imports. The *musharakah* structure is applicable when a margin is deposited for opening a Letter of Credit (LC). Once the imported goods are sold, the sales proceeds are distributed between the importer and the financier based on a predetermined ratio. When employing *musharakah* as a financing structure for a single import transaction, the financier may retain ownership of the imported goods in proportion to their investment. The *musharakah* arrangement in this regard may have a specific limitation to a set of terms, and if the goods remain unsold upon expiration of the terms, the importer can acquire the financier's share and assume sole ownership. The sale of goods in a *musharakah* arrangement must take place at either the prevailing market rate or an agreed-upon price between the parties at the time of sale rather than at a predetermined price established at the onset of the *musharakah*. If a predetermined price was established, the financier is not authorised to compel the importer to purchase the goods at that price (Usmani, 2008).

Export financing can also be structured using *musharakah*. In situations where an exporter has a confirmed export order and a predetermined price, the financier can assess the expected profit and offer to finance the exporter based on a previously agreed-upon percentage. In order to safeguard themselves against any potential negligence by the exporter, the financier may stipulate that the exporter must comply with all conditions of the Letter of Credit (LC) when exporting the goods. In the event of any discrepancies, the exporter assumes full responsibility, while the financier is shielded from any losses resulting from the exporter's negligence. Nevertheless, as a partner of the exporter, the financier will assume responsibility for any losses incurred that are not a result of the exporter's negligence or misconduct.

2.8.4 Financing for Working Capital

A business owner and the financier can enter into a *musharakah* agreement where the financier provides funds for the working capital of the business. The profit or loss is shared based on a pre-agreed ratio, and the financier becomes a partner in the business operations. The financier also has a right to take part in important business decisions and receives a share of the profits. The following methods can be considered in this case:

In a business that is already operational, the value of the capital can be established by mutual consent. In the Islamic finance framework *of musharakah*, the capital must be in the form of cash, according to Imam Malik. However, non-liquid assets may also be considered as part of the capital through a process of evaluation. In the context of *musharakah*, the value of a business can be regarded as the investment made by the party seeking finance. The financier's contribution can be seen as their share of the investment. The partnership can be established for a specific duration, such as six months, one year, or less, during which both parties agree on a profit percentage to be given to the financier. This percentage should not exceed the financier's investment percentage as they do not participate in business operations. When the term of the *musharakah* ends, all the assets of the business, both liquid and non-liquid, are re-evaluated, and the profit is distributed according to this evaluation. However, according to traditional mechanisms, profit cannot be determined until all business assets are liquidated. However, with mutual consent, asset valuation can be considered as "constructive liquidation" as there is no Shari'ah prohibition against it. This means the working partner has bought the financier's share in the trade assets, and their share value can be fixed through valuation while considering the profit ratio allocated to the financier under the *musharakah* terms.

However, the financing method based on *musharakah*, as described above, may induce challenges in a business with many fixed assets, particularly in operating industries. The valuation and calculation of depreciation or appreciation for all assets can result in accounting difficulties and lead to disputes. In such scenarios, *musharakah* can be implemented in an alternative manner. One of the primary challenges in such situations is the computation of indirect expenses like machinery depreciation and staff salaries. To overcome this, the parties involved can opt for a solution where they divide the gross profit instead of the net profit. This approach ensures that the indirect expenses are not deducted from the distributable profit. In this process, the industrialists bear the responsibility of covering all indirect expenses voluntarily on their shoulders. Meanwhile, the *musharakah* partnership only covers direct expenses such as raw materials, direct labour, and utilities. Considering that since the industrialists are providing their pieces of machinery, infrastructures, and staff to the *musharakah* partnership voluntarily, hence, it can be reasonable to increase the profit percentage to some scale as compensation for their contribution (Usmani, 2008).

2.9 Dispute Over *Musharakah* and Responses

Though *musharakah* is one of the significant products in the contemporary IBF industry, it is still assumed that it generates some drawbacks. This section will highlight a few of them and rational responses to them.

2.9.1 Possibility of Incurring a Loss

This is argued that in a *musharakah* financing contract, losses from the business are more likely to be passed on to the financing bank or institution, affecting depositors as well. This loss exposure may deter depositors from investing their capital in banks, firms, or other entities that provide various financial services, leading to idle savings or the use of money in non-banking transactions, which could hinder national economic growth. This argument, however, is flawed. This is because before financing through *musharakah*, the proposed fund-seeking business must undergo a rigorous viability assessment. This is also done in the current interest-based loan system, where all applicants are not entertained with a loan. Banks only approve loans after evaluating the potential of the business and rejecting it if it is deemed unprofitable and risky. Besides, banks or financial institutions cannot limit themselves to just one form of *musharakah* financing. They must have a diverse portfolio of *musharakah* investments. If a bank has approved *musharakah* financing for 100 clients after reviewing each proposal, it is unlikely that all or most of the investments will fail. Although some may not be successful, profitable investments are expected to generate higher returns compared to interest-based loans, as the real profit is shared between the customer and the bank. Hence, the *musharakah* portfolio is considered to have a low risk of loss, as its diversified nature compensates for any potential losses in one investment. The possibility of loss is just a theoretical scenario and is less likely to occur compared to investing in a joint stock company with limited business activities. Despite the theoretical possibility of loss, people still invest in joint stock companies, so it is expected that they would not be discouraged from investing in the bank and financial institutions offering the *musharakah* portfolio (Usmani, 2008).

In addition, a key aspect of an Islamic economy is to foster a mindset that views any profit made through business ventures as a reward for accepting the risk involved. Though the risk can be reduced through business expertise and diversifying investments, it cannot be completely eliminated. Those seeking profit must acknowledge and accept this minimal level of risk. This concept is already established with traditional joint stock companies and is not seen as an issue, as it is understood that the shareholders' money may be at risk of loss.

2.9.2 Fraudulence

A further issue of *musharakah* investment is the client's fraudulence, which creates the probability of abuse of the contract by not paying back financiers claiming that the venture failed to craft a profit or suffered a loss, which puts both the profit and the principal amount at risk. The problem of dishonesty in banks can be effectively addressed in a country where the entire financial institutions are operated based on Shari'ah rulings through the overwhelming support of the central bank and government. In order to mitigate this hindrance, a comprehensive auditing system should be implemented to maintain and monitor clients' accounts. Profits should only be calculated based on gross margins, which reduces the potential for disputes and fraud. If a client is found guilty of any immoral conduct, fraudulence, or negligence, he must face punitive measures and may be banned from using any bank in the country for a specified period (Usmani, 2008).

2.9.3 Issue with Business Privacy

One vibrant issue of *musharakah* financing is that the involvement of the financier as a partner in the client's business may frustrate the business confidentiality and trade secrets keeping.

Actually, the solution to this concern seems uncomplicated. The client can include a provision in the *musharakah* agreement stating that the investing partner will not be allowed for any form of interference with the managing parties of the business as well as prohibited from publicly disclosing any business information without the client's prior consent. This type of confidentiality agreement is typically practised by reputable institutions, including banks and financial institutions, whose business relies heavily on maintaining confidentiality.

2.9.4 Issue with Client's Unwillingness to Share Profits

A frequent objection regarding the *musharakah* contract is the dishonesty of the client in sharing the actual profit margin with the financer, i.e. banks or institutions. Usmani (2008) cited two reasons for such conduct. For instance, critics believe that the bank should not be eligible to be informed about the significant profits of the business since it does not play a role in its management or operation. They argue that it is unjust to disclose the fruits of their labour with the bank, which only provides funds. Conventional financing entities limit their earning desire with a low rate of interest, and therefore, clients feel that Islamic banks should also offer the same privilege. However, clients are often reluctant to expose the true profits to the banks due to the fear that the disclosure may be channelled to the tax authorities, leading to an increase in their tax liability.

Usmani (2008) hence, responds that the solution to the first part of the issue is not necessarily straightforward but can still be achieved. Such clients need to be convinced and motivated to understand that borrowing with interest is considered a major sin unless it is absolutely necessary. Simply expanding a business is not considered a valid reason for interest-based borrowing. By choosing to obtain funds for their business through the *musharakah* arrangement, clients earn not only the satisfaction of Allah (SWT) but also a legitimate profit for themselves and the Islamic banks. Regarding the second factor, it should be noted that in some Muslim countries, tax rates are unjust and prohibited. Islamic banks and clients should advocate for change by lobbying their governments and striving to alter laws that hinder the development of Islamic banking. Governments should understand that if tax rates are fair and taxpayers believe they will benefit from paying their taxes honestly, this would lead to an increase, not a decrease, in government revenue.

2.10 Application of the Above Using an Example Case Study

Ahmed and Fatima, both sound-minded adults, decide to enter into a *shirkah* (partnership) contract for a real estate investment venture. They have carefully considered the necessary conditions of the contract and aim to abide by the principles of Shari'ah in their business dealings.

- Qualifications of the Partners: Ahmed and Fatima fulfil the necessary conditions to be partners in the *shirkah* contract. They are mentally sound, responsible individuals who are of mature age and legally capable of entering into contracts. They are not restricted in dealing or doing business and are not bankrupt.
- Contractual Obligations: Ahmed and Fatima draft a partnership agreement that outlines the terms and conditions of their partnership. They ensure the following necessary conditions are met:
  (a) Distribution of Investment and Profit: They agree that their investment and subsequent profit-sharing will be proportionate to their respective contributions. Ahmed invests $100,000, and Fatima invests $50,000. They decide that the profit will be distributed in the ratio of 2:1, reflecting their investment proportions.
  (b) Clear Statement of Investment and Profit Shares: The partnership agreement clearly states the percentage of investment and profit for each partner. It is explicitly mentioned that Ahmed holds a 66.67% share, and Fatima holds a 33.33% share in the partnership.
  (c) Contribution of Capital: Both partners contribute their capital as agreed upon in the partnership agreement. Ahmed provides cash, while Fatima contributes a non-monetary asset in the form of commercial property.
- Asset Selection: Ahmed and Fatima carefully choose the property to be included in their partnership. They ensure the following conditions are met:
  (a) Existence and Specified Address: The property they select for investment exists and can be identified by its precise address, ensuring transparency and clarity.
  (b) Halal and Permissible: The chosen property complies with Shari'ah principles, free from any prohibited elements or

activities. It is suitable for lawful and permissible purposes, aligning with Shari'ah guidelines.
(c) Ownership and Identification: The property's ownership is legitimate, known, and verified by both partners. Ahmed and Fatima have conducted the necessary due diligence to ensure legal ownership.

- The benefit of the Asset: The selected property fulfils the following necessary conditions:
  (a) Value and Quality: The property holds substantial value in terms of its quality and appearance, ensuring that it will be a valuable asset for the partnership.
  (b) Shari'ahCompliance: The intended use of the property is in line with Shari'ah principles, adhering to AAOIFI Shari'ah Standard No. (9). It will not be utilised for any activities prohibited by Shari'ah, such as selling prohibited substances or engaging in haram practices.
  (c) Known and Identified Asset: The property is well-known and identifiable to both partners. They are fully aware of its characteristics, location, and potential benefits.

By carefully considering and fulfilling these necessary conditions, Ahmed and Fatima establish a *shirkah* contract for their real estate investment venture, ensuring transparency, fairness, and adherence to Shari'ah principles throughout their partnership.

Problems and Solutions for the Example Case Study

Problem 1:
Ahmed and Fatima want to enter into a *shirkah* partnership, but Ahmed is only 16 years old. What necessary condition is not being met, and what should they do to resolve this issue?

Solution 1:
The necessary condition of acquiring maturity (rushd) and puberty (bulugh) of age is not being met. Ahmed should wait until he reaches the legal age required to enter into contracts, usually 18 years old, before participating in the *shirkah* partnership with Fatima.

Problem 2:
Ahmed and Fatima are considering investing in a property, but they are unsure if it is owned by an actual owner. What necessary condition is causing concern, and how can they address it?

Solution 2:
The necessary condition of the property being owned by an actual owner and known to all partners is causing concern. Ahmed and Fatima should conduct due diligence to verify the ownership of the property by obtaining legal documentation and conducting title searches. This will ensure that the property is legitimately owned and reduce any potential risks or disputes in the future.

Problem 3:
Ahmed and Fatima have agreed to distribute profits in their *shirkah* partnership, but they haven't clearly stated the percentage of investment and profit for each partner. What necessary condition is missing, and what should they do to rectify the situation?

Solution 3:
The necessary condition of clearly stating the percentage of investment and profit for each partner is missing. Ahmed and Fatima should draft a written agreement or contract that clearly specifies the proportionate distribution of investment and profit for each partner. This will ensure transparency, avoid misunderstandings, and provide a clear framework for the partnership.

Problem 4:
Ahmed and Fatima have entered into a *shirkah* partnership, but they discover that the property they invested in is being used for a purpose that is prohibited in Shari'ah. What necessary condition is being violated, and what action should they take?

Solution 4:
The necessary condition of the purpose of use being in line with Shari'ah is being violated. Ahmed and Fatima should immediately cease involvement in the partnership and seek a lawful alternative investment. Engaging in activities that are prohibited by Shari'ah is

not permissible, and they should ensure that their investments align with Islamic principles.

Chapter Review Questions

1. Which contract serves as the first essential contract in the structure of Hire Purchase under *Shirkah al-Milk* (HPSM)?
   a. *Ijarah* (lease) contract
   b. Shirkah (partnership) contract
   c. Salam (forward sale) contract
   d. Murabaha (cost plus financing) contract
2. What is the literal meaning of the term "*musharakah*" in Arabic?
   a. Sharing
   b. Partnership
   c. Financing
   d. Negotiation
3. Which of the following best describes the concept of *musharakah* according to the BNM Shari'ah resolution?
   a. It is a contract between two parties or more to finance a particular business joint venture.
   b. It is a contract between a lender and borrower for working capital financing.
   c. It is a contract between a buyer and seller for trade financing.
   d. It is a contract between a lessor and a lessee for asset financing.
4. Which of the following classifications of *musharakah* is based on a diminishing partnership contract?
   a. Commercial *musharakah*
   b. Decreasing participation *musharakah*
   c. Permanent participation *musharakah*
   d. None of the above
5. Which classification of *musharakah* is based on the division of capital into equal units of commercial shares with limited liability for each shareholder?
   a. *Musharakah* based on a stock company
   b. *Musharakah* based on joint liability company
   c. *Musharakah* based on financing partnership
   d. *Musharakah* based on company limited by share

6. Which classification of *musharakah* requires partners to publicly declare as a registered company and hold personal responsibility for the company's obligations and liabilities?
   a. *Musharakah* based on a stock company
   b. *Musharakah* based on joint liability company
   c. *Musharakah* based on financing partnership
   d. *Musharakah* based on company limited by share
7. In which classification of *musharakah* are operating partners treated differently in terms of ownership determination, with ownership calculated based on disproportionate lots of shares?
   a. *Musharakah* based on a stock company
   b. *Musharakah* based on joint liability company
   c. *Musharakah* based on financing partnership
   d. *Musharakah* based on company limited by share
8. Which classification of *musharakah* is similar to a financing partnership but with participation based on equal numbers of shares?
   a. *Musharakah* based on a stock company
   b. *Musharakah* based on joint liability company
   c. *Musharakah* based on financing partnership
   d. *Musharakah* based on company limited by share
9. In the *musharakah* mutanaqisah concept, what happens to the client's share ratio after each rental payment?
   a. It decreases
   b. It remains the same
   c. It increases
   d. It fluctuates
10. What is the key characteristic of the *musharakah* mutanaqisah or diminishing partnership contract?
    a. The bank collects a portion of the profit according to the agreement
    b. The bank provides banking services and progress monitoring
    c. The partner pays an initial share to co-own the asset
    d. The partner is responsible for the management and supervision of the venture

Answers

1. b
2. a

3. a
4. b
5. a
6. b
7. c
8. d
9. c
10. a

References

AAOIFI. (2017). *Shari'ah standard*. Accounting and Auditing Organisation for Islamic Financial Institutions.

Abu Yahya, M. (2003). *Al-Ijma Inda A'immah ahl Sunnah al-Arba'ah*. Maktabah al-Ubaikan.

Al-Sharbini, M. Ibn Muhammad al-Khatib. (1994). *Mughni al-Muhtaj* (Vol. 2). Matba'at al-Babi al-Halabi.

Arshad, N. C., & Ismail, A. G. (2010). Shariah Parameters for Musharakah Contract: A Comment. *International Journal of Business and Social Science, 1*(1), 145–162.

BNM. (2010). *Shariah Resolutions in Islamic Finance, Part 1* (2nd ed.). Bank Negara Malaysia.

Daruqutni, Abu al-Hasan D. (2004). *Sunan al-Daruqutni* (Vol. 3). Mu'assasah al-Risslah.

Fatma, A. (n.d.). *Meaning of ijarah*. https://www.academia.edu/3583126/meaning_of_ijarah. Accessed 29 December 2022.

Ibn Qudamah, Muwaffaq al-Din. (1994). *Al-Mughi* (Vol. 4). Dar al-Fikr.

Kenton, W. (2020). *What Is Musharakah? Meaning and How It Works in Finance*. https://www.investopedia.com/terms/m/musharakah.asp. Accessed 22 December 2022.

Lahore, A. (2009). *The Concept of Musharakah*. https://www.scribd.com/doc/17223453/The-Concept-of-Musharakah. Accessed 29 December 2022.

Mundhir, I., & Abu, B. M. (2003). *Al-Ijma'* (2nd ed.). Dar al-Alam al-Kutub.

Saad, N. M., & Razak, D. A. (2013). Towards an Application of Musharakah Mutanaqisah Principle in Islamic Microfinance. *International Journal of Business and Society, 14*(2), 221–234.

Saeed, A. (1996). *Islamic Banking and Interest: A Book of the Prohibition of Riba and Its Contemporary Interpretation* (R. Peters, B. Weiss, & B. J. Brill, Eds.). Studies in Islamic Law and Society.

San'ani, Abd al-Razzaq Abu Bakar. (1983). *Musannaf Abd al-Razzqa* (Vol. 8). al-Maktabah al-Islami.

Tamer, S. (2005). *The Islamic Financial System*. Peter Lang.
Usmani, M. T. (2008). *An Introduction to Islamic Finance*. Idarah Isha'at-E-Diniyyat (P) Ltd.

CHAPTER 3

Ijarah: The Second Contract in HPSM

Abstract *Ijarah* plays a vital role in the HPSM contract. It refers to Islamic leasing, which involves the transfer of the right to use an asset or property from the lessor to the lessee for a specified period in exchange for rental payments. This chapter will delve into the fundamental principles and key elements of the *ijarah* contract and examine the conditions that must be fulfilled by the contracting parties. It will explore the requirements pertaining to the property or asset, ensuring its ownership, readiness for use, and specification. Moreover, it will explore the concept of benefit in the context of *ijarah*, emphasising the importance of adhering to Shari'ah guidelines regarding permissible usage and the distinction between the material part of the property and the usufruct derived from it. Furthermore, it will highlight the necessity of specifying the currency and the absolute amounts in accordance with Shari'ah principles. It will also address practical issues and challenges that may arise in its implementation by examining scenarios where ambiguity or inadequate provisions may lead to disputes and suggest solutions to overcome these challenges while ensuring Shari'ah compliance.

Keywords *Ijarah* · *Ijarah al-ʿain* · *Ijarah al-ʿamal* · *Forward ijarah* · *Lease*

M. K. Hassan et al., *Hire Purchase Under Shirkah al-Milk (HPSM) in Islamic Banking and Finance*,
https://doi.org/10.1007/978-3-031-50105-0_3

Preview

The role of *ijarah* within the HPSM contract is vital. *Ijarah*, or Islamic leasing, signifies the transfer of the utilisation rights of an asset or property from the lessor to the lessee for a defined timeframe, in return for stipulated rental payments. This chapter undertakes an in-depth exploration of the core tenets and crucial components of the *ijarah* contract. It delves into the requisite conditions that necessitate fulfilment by the involved parties, examining the specific prerequisites associated with the asset or property. This encompasses aspects such as ownership verification, suitability for usage, and detailed specifications.

Furthermore, the chapter delves into the concept of benefit within the context of *ijarah*, placing a strong emphasis on the adherence to Shari'ah guidelines governing permissible utilisation. It underscores the significance of distinguishing between the tangible aspects of the property and the benefits derived from its utilisation.

A pivotal aspect addressed in this chapter is the meticulous specification of currency and exact amounts in alignment with Shari'ah principles. Additionally, it tackles practical challenges and potential complications that might arise during the execution of *ijarah* agreements. By exploring scenarios where ambiguities or inadequate provisions could lead to disputes, the chapter provides insightful solutions to overcome such challenges while upholding strict adherence to Shari'ah compliance.

In essence, this chapter contributes to a comprehensive understanding of the pivotal role of *ijarah* within the HPSM framework. It delves into the intricacies of the contract, highlighting its various dimensions, principles, and practical implications, and offers valuable insights into ensuring a harmonious and Shari'ah-compliant implementation.

3.1 What Is an *Ijarah* Contract?

The definitions of *ijarah* are diverse according to the different Muslim jurists. From the practical perspective, *ijarah* denotes the concept of transferring the right to use and enjoy the benefit of a property in exchange for a payment or "possessing of a usufruct for a consideration" (Sarakhsi, 2013; Shafi'i, 2000). In the Hanafi school, *ijarah* is defined as an agreement or contract where one party grants the use of a property or asset to another party in exchange for a specific payment or price (Nizam, 2000; Sarakhsi, 2000). This payment serves as compensation for the usufruct, which refers to the right to use and enjoy the benefits or income generated by the property or asset. According to the interpretations of the Malikis and Hanbalis, *ijarah* is defined as the act of transferring the privilege to utilise the benefits and advantages of a permissible object in return for a clearly defined and specified compensation (Al-Dasuqi, 1996). In this context, the term "usufruct" refers to the right to enjoy the benefits and produce income from the object or property. The counter value represents the agreed-upon compensation for the temporary transfer of the usufruct. According to the Shafi'i school, *ijarah* is an agreement where a permissible, determined, and known usufruct, which can be utilised and consumed, is leased out in exchange for a specified and known counter value or price (Al-Shiribini, 2000). AAOIFI Shari'ah Standard No. (9) defines *ijarah* as:

> leasing of property pursuant to a contract under which a specified permissible benefit in the form of a usufruct is obtained for a specified period in return for a specified permissible consideration.

Although the wording may differ in the *ijarah* contract, however, all schools of jurisprudence agree on the fundamental meaning of *ijarah*. It is universally understood as a contract that involves the utilisation of the usufruct of a specific object in exchange for an agreed-upon consideration or counter value. In practical terms, *ijarah* can be categorised into two distinct subject matters (Usmani, 2001). The first category of *ijarah* involves hiring the services of an individual who is compensated with a wage for the work. In this regard, the employer is referred to as the *musta'jir*, the employee as the *ajir*, and the payment for the services rendered as *'ujrah*. For instance, if Ahmad hires Ali as a manager or clerk in his office and provides Ali with a monthly salary, Ahmad, in this process, would be the *musta'jir*, and Ali would be the *ajir*. Likewise, if Ahmad engages the services of a haulier to transport his luggage to the airport, Ahmad, in this contract, is considered the *musta'jir*, while the haulier would be the *ajir*. In both cases, these transactions fall under the category of *ijarah*. This form of *ijarah* encompasses any transaction where one party hires the services of another individual, whether it be a doctor, lawyer, teacher, labourer, or any other person capable of providing valuable services. Hence, each individual mentioned above, in line with Islamic transactional law, can be referred to as an "*ajir*". The person who hires their services is known as a "*musta'jir*", and the compensation provided to the "*ajir*" is termed as "*ujrah*".

The second category of *ijarah* pertains to the usufructs of assets or properties rather than human services. In this context, *ijarah* involves transferring the right to use a specific property to another person in return for a rental payment. In this case, the term "*ijarah*" can be likened to the English term "leasing". In this arrangement, the party granting the lease is known as the "*mu'jir*" or lessor, while the party receiving the lease is called the "*musta'jir*" or lessee. The payment made to the lessor as rent is referred to as "*ujrah*".

In the Islamic commerce spectrum, *ijarah* denotes a contractual association involving the owner of a property and an individual desiring to lease said property. The involved parties will engage in a lease agreement, commonly known as a hire contract (Abdullah, 2005). However, from the perspective of Islamic banking, *ijarah* represents a lease contract in which a bank or financial institution leases out equipment or a building to a client in exchange for a predetermined fee. Upon the termination of the lease period, the bank typically seeks to rent out the property again, ensuring its continuous utilisation and preventing prolonged periods of vacancy. In this case, the ownership title of the property remains with the bank, thereby placing the associated risks, such as economic downturns and other potential risks, to be held by the bank as the owner (Abdullah, 2005).

Islamic jurisprudence at larger, and especially its transactional law, extensively covers both forms of *ijarah* in the works of literature, each with its own set of rules. However, the second type of *ijarah* holds greater relevance to the modern Islamic banking and finance industry. It is commonly employed as an investment tool and a means of financing.

3.2 Authenticity of *Ijarah*

Ijarah is fundamentally considered a permissible transaction, and its legitimacy is derived from various sources, including the Qur'an, the Sunnah, the consensus (*ijma'*) of the legal authority, and reasoning. The legality of *ijarah* is explicitly mentioned in several verses of the Qur'an. Examples of them are the no. 26 of surah al-Qasas, where Allah (SWT) says:

قَالَتْ إِحْدَاهُمَا يَا أَبَتِ اسْتَأْجِرْهُ ۖ إِنَّ خَيْرَ مَنِ اسْتَأْجَرْتَ الْقَوِيُّ الْأَمِينُ

Said one of them (the two women), O my father! Hire him! Verily, the best of men for you to hire is the strong, the trustworthy.

In verse no. 8 of Surah al-Talaq He (SWT) says:

ﵟفَإِنْ أَرْضَعْنَ لَكُمْ فَآتُوهُنَّ أُجُورَهُنَّ

Then if they give suck to the children for you, give them their duo payment.

In verse no. 66, Surah al-Kahaf, Allah (SWT) says again:

ارْجَأ ِهْيَلَع َتْذَخَّتال َتْئِش ْوَل َلاَق

He said, if you had wished, surely you could have exacted some recompense for it.

The legality of *ijarah* is mentioned in several places in hadiths; among them are,

His (SAW) sayings:

من استأجر أجيرا فليعلم أجره

Whoever hired a worker must inform him of his wages (Ibn Majah, 2007).
He (SAW) again says

إعطوا الأجير أجره قبل أن يجف عرقه

Pay the employee's wages before his sweat (body odour) is dried. (Ibn Majah, n.d.)

The *ijarah* transaction is universally permissible across all schools of thought, as there exists a consensus among scholars of the Muslim community, spanning from the era of the Prophet's (SAW) companions to the present day, "no one disputed this consensus except *Adul Rahman Ibn al-'Assam* who opined that it is prohibited due to *gharar* as it is a contract on usufruct which to be materialised later, but jurists refuted his argument indicating that *gharar* in this matter is avoided because the contract on usufruct is not permissible after the existence of usufructs as usufructs perish as time passes, so a contract must be taken place before they exist alike *Salam* contract of assets" (Abu Ghuddah, 1998).

According to AAOIFI Shari'ah Standard No. (9), the legitimacy of *ijarah* is established through reasoning, as it serves the purpose of enabling individuals to obtain the right to utilise assets, especially for those who do not possess assets due to their financial barriers; hence *ijarah* is such a contract which incorporates the usufruct to some extent towards the deprived ones by easing their needs attainable despite financial burdens. Sarakhsi (2013), thus, utters the view that *ijarah* serves as a means of supporting livelihoods by allowing individuals to access and benefit from the use of assets that do not belong to them. The significance of the benefits derived from these assets is comparable to the importance of the assets themselves. This is because economically disadvantaged individuals rely on the wealth of financially prosperous individuals, while affluent individuals depend on the labour of the less fortunate. Addressing people's needs constitutes a fundamental principle underlying any contract in order to be legislated from the *maqasid al-Shari'ah* approach (objective of Shari'ah) as to be the *maslahah*, especially in the context of contracts governed by the Shari'ah rulings. And the evident fact is that each individual is not privileged to possess his own house and cannot afford personal transportation, but a house, for instance, as shelter and transportation for necessary rides and daily needs, is inevitable. Thus, *ijarah* is one of the significant means to meet such types of needs in people's lives. Moreover, experts are not frequently attainable everywhere, and everyone cannot be skilled to do any form of job or to provide any type of service, and those who are skilled, typically do not serve free of charge always. Hence, the required service may be attainable in exchange for labour and skill with money which is *'ujrah*, derived from an *ijarah* contract.

3.3 Classification of *Ijarah*

The classification of *ijarah* encompasses several categories based on its concept and process of implementation. Essentially, *ijarah* can be categorised into two distinct types. The first classification is based on the subject matter of the contract, while the second classification is centred on the contractual relationship between the institution and the customer (Slide Share, 2011).

3.3.1 Types of Ijarah *Based on Its Subject Matter*

Ijarah, based on its subject matter, consists of the following contracts:

1. ***Ijarah al-'Ain***: This *ijarah* contract establishes through the leasing of the usufruct of a specific good or asset. The rental payment can either be fixed and made at the beginning of the lease contract or deferred. The *ijarah* asset or good can encompass tangible

and movable items, as well as certain intangible assets, such as properties, transportation, facilities, and factories. In such type of *ijarah* contract, the leased asset is not transferred to the lessee, and instead, the ownership of the property remains with the lessor, who is the actual owner of the property. For instance, Ahmad rented out his property or transportation (such as a car, bus, or any other form of vehicle) to Ali for a period of one year, with a monthly rent of USD1000. In this agreement, Ahmad acquires the benefit of receiving the rent amount from Ali, while Ali benefits from utilising and enjoying the usufruct of the property or transportation. It is important to note that the ownership of the property/transportation remains with Ahmad as the rightful owner throughout the contract duration.

2. ***Ijarah al-'Amal***: *Ijarah al-'amal* refers to the engagement of an individual's services or skills in exchange for wages. This type of contract involves two categories of workers. The first category consists of employees who work exclusively for their employers' benefit and are not permitted to serve other individuals or employers during the agreed-upon contract period. For instance, this could include hiring a full-time domestic worker or a babysitter for the entire day. The second category of *ijarah al-'amal* encompasses independent contractors or service providers who operate similarly to a freelancing job. An instance in this regard is, Ahmad engages a painter to provide painting service for his house. In this state, Ahmad hires the painter's specific service or skill, which is painting, and the act of painting serves as the "*'amal*" or the work being performed as a freelancer instead of a full-timer.
3. ***Ijarah Mawsufah Fi al-Dhimmah*** (***Forward Ijarah***): Abu Ghuddah (2007) states *ijarah mawsufah fi al-dhimmah* as a contract in which the lessor (*mu'ajjir*) commits to providing the specified usufruct, considering the subject matter qualifying the *salam*[1] in order to prevent any potential conflicts regarding its usufruct. This can include leasing a designated car or availing the services of an individual, such as tailoring or teaching. The implementation

[1] *Salam* is a contract of sale of an object, which is not available at time of the conclusion of the sale, but will be delivered in the future on a fixed future date. The price is however, to be paid immediately during the session of the contract (Muhammad & Chong, 2007), which in other word is a contract with spot payment for a deffred product.

of this *ijarah* complements the *musharakah mutanaqisah*-based financing for houses that are currently under the construction phase. In this financing arrangement, both the customer and Islamic financing institution (IFI) jointly hold rights to the asset under construction through a *musharakah* mutanaqisah contract. Subsequently, the IFI leases its portion of the asset, which is still being built, to the customer using an *ijarah mawsufah fi al-dhimmah* contract. During the construction phase, the customer makes advance rent payments. Once the asset is completed, the customer transitions to paying the full rent amount to enjoy the benefits of the asset's usufruct (BNM, 2010). The *ijarah mawsufah fi al-dhimmah* is alternatively known as forward *ijarah* too. A further discussion of this *ijarah* will be carried out in Chapter 7.

3.3.2 Ijarah *Pertaining to Its Contractual Features*

Ijarah, pertaining to its contractual features, is carried out through two distinct contracts known as operating *ijarah* and financing *ijarah*.

The operating *ijarah* evolved from the concept of *ijarah 'ain*, wherein the lessor and lessee mutually agree upon a specified lease duration. In this contract, the lessor benefits from the rent payments made by the lessee, while the lessee enjoys the privilege of utilising the usufruct of the leased asset in exchange for the rent payment. This agreement can be established for either a short or long-term period, with the possibility of renewing or extending the contract upon its expiration. Nevertheless, the operating *ijarah* contract does not involve the transfer of ownership to the lessee, nor is there any prior commitment for such a transfer. The lessor in *ijarah 'ain* abides by the responsibility for covering administrative and maintenance costs, while the lessee is only responsible for maintenance expenses directly resulting from their use of the leased asset.

The feature of a financing *ijarah*, on the other hand, is diverse from the feature of an operating *ijarah*. Financing *ijarah* is a hybrid variant of *ijarah* contract that has been introduced by the modern Islamic banking and finance industry, combining elements of both *ijarah* and sale contracts. This form of *ijarah* extends over a significant period, with rental instalments for the asset being higher than the prevailing market price. This ensures that the accumulated rent payments can eventually cover the cost of the leased asset within the estimated timeframe.

Nevertheless, under this payment structure, the lessor is obligated to transfer the ownership of the leased asset to the lessee after the lease period. This transfer occurs once all the agreed-upon instalments have been paid in full. In this financial *ijarah*, it is essential to clearly state the method of transferring the ownership or legal title of the leased asset upon the conclusion of the agreed tenure. Transparency regarding this aspect is crucial in this type of arrangement (Kamali, 2007). This is because various methods can be employed to transfer the ownership or legal title to the lessee. These methods may include gradual sale, gift or *hibah*, nominal price or token consideration, or sale with a specific amount.The financing *ijarah* is also recognised as *ijarah thumma al-bay'*, *al-ijarah wa al-iqna'* or *al-ijarah muntahiyyah bi al-tamlik* (Abdullah, 2005; Kamali, 2007). However, there are a few more different modes of *ijarah* that have recently been developed in modern IBFIs, such as *ijarah*-based credit cards, *ijarah sukuk,* and *ijarah* renewal swaps and are being applied in several Islamic banks and financial institutions in many countries.

In an *ijarah*-based card process, customers acquire an asset and make rental payments for a specified duration until the total rental amount is fully paid. Once the payment is complete, the obligation on the asset is released. However, there are certain limitations to this structure. Only specific merchants are authorised to accept this card for leasing purposes. The list of these merchants is periodically updated and made available to customers through a booklet or website. The usage of this card is restricted, and it does not provide a cash advance facility (Islamic Bankers Resource Centre, n.d.).

Ijarah sukuk is a type of security that represents equal ownership in the usufruct of a well-defined and existing asset. It is based on an *ijarah* contract in accordance with Islamic principles. This *sukuk* grants the owners the right to possess the underlying assets, earn rental income, and freely sell the *sukuk* without affecting the issuer's right to use the asset. Chapter 7 will hold a detailed discussion on *ijarah sukuk*. Figure 3.1 represents the classifications of *ijarah*.

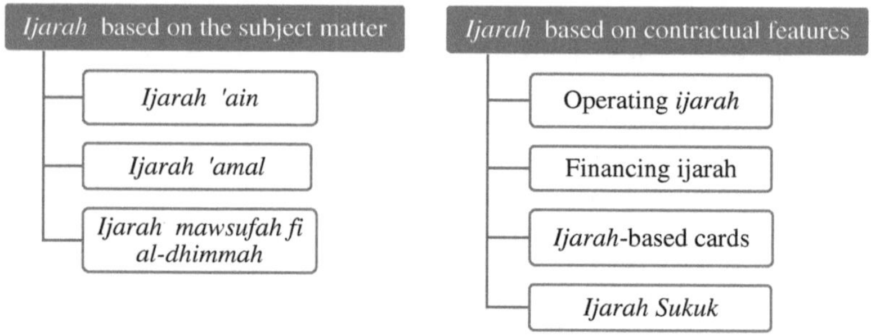

Fig. 3.1 Classification of *Ijarah* (*Source* Author's own)

3.4 Elements and Conditions for an *Ijarah* Contract

Ijarah, as one of the prominent contracts in Islamic finance and transactions, has been subject to thorough examination due to its significant involvement in both classical and modern financial activities. Therefore, Muslim jurists have widely discussed the requirements of *ijarah*. In *ijarah*, like other contracts, the offer *(al-ijab)* and acceptance (*al-qabul*) (al-Kasani, 1998) are the fundamental requirements to make the contract lawful. However, mainstream Muslim jurists determined four fundamental components to validate an *ijarah* contract, and they are as follows:

a. **The contracting parties:** consist of the lessor (*mu'ajjir*) and lessee (*musta'jir*).
b. **The content of the contract:** comprises the elements of offer (*ijab*) and acceptance (*qabul*).
c. **The subject matter of the contract:** encompasses two key components: the payment of rent (*ujrah*) to be given to the lessor and the provision of usufruct (*manfa'ah*) to be given to the lessee.
d. **The property.**

a. **The Contracting Parties of the *Ijarah* Contract: The Lessor and the Lessee**

Before a contract takes place, the contracting parties are fundamental and indispensable components of the contract. While certain financial transactions may involve more than two parties, and some may require a minimum of two, the *ijarah* contract specifically necessitates the engagement of two parties. One party is referred to as the lessor, who assumes the role of the giving or offering party, while the other party is known as the lessee, who assumes the role of the taking or accepting party. Furthermore, both contracting parties must possess the necessary eligibility and legal status to enter into the contract. They should be of sound mind, adults (meeting the age requirement stipulated by Shari'ah), and free from enslavement. The parties must not be prohibited from managing their own properties, meaning they should not be declared bankrupt or deemed prodigal. Consequently, any contract involving an immature[2] child or an individual lacking mental capacity would not be considered valid to enter the contract, as stated by Prophet (SAW), which has been narrated by Ali Ibn Abi Talib and cited by al-Nasa'i (1991):

رفع القلم عن ثلاث عن النائم حتى يستيقظ، وعن الصبي حتى يبلغ، وعن المجنون حتى يعقل أو يفق

Three are free from obligations of Shari'ah, the sleeping person until he wakes up, the child until his adulthood, the insane until his sense is back.

However, it is important to note that the contract can be valid if it is entered into by a legal representative or guardian (*wali*) on behalf of a child. Additionally, it is crucial that both parties willingly and voluntarily agree to enter into the contract. If any party or parties are forced by the other, the contract cannot be executed in line with Shari'ah. This is because the leasing contract, being a business agreement, necessitates the mutual agreement of all contracting parties in accordance with the principles outlined in the Qur'an 4:29 "o you who have believed, do not consume one another's wealth unjustly but only [in lawful] business by mutual consent" and the hadith where Prophet (SAW) said, "verily, the contract of sale based on mutual consent" (Ibn Majah, n.d.).

Similarly, to carry out a fair and lawful *ijarah* transaction, there are certain conditions to be retained by both parties. So, the lessor, in the *ijarah* contract, must comply with the following stipulations.

i. Before entering into the *ijarah* contract, the lessor is required to possess complete authority over the utilisation and legal right of the leased asset (Khafif, n.d.).

[2] Most of scholars are agree that the child who is matured and can compare between good and bad is allowed to execute any transactional contract.

ii. The owner (lessor) is obliged to deliver the leased asset to the tenant at the agreed-upon time (Abdullah, 2005), yet the possession of the leased property and its legal title will remain under the ownership of the lessor. However, it is important to note that items that cannot be used without being consumed are not eligible for leasing. Therefore, objects such as money, perishable food items, fuel, and ammunition cannot be leased, as their use necessitates consumption. If such items are mistakenly leased, the transaction would be considered a loan, subject to the rules pertaining to loans. Any rental charges imposed on such an invalid lease would be regarded as interest charged on the loan (Usmani, 2001).
iii. The owner is responsible for providing all essential items that can be utilised by the lessee (Abdullah, 2005).
iv. During the rental period, the owner is responsible for maintaining the property in its usual condition, ensuring that it generates the intended benefit for which the lessee is paying rent. On the other hand, the owner assumes all liabilities associated with ownership, including government taxes, management fees, and insurance. As stated by Al-Rajihi Bank (n.d.), the lessor also bears most liabilities related to the leased object, such as damages, replacement costs of durable parts, and basic maintenance expenses. The lessor can authorise the lessee to undertake these liabilities, but the costs must still be borne by the lessor.
v. Throughout the lease period, the leased asset remains the responsibility and risk of the lessor. This means that any harm or loss resulting from factors beyond the control of the lessee will be borne by the lessor (Usmani, 2001).
vi. The lessor is not permitted to unilaterally increase the rent, and any agreement attempting to do so is considered invalid (Usmani, 2001).

The lessee must fulfil the following conditions when entering into the *ijarah* contract (Abdullah, 2005):

i. The lessee is entrusted as a trustee to the lessor in utilising the property.
ii. The lessee is responsible for maintaining the property in its usual condition and ensuring it is not used in a harmful or unlawful manner.

iii. The lessee is obligated to cover the customary maintenance costs associated with the property's use, as well as utility bills such as electricity and water expenses. If the lessee rents a car, for example, he is responsible for fuel and engine oil expenses. Essentially, any liabilities arising from the use of the property are to be borne by the lessee too.
iv. The lessee is granted exclusive permission to use the property for the designated purpose as stated in the agreement. For example, if the property is rented solely for personal use as specified in the agreement, the lessee is not allowed to convert it into a shop or any other purpose not mentioned in the agreement. In such cases, the lessee is obligated to seek prior permission from the lessor.
v. The lessee bears the responsibility to compensate the lessor for any harm or damage caused to the leased asset due to misuse or negligence on the part of the lessee (Usmani, 2001).

b. **The *Sigah* or (*Ijab* and (*Qabul*) in *Ijarah* Contract**

Muslim jurists have frequently uttered their judgement regarding the underlying issues of offer and acceptance in the *ijarah* contract. According to their viewpoints, the following conditions are necessary for the offer and acceptance to justify the contract as valid:

i. The offer must be made by the lessor (or on their behalf), and the acceptance must come from the lessee (or on his behalf). However, scholars like Hanafis permit the offer and acceptance to be initiated by either the lessor or the lessee (Nizam, 2000).
ii. The expression of the offer and acceptance should be clear, demonstrating the intention of the contracting parties (Kamali, 2007).
iii. The offer and acceptance can be communicated through written, symbolic, or oral means, signifying the execution of the lease contract (Abdullah, 2005).
iv. The duration of the lease contract should be explicitly stated and determined (Usmani, 2001) during the offer and acceptance.
v. The lease period officially begins from the date on which the leased asset is delivered to the lessee, irrespective of whether the lessee has commenced using it or not (Hama, 2007; Usmani, 2001).

vi. If the leased asset becomes unusable for its intended purpose and cannot be repaired, the lease contract will terminate on the day the damage occurs. However, if the loss/damage is due to the misuse or negligence of the lessee, they are liable to compensate the lessor for the diminished value of the asset prior to the loss (Usmani, 2001).
vii. The offer and acceptance should be unequivocal and expressed in clear and decisive language. They should not be contingent upon any conditions, and they must be formulated in the present or past tense rather than the future tense or imperative form. However, the acceptance must align with the terms of the offer. Moreover, both the offer and acceptance must be made during the same gathering, known as the "*majlis al-'aqd*" (Fatma, n.d.).

c. **The Subject Matter of the Contract, the Rent (*'Ujrah*) and Usufruct (*Manfa'ah*)**

The fundamental objectives of the *ijarah* contract are rent (*'ujrah*) and usufruct (*manfa'ah*). Scholars have emphasised the importance of specific conditions related to both rent and usufruct to ensure that the contract is executed fairly and eliminates any potential issues in the future. The following conditions are related to the rent:

i. It is essential to specify in the contract whether the rent will be fixed or subject to variation throughout the entire duration of the *ijarah* contract. This clarification is important because the rental rate can either remain constant or be tied to a mutually agreed variable for a specified period (Usmani, 2001).
ii. The currency name must be specified when stating an amount, such as Ringgit Malaysia (MYR) or US Dollars (USD) and must be in absolute amount. Merely stating a number, like five hundred (500), without mentioning the currency is not sufficient to finalise the contract (Fatma, n.d.).
iii. The BNM Shari'ah regulatory, during its 35th meeting held on 22 May 2003 and the 38th meeting held on 28 August 2003, established that there should be an option for renewal based on prevailing market fluctuations. If the contract is renewed, the specific timing for the action and the tentative percentage of rent increase or decrease must be clearly stated.

iv. The agreement must clearly state the intervals of payment, whether they are on a daily, weekly, or monthly basis. Additionally, the methods of payment, such as cash, banking cheques, or banking transfers, should be explicitly mentioned. In the absence of specified methods, local customs relating to payment will be considered as per BNM 35th meeting's resolution held on 22 May 2003 and the 38th meeting held on 28 August 2003.

v. Usufruct (*manfa'ah*) can only be assumable when the underlying asset exists. For instance, in the case of renting a house, the house must physically exist for the rental arrangement. If the house does not exist, the leasing contract to that specific house becomes irrelevant. However, in such cases, the *ijarah* contract can be transformed into a forward *ijarah*, where the customer and the Islamic financial institution jointly share rights over the asset under construction through a *musharakah mutanaqisah* contract. The Islamic financial institution then leases its portion of the asset to the customer under the contract of forward *ijarah* (*ijarah mawsufah fi al-dhimmah*), as the asset is still being constructed. During the construction period, the customer pays advanced rent. Once the asset is completed, the customer continues to pay the full rent to enjoy the usufruct of the asset.

vi. The usufruct must adhere to Shari'ah principles and be acknowledged by both parties involved in the contract.

vii. The benefit derived from the leased asset must be fully prepared and ready for delivery to the lessee without any hindrances.

viii. The duration of asset use is limited, and the corpus that generates the usufruct must be tangible property (Qurtubi, 2001). Therefore, items that cannot be used without being consumed, such as money, food, fuel, or ammunition, cannot be leased. Leasing such items would be considered a loan, subject to the rules governing loan transactions. Any rent charged in such an invalid lease would be deemed interest charged on the loan (Usmani, 2001).

ix. The leased asset must be utilised for the specified purpose stated in the contract. However, it is permissible to lease the asset for any other customary usage that is not prohibited by Shari'ah.

x. The subject matter of the lease must possess the necessary qualifications to provide valuable usufruct. An asset that lacks usufruct is not appropriate for a lease contract. Hence, the *ijarah* contract must be terminated if the leased asset becomes non-functional, loses its usufruct, if the contracting parties fail to comply with the terms and conditions, or if both parties mutually agree to terminate the contract. Precise identification of the leased property is also a necessary component of the contract to be valid (Doyan, 1989).

xi. The period of use must be fixed and agreed upon by both parties. Renewal terms must also be stated clearly and should not be left to the lessor's discretion (Usmani, 2008).
xii. The benefit derived from the property should be in the form of usufruct, emphasising that the benefit obtained is not the physical or material part of the property itself (Fatma, n.d.).

d. Property

The following element in the *ijarah* contract pertains to the property or asset being leased, and it must satisfy the following four essential conditions, as outlined by Fatma (n.d.):

i. The property must be owned by the lessor and be in an appropriate condition and ready for immediate use.
ii. The property must be capable of being delivered to the lessee and clearly identified through its address, description, or specifications.
iii. The property can have a fixed value and should possess qualities and appearance that reflect its full value, and the lessor must have the legal capacity to provide the benefit and grant the lessee permission to use the property.

3.5 *Shari'ah* Standards of *Ijarah*

Despite many Shari'ah standards of *ijarah* that have been developed by several financial regulatory bodies in many jurisdictions, which seem to be similar to the several existing stipulations of *ijarah* which are proposed by classical and contemporary scholars individually what we have seen earlier, yet, the Shari'ah standards in some cases are unique and shaped pertaining to the current financial spectrum that guarantees the transparency of the contracts having many modern features in their contemporary practice. The Accounting and Auditing Organization for Islamic Financial Institutions (AAOIFI) is one of the largely recognised standards-setting organisations whose standards are trailed by many Islamic financial institutions across the world. For the *iajarah* contract AAOIFI sets its Shari'ah Standard No. (9). Some of its key adoptions are as follows:

3.5.1 *Security Deposit in* Ijarah

In a lease contract, the lessor has the right to request a security deposit from the lessee as a guarantee of fulfilling the lease agreement and to cover any subsequent expenses. However, it is important to note that the lessor is not allowed to regard the security deposit as equivalent to the monthly rent. As mentioned in the standard:

> It is permissible for the institution to require the lease promisor (customer) to pay a sum of money to the institution to guarantee the customer's commitment to accepting a lease on the asset and subsequent obligations, provided no amount is to be deducted from this sum except on proportion to the actual damage suffered by the institution.

On the other hand:

> The amount of money deposited by the customer as security for his commitment can be either held on trust in the custody of the institution in which case the latter cannot invest it, or it may be held on an investment trust basis in which case the customer permits the institution to invest it on the basis of *mudarabah* between the customer and the institution. It is permissible to agree with the customer, upon the execution of the contract of lease, that this amount shall be treated as an advance payment of the instalments of the lease rental.

3.5.2 *Issues of Lease Back to the Lessor Based on Spot Dealing*

The lessee is permitted to sub lease the asset back to the lessor. The rental amount in this sublease contract can be the same, lower, or higher than the original lease. However, both rental payments must be made on a spot basis. Failure to do so could result in the contract being considered *bay' al- 'inah*.[3] As stated in the standard:

> The lessee may lease the asset back to its owner in the first lease period for a rental that is lower, same or higher than what he is paying if the two rentals are paid on a spot basis. However, this is not permissible if it should lead the contract to *'inah* varying the rent of duration. For example, it is not permissible, if the first rental is one hundred *dinars* payable on a spot basis, for the lessee to sublet it to the lessor for one hundred and ten *dinars* payable on a deferred basis or if the first rental is one hundred and ten *dinars* payable on a deferred basis, for the second to be for one hundred *dinars* payable instantly, or if the two rentals are of the same amount, but the payment of the first rental is deferred for one month and the second rental is deferred for two months.

In situations where an asset is co-owned by an institution and its customer, and the customer wishes to lease their portion of the asset, the rental amount will apply only to the customer's proportionate share. No rent will be charged for the share owned by the customer in such cases as adopted in the standard:

> An institution's customer may jointly have an asset that he wishes to lease with the institution, and then he takes lease the institution's share of the asset from the institution. In this case, the rental specified as receivable by the institution should only be in proportion to its share in the ownership of the asset, since the lessee is a co-owner of the asset and therefore has to pay rent only on the share that he does not own.

3.5.3 *Issues While Customer Acts as an Agent in the* Ijarah *Contract*

In the modern practice of the *ijarah* contract, it is permissible for an institution to appoint its customer as an agent to identify and find an asset that the customer intends to lease. However, in this case, it is important to establish a fixed description and price for the asset. As said in the standard:

[3] In this contract, an amount of *Shari'ah*-compliant asset will be sold by a financier to the receiving financial institution at X price on credit. Subsequently, the receiving financial institution will sell back it to the financier on cash basis at Y price. The X price is higher than the Y price. Both sales contracts are executed separately.

> an institution may appoint one of its customers to act as an agent in acquiring an asset on its behalf that is desired by that customer such as equipment or machinery whose description and price are fixed with a view to the institution's leasing such asset or assets to the customer after it has acquired their ownership through either actual or constructive possession.

3.5.4 Issues Related to the Advance Rental and Asset Delivery

In the event of a possible delay in delivering the asset to the lessee due to any unforeseen circumstances or incidents involving the lessor, no rent will be charged to the lessee. Additionally, no rent will be due for the period between the execution of the contract and the actual delivery of the asset. The rental amount must be adjusted accordingly, taking into account the deduction for the period of delay.

> If the lessor fails to deliver the asset to the lessee on the date specified in the *ijarah* contract, no rental is due for the period between the contract date and the date of actual delivery, and the rental should be reduced accordingly unless it is agreed that the lease be extended by an equivalent period after its original expiry date.

On the other hand, the lessee has the option to make full payment of the rental amount for a specified period in advance. In such a case, the advanced rental payment made by the lessee is considered an advance payment. However, if the contract cannot be implemented due to any reasons attributable to the lessee, the lessor has the right to retain the advance rental amount with him.

> *'Urbun* may be taken in respect of the lease at the execution of the contract of lease and this is treated as an advance payment of the rental. If the *ijarah* contract is not executed for a reason attributable to the lessee, the lessor may retain the '*urbun*'.

The *ijarah* contract also takes into consideration the possibility of dividing the total rental payment into two parts, subject to an agreement between the lessor and the lessee. One part of the rental payment is made directly to the lessor, while the other part can be retained by the lessee with the lessor's approval. This retained portion of the rental serves to cover significant expenses such as insurance and essential maintenance. In this case, the second part of the rental payment is treated as an advance payment to the lessee by the lessor, recorded on account.

3.5.5 *Multiple* Ijarah *Agreement*

The lessor is not permitted to lease the property to a lessee for a specific duration if the property is already leased to another lessee for the same duration.

> if the lessor signs an *ijarah* contract for a particular asset for a specified period, he cannot sign another *ijarah* contract with another lessee for the duration of the existing *ijarah* period or for any remaining period thereof.

However, the lessor is allowed to lease the asset to multiple lessees for different periods and with different rental amounts as long as it is for a specific right to use the asset. Each lessee can enjoy the benefits of the asset during their assigned time period, following the applicable rules. As cited in the standard.

> An *ijarah* contract may be signed with several lessees being entitled to the same specified usufruct of a particular asset and duration of rent, without specifying a particular period for a particular person. In this case, each lessee may benefit from the property during the time assigned to him in accordance with specified rules.

When a tenant enters into a lease contract, they gain the right to possess and use the rented property. Generally, as the lawful occupant, the tenant has the option to sub lease the property to another tenant. However, there is a condition that the sub-tenant's use of the property should not exceed the usage of the current tenant. The tenant's privilege to sub lease is subject to the terms specified in the contract. Therefore, if subleasing is prohibited, the tenant must comply with the conditions regarding subleasing.

> The lessee may invite co-lessee to share with him in the usufruct to which he has a right, by assigning them shares in the usufruct before entering into a sub-lease. In this case, they become his shares in the usufruct of the leased property. If the property is sub-leased, each co-share is entitled to a share in the sub-lease rental pro rata to his share in the usufruct.

3.5.6 *Usage Rules of the Asset*

The property's purposes of use must align with Shari'ah principles. Thus, if any usage of the property contradicts Shari'ah principles, the contract would be deemed invalid due to this impediment.

> The benefit from an *ijarah* must be lawful in Shari'ah.

As an example, if a property is leased to a company engaged in interest-based transactions or to a shopkeeper who sells and stores prohibited items such as pork, wine, and alcoholic beverages that are harmful to human beings, it would be considered a violation of Shari'ah principles. In such cases, the leasing contract would be deemed invalid.

3.6 *IJARAH* AS A MODE OF FINANCING AND ITS UNDERLYING HINDRANCES

Although *ijarah* remains a prominent contract in contemporary transactional practices, it still encounters various potential challenges. According to Usmani (2008):

> some requirements of Shari'ah are often overlooked.

In the real practice of *ijarah* transactions, a potential issue arises when an unforeseen event leads to damage to the asset, yet the lessee remains obligated to pay rent. This scenario contradicts the principle that the lessor bears the responsibility of asset ownership and provides its benefits to the lessee. Challenges in *ijarah* within the context of Islamic finance extend beyond Shari'ah non-compliance and encompass drawbacks in terms of cost and consumer protection when compared to conventional finance. El-Gamal (2006) highlights certain challenges associated with *ijarah*. One such challenge is the additional cost borne by banks or financiers in *ijarah* due to the need to maintain a substantial level of property ownership throughout the lease term, in contrast to the financial leases utilised in conventional finance. Another issue arises in *ijarah*, where customers may encounter the risk of losing the property if the financier faces legal action and is declared bankrupt, even if the customer has already made considerable payments towards the property price (e.g. 90%). To address this issue, a potential solution, despite entailing extra expenses, is the establishment of "bankruptcy-remote" special-purpose entities. These entities would hold the property title and serve as parties involved in agreements concerning maintenance and insurance obligations (el-Gamal, 2006).

According to Ahmad (2010), in certain jurisdictions, the legal position of an *ijarah wa iqtina'*, the lessee (house purchase borrower), is comparatively weaker when compared to a conventional mortgage payer. The *ijarah wa iqtina'* lessor (lender) retains the authority to evict the borrower in case of payment defaults since the borrower is considered a tenant rather than an owner. Conversely, a conventional mortgage borrower enjoys the security of tenure and is protected against eviction. In the event of foreclosure, the conventional mortgage lender is legally obligated to obtain the best possible price for the property and provide a comprehensive account of the resale to the foreclosed borrower. However, in an *ijarah wa iqtina'* contract, the lessor is not bound by any such obligation to the lessee. Khan (2013) and Visser (2009) raise concerns regarding the relatively weaker customer protection provided by *ijarah* in comparison to conventional interest-bearing loans. They present an illustrative example of a car purchase to emphasise their point. In a conventional bank, if an individual obtains a five-year interest-bearing loan to buy a car, they have the option to sell the car and repay the loan after two years if they deem it economically unfavourable. However, such flexibility is absent in *ijarah* finance, as premature termination is not allowed.

Nonetheless, the *ijarah* contract holds significant importance as a crucial element within the Islamic banking and finance system, presenting a distinct alternative to conventional interest-based lending. It is deeply rooted in the principles of justice, equity, and fairness, offering a morally and ethically sound approach to financing assets for individuals who strive to harmonise their financial practices with their religious convictions.

Ijarah serves as a means for customers to access financing for assets like homes or cars while adhering to the principles of Islamic finance that prohibit the payment of interest, deemed usury. This financing structure revolves around the concept of leasing the asset to the customer, with the intention of transferring ownership at the end of a specified period. By adopting this structure, both the lender and the borrower partake in the risks and benefits associated with the underlying asset, fostering a more equitable relationship compared to conventional lending practices.

Although criticisms regarding customer protection in *ijarah* compared to conventional loans exist, it is essential to contextualise these criticisms within the framework of comparison to interest-based systems. The Islamic finance industry operates on a distinct set of values and principles that prioritise the avoidance of exploitation and the advancement of social justice. Consequently, evaluating *ijarah* solely through the lens of conventional finance may not fully capture its intended objectives and the underlying ethical considerations.

To summarise, the *ijarah* contract serves as a valuable instrument for individuals seeking financing in adherence to Islamic finance principles. It offers a means for customers to obtain financing while upholding their religious beliefs and fosters a more equitable relationship between lenders and borrowers. The increasing growth and popularity of *ijarah* within the Islamic banking and finance industry underscore its significance and role in providing a morally and ethically aligned alternative to conventional lending practices.

3.7 Application of the Above Using an Example Case Study

A financial institution, XYZ Bank, owns a commercial property and wishes to lease it to a business entity, ABC Corporation, for a specified period. Both parties engage in negotiations and agree to enter into an *ijarah* contract. Let us analyse the compliance of this contract with the essential elements of an *ijarah* contract.

- Contracting Parties: The lessor is XYZ Bank, a reputable financial institution, and the lessee is ABC Corporation, a legally recognised business entity. Both parties fulfil the necessary conditions for entering into the contract. They are sound-minded, have reached the age of puberty and maturity, and are not declared bankrupt or prodigal. There is no coercion involved in the contract.
- Property or Asset: The property, a commercial building, is owned by XYZ Bank, satisfying the first condition. It is ready for use and can be delivered to the lessee as per the second and third conditions. The property is properly specified by its address, description, and specification, fulfilling the fourth condition.
- Benefit (Use or Usufruct): The benefit derived from the property, i.e. the use or usufruct, complies with Shari'ah principles. It is

permissible to use the property for the intended commercial activities, adhering to Shari'ah guidelines. The lessor, XYZ Bank, has the legal capacity to provide the benefit and allow the lessee, ABC Corporation, to utilise the property. The benefit is specified, and it represents the right to use the property without transferring its ownership.

- Rental: The rental amount specified in the contract is denoted in a known currency, such as Ringgit Malaysia (MYR) or US Dollars (USD), satisfying the first condition. The rental amount is defined explicitly, without ambiguity, fulfilling the second condition. It is an absolute amount payable by the lessee to the lessor for the use of the leased property.
- Contract: The offer and acceptance between XYZ Bank and ABC Corporation are absolute and conveyed in definite and decisive language. The contract does not contain any conditional clauses, future tense, or imperative statements. The acceptance aligns with the offer, ensuring mutual agreement. The offer and acceptance were made at the same meeting (*majlis al-ʿaqd*), adhering to the third condition.

Based on the analysis of the *ijarah* contract between XYZ Bank and ABC Corporation, it can be concluded that the contract complies with the essential elements and conditions required by Shari'ah principles. The contracting parties fulfil the necessary criteria, the property meets the required conditions, the benefit adheres to Shari'ah guidelines, the rental is appropriately specified, and the contract itself aligns with Shari'ah requirements.

Problems and Solutions for the Example Case Study

Problem 1: Lack of Detailed Maintenance Cost Provision
In the case study, it is mentioned that the responsibility for maintenance costs is not clearly addressed in the *ijarah* contract. This ambiguity may lead to disputes between the lessor and lessee regarding the payment of maintenance expenses.

Solution:
To address this issue, XYZ Bank and ABC Corporation should include a specific provision in the contract outlining the responsibility for

maintenance costs. They can either agree that the lessor (XYZ Bank) will bear all maintenance expenses or negotiate a shared responsibility based on mutually agreed terms. Clearly defining the maintenance cost provisions in the contract will help avoid future conflicts.

Problem 2: Currency Ambiguity in Rental Amount
The case study mentions that the rental amount is specified, but the currency is not clearly mentioned. This lack of currency clarification can create confusion and ambiguity regarding the payment terms.

Solution:
To resolve this problem, XYZ Bank and ABC Corporation should explicitly state the currency in which the rental amount is denoted. They can specify whether the rental is in Ringgit Malaysia (MYR) or any other agreed-upon currency, ensuring clarity and avoiding any misunderstandings regarding the payment terms.

Problem 3: Inadequate Documentation of Offer and Acceptance
The case study does not provide information on how the offer and acceptance were documented during the contract negotiation process. Without proper documentation, there may be challenges in proving the agreement and enforcing the terms in case of any disputes.

Solution:
XYZ Bank and ABC Corporation should ensure that the offer and acceptance are documented appropriately. They can prepare a written agreement or contract that clearly outlines the terms and conditions agreed upon by both parties. This documentation will serve as evidence of the mutual agreement and help resolve any potential disagreements in the future.

Problem 4: Incomplete Contingency Plan
The case study does not mention any provisions or contingencies in case of unexpected events or breaches of contract. This lack of a contingency plan can leave both parties vulnerable to unforeseen circumstances.

Solution:
XYZ Bank and ABC Corporation should include clauses in the contract that address contingencies and provide solutions for situations

such as default, force majeure events, or breaches of contract. By incorporating contingency provisions, both parties can better protect their interests and have a clear course of action in case of unexpected events.

Chapter Review Questions

1. What is the literal meaning of *ijarah*?
   a. Sale of property
   b. Possessing a property for consideration
   c. Leasing of property
   d. Transfer of ownership
2. Which school of jurisprudence defines *ijarah* as a contract for the use of the usufruct for a counter value or price?
   a. Hanafi
   b. Shafi'i
   c. Maliki
   d. Hanbali
3. According to AAOIFI Shari'ah Standard No. (9) what is the definition of *ijarah*?
   a. Transfer of ownership for a specified period
   b. Lease of property for a specified period in return for a specified consideration
   c. Sale of a usufruct for a known counter value
   d. Hiring of services for a determined wage
4. From the Islamic banking perspective, what happens to the property in an *ijarah* contract?
   a. It is sold to the lessee
   b. It remains unutilised for a long period
   c. It is owned by the bank or financial institution
   d. It is transferred to the lessor
5. What is another term for *ijarah* mawsufah fi al-dhimmah?
   a. Forward *ijarah*
   b. Financial *ijarah*
   c. Operating *ijarah*
   d. Hybrid *ijarah*
6. Which type of *ijarah* involves the transfer of usufruct stipulated by the qualities of salam?
   a. *Ijarah ʿain*

   b. *Ijarah ʿamal*
   c. *Ijarah mawsufah fi al-dhimmah*
   d. Operating *ijarah*
7. What does *ijarah* ʿain refer to?
   a. Leasing the services of a person
   b. Leasing tangible assets or goods
   c. Leasing assets under construction
   d. Leasing assets for a specified period
8. What are the conditions for the benefit (use or usufruct) in the *ijarah* contract?
   a. Must be permissible by Shari'ah
   b. Must be the material part of the property
   c. Must be specified in quantity and quality
   d. Must be owned by the lessee
9. What are the necessary conditions for the property or asset in the *ijarah* contract?
   a. Must be owned by the lessee
   b. Must be specified by address, description, or specification
   c. Must be ready for use
   d. Must be in a known currency
10. What are the necessary conditions for the contracting parties in the *ijarah* contract?
    a. Must be of legal age and sound mind
    b. Must not be declared bankrupt or prodigal
    c. Must not be coerced into the contract
    d. All of the above

Answers

1. b
2. a
3. b
4. c
5. a
6. c
7. b
8. a
9. b
10. d

References

Abdullah, N. I. (2005). *Islamic Hire-Purchase in Malaysian Financial Institutions: A Comparative Analytical Book*. Loughborough University.

Abu Ghuddah, Abd al-Sattar. (2007). Al-tatbiqat al-amaliyyah li al-ijarah al-mawsufah fi al- dhimmah. Paper presented *at the 28th al-Barakah Symposium on Islamic Economics*. Jeddah.

Abu Ghuddah, Abd al-Sattar. (1998). *Ijarah*. al-Barakah Banking Group.

Ahmad, A. U. F. (2010). *Theory and Practice of Modern Islamic Finance: The Case Study from Australia*. Brown Walker Press.

Al-Dasuqi, Mohammad Ibn Ahmad Ibn Arafa. (1996). *Hashiyyah al-Dasuqi ala al-Sharh al-Kabir* (Vol. 4). Dar al-Kutub al-'Ilmiyyah.

Al-Kasani, A. B. Ibn Muhamad. (1998). *Bada'i' al Sana'i fi Tartib al-Shara'i'* (Vol. 4). Dar Ihya al-Turath al-Arabi.

Al-Nasa'i, A. Ibn Shuayib. (1991). *Sunan al- Nasa'i al-Kubra* (Vol. 3). Dar al-Kutub al-'Ilmiyyah.

Al-Rajihi Bank. (n.d.). *The Resolution of the Shariah Board of Al-Rajihi Banking and Investment Corporation*. Al-Rajihi Bank.

Al-Sarakhsi, M. Ibn Ahmad. (2013). *Al-Mabsut* (Vol. 5). Dar al-Nawadir.

Al-Shiribini, M. Ibn Muhammad al-Khatib. (2000). *Mughni al-Muhtaj ila Ma'rifat Maani Alfaz al-Minhaj* (Vol. 3). Dar al-kutub al-'llmiyyah.

BNM. (2010). *Shariah Resolutions in Islamic Finance, Part 1* (2nd ed.). Bank Negara Malaysia.

Doyan, Ibrahim Ibn M. Ibn Salim. (1989). *Manar al-Sabil* (7th ed., Vol. 1). al-Maktab al-Islami.

El-Gamal, M. A. (2006). *Islamic Finance: Law, Economics, and Practice*. Cambridge University Press.

Fatma, A. (n.d). *Meaning of ijarah*. https://www.academia.edu/3583126/meaning_of_ijarah. Accessed 29 December 2022.

Hama, A. O. (2007). *Islamic Hire-Purchase Transaction*. International Islamic University Malaysia.

Ibn Majah. (2007). *Sunan Ibn Majah* (Vol. 2). Dar al-salam. Riyad.

Ibn Majah (n.d.). *Sunan Ibu Majah* (Vol. 2). Dar al-Fikr.

Islamic Bankers Resource Centre. (n.d.). *Discussions on Islamic Banking*. https://islamicbankers.me/islamic-banking-islamic-contracts/credit-cards-ujrah/. Accessed 4 June 2023.

Kamali, M. H. (2007). A *Shariah* Analysis of Issues in Islamic Leasing. *J.KAU: Islamic Econ, 20*(1), 3–22.

Khafif. A. (n.d). *Ahkam al-Mu'amalat al-Shar'iyyah*. Bank al-Barakah.

Khan, M. A. (2013). *What Is Wrong with Islamic Economics? Analysing the Present State and Future Agenda*. Edward Elgar Publishing.

Muhammad, M. Z., & Chong, R. (2007). The Contract of bay'Al-Salam and Istisna'in Islamic Commercial Law: A Comparative Analysis. *Labuan e-Journal of Muamalat and Society (LJMS)*, *1*, 21–28.

Nizam, Al-Sheikh. (2000). *Al-Fatawa al-Hindiyyah* (Vol. 4). Dar al-Kutub al-'llmiyyah.

Qurtubi, M. Ibn Ahmad Ibn Rushd. (2001). *Bidayat al-Mujtahid wa Nihayat al-Muqtasid*. Dar al-Kutub al-'Ilmiyyah.

Sarakhsi, M. Ibn Ahmad. (2000). *Al-Mabsut* (Vol. 8). Dar al-Fikr.

Shafi'i, M. Ibn Idris. (2000). *Kitab al-'Umm* (1st ed., Vol. 2). Dar Ihya al-Turath al-Arabi.

Slide Share. (2011). *Al-Ijarah*. http://www.slideshare.net/emkay84/isb540-ijarah. Accessed 22 December 2022.

Usmani, M. T. (2001). *An Introduction to Islamic Finance*. Brill.

Usmani, M. T. (2008). *An Introduction to Islamic Finance*. Idarah Isha'at-E-Diniyyat (P) Ltd.

Visser, H. (2009). *Islamic Finance: Principles and Practice*. Edward Elgar.

CHAPTER 4

Sale: The Final Contract in HPSM

Abstract The role of the sale contract within HPSM is vital, serving as the conclusive and pivotal element that facilitates lawful economic transactions in adherence to Islamic law. This chapter intricately explores the essential aspects, principles, and conditions inherent in the sale contract within Islamic finance. It sheds light on the multifaceted dimensions governing its execution—legal, ethical, and economic. Understanding the complexities of the sale contract empowers individuals and businesses to ensure Shari'ah compliance, fostering ethical and equitable transactions that uphold justice and mutual benefit. This chapter provides insights into the philosophical underpinnings of sales in Islamic finance, enabling readers to navigate modern economic complexities while adhering to Islamic teachings. Furthermore, the chapter serves as a comprehensive guide to the diverse types of sale contracts within HPSM. By delving into the intricacies of this vital contract, readers gain a deeper understanding of the ethical and legal foundations that form the bedrock of commercial activities in the realm of Islamic banking and finance.

Keyword Sale · *Bay'* · Contract · *'uqud* · *'Aqd*

M. K. Hassan et al., *Hire Purchase Under Shirkah al-Milk (HPSM) in Islamic Banking and Finance*,
https://doi.org/10.1007/978-3-031-50105-0_4

Preview

The concept of sale holds great significance in the realm of Islamic finance and transactions. In HPSM, the sale is recognised as the final essential contract that plays a pivotal role in facilitating lawful economic activities. It is through the mechanism of sale that individuals and businesses engage in the exchange of goods and services, adhering to the principles and guidelines prescribed by Islamic law.

This chapter explores the fundamental aspects, principles, and conditions associated with the sale contract within the context of Islamic finance. It delves into the intricate details of this essential contract, shedding light on the legal, ethical, and economic dimensions that govern its execution.

By understanding the intricacies of the sale contract in HPSM, individuals and businesses can ensure compliance with *Shari'ah* principles, fostering a system of fair and ethical transactions that promote justice and mutual benefit. Through the study of this chapter, readers gain valuable insights into the underlying philosophy of sale in Islamic finance, enabling them to navigate the complexities of modern economic transactions within the bounds of Islamic teachings.

The chapter also serves as a comprehensive guide types of sale contracts within the framework of HPSM. By delving into the nuances of this essential contract, readers develop a deeper appreciation for the ethical and legal foundations that underpin commercial activities in the Islamic banking and finance spectrums.

4.1 Understanding of Sale (*Bay'*)

Sale is the core contract among all contracts, both in conventional and Islamic spectrums, that is practised in the banking and finance industry. Especially this is the foremost contract in the Islamic commercial domain which is incorporated in nearly every contract in economic activities (Hasan, 2007) because of its significance compared to other contracts. Hence, this is vital to clarify the definition and legitimacy of the sales contract from a Shari'ah perspective.

The term "sale" is derived from the Arabic word "*bay'*", which encompasses both the concepts of buying and selling. It can be described as the act of swapping one commodity for another commodity, commonly known as barter trading, or the transaction involving the

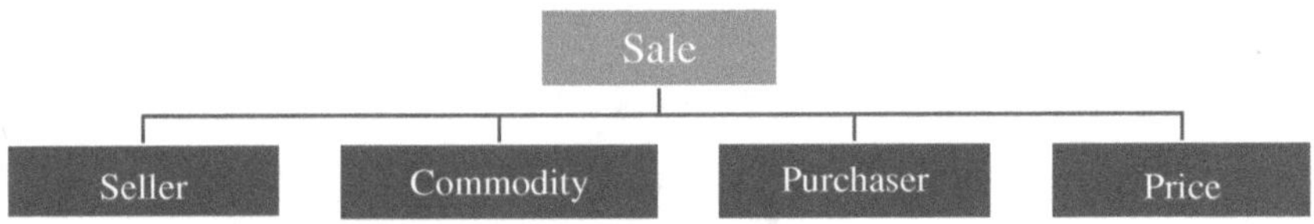

Fig. 4.1 Sale contract execution process (*Source* Author's own)

exchange of a commodity for money (typical sale) or money for money (*sarf*) (Abdullah, 2005). In essence, a sale is a mutual agreement to exchange one item for another (al-Zuhayli, 2003). According to the Hanafi school, a sale entails the exchange of a possessed commodity for another in a prescribed manner. Conversely, according to the Shafi'i school, a sale is viewed as the transfer of ownership and possession of an owned commodity to a new owner in conjunction with the exchange for another commodity (al-Zuhayli, 2003).

The notion of a sale can also be comprehended as a contractual agreement between two parties involving the exchange of properties, taking into account the ownership of both the price and the commodity involved (Moustafa, 2001). This entails a transfer of ownership from the seller to the buyer, whereby the seller's property, in the form of a commodity, is transferred to the buyer, and in exchange, the buyer's property, which can be in the form of cash or goods, is transferred to the seller. Qurtubi describes the nature of sale as the exchange of two properties, which can be tangible assets, an exchange of a tangible asset for a corresponding liability, or an exchange of liabilities. These exchanges can be immediate or delayed. A sale contract comprises four fundamental elements: the seller (*al baa'i*), the purchaser (*al-mubta'*), the price (*al-thaman*), and the valued commodity (*al-muthamman*) (Hasan, 2007). Figure 4.1 represents the elements of a sale contract.

4.2 Authenticity of Sale Contract

When *bay'* or sale contracts are implemented according to their rules and in compliance with Shari'ah, they are considered legal and permitted. The Qur'an supports the legitimacy of such contracts and explicitly approves them in multiple verses. Instances are verse no. 275 and 282 of Surah al-Baqarah and verse no. 29 of Surah al-Nisa:

وَأَحَلَّ اللَّـهُ الْبَيْعَ وَحَرَّمَ الرِّبَا

Allah has allowed trading and forbidden usury.

Undoubtedly, this verse is the fundamental basis that permits the *bay'* or sale unanimously; however, business transactions that involve any form of *riba* (interest or usury) are not permitted and are, in fact, prohibited according to Islamic teachings. *Riba* is explicitly condemned in the Qur'an, and any business that includes elements of *riba* is considered impermissible in Shari'ah.

Likewise Allah (SWT) says:

أَيُّهَا الَّذِينَ آمَنُوا إِذَا تَدَايَنتُم بِدَيْنٍ إِلَىٰ أَجَلٍ مُّسَمًّى فَاكْتُبُوهُ ۚ وَلْيَكْتُب بَّيْنَكُمْ كَاتِبٌ بِالْعَدْلِ

O you, who believe! When you contract a debt for a fixed period, write it down. Let a scribe write it down in justice between you.

This verse in the Qur'an not only permits sale transactions but also provides guidelines for conducting them. If the transaction involves deferred payment, it emphasises the importance of documenting it through a written contract as evidence. These conditions outlined in the verse aim to ensure that the transaction is fair and suitable for all parties involved while also minimising the potential for disputes, fraud, and conflicts in the future.

In another verse He (SWT) instructs:

يَا أَيُّهَا الَّذِينَ آمَنُوا لَا تَأْكُلُوا أَمْوَالَكُم بَيْنَكُم بِالْبَاطِلِ إِلَّا أَن تَكُونَ تِجَارَةً عَن تَرَاضٍ مِّنكُم

O you who have believed! do not consume one another's wealth unjustly but only [in lawful] business by mutual consent.

The verse allows for the generation of profits through sale transactions, but it emphasises that these profits must be acquired through lawful means. This implies that the sale must be conducted in a proper manner, adhering to the guidelines and principles of Shari'ah. Additionally, any conditions or stipulations attached to the sale contract must be mutually agreed upon by all parties involved.

In contrast, many hadiths from Prophet (SAW) indicate the legal authorisation of a sale contract. Moreover, He, the Prophet (SAW), was born in a place and time where several sales transactions were in practice, and he has not been reluctant into them except for usury-based transactions; however, the Prophet (SAW) himself has been engaged in several sale transactions. As a principle of a business, He utters:

إنما البيع عن تراض

Verily, the contract of sale based on mutual consent. (Ibn Majah, n.d.)

This hadith specifically permits a sale contract; however, it stipulates mutual consent of all parties who are involved in the sale contract.

Prophet (SAW) says in another hadith:

التاجر الصدوق الأمين المسلم مع الشهداء يوم القيامة

A trustworthy and honest Muslim trader (or whoever involves in trade) will be positioned amongst the martyrs on the day of judgement. (Daruqutni, 1966)

In this hadith, Prophet (SAW) encourages people to conduct businesses which are naturally cannot be materialised without a sale contract. Thus, this hadith also is another piece of evidence that strengthens the legitimacy of a sale contract.

He (SAW) says in another hadith:

لا تبع ما ليس عندك

Do not sale anything you do not possess. (Abadi, 2001; Mubarakpuri, 2001)

In this saying, Prophet (SAW) prohibits a person from being engaged in such a sale transaction which he does not possess; however, if a person possesses the subject matter, he is allowed to make a sale transaction if the transaction does not abuse the Shari'ah stipulations.

Muslim jurists unanimously agree that a sale transaction is permissible when all conditions are met, and both parties adhere to the terms of the sale contract. They emphasise that a lawful sale should avoid elements of interest (*riba*), uncertainty (*gharar*), and ignorance (*jahalah*), as these can lead to uncertainty and disputes (Abdullah, 2005). Scholars, moreover, assert that the permissibility of sale allows individuals to fulfil their own needs while cooperating with others who are also striving to meet their own needs. Consequently, there is no general prohibition on sales, according to them. Imam Al-Shafi'i specifically stated that the general rule for all sales is permissible as long as they are executed with the consent of both parties, except for what has been explicitly forbidden in the Qur'an and by the Prophet Muhammad (SAW) (al-Zuhayli, 2003).

4.3 Sale Contracts and Their Nature

The term "contract" or "'*aqd*" in Arabic carries the meaning of "to tie", "to bind", or "to combine". In a general sense, it refers to an agreement between two parties that is intended to have legally enforceable consequences. Technically, a contract can be defined as an obligation that connects an offer and acceptance, leading to legal effects on the subject matter of the contract. In Islamic law, the concept of "*'aqd*" encompasses both unilateral and bilateral contracts. Unilateral contracts are those in which a single party makes a promise or agreement without requiring consent from the recipient party. Such contracts often involve transactions of a gratuitous nature, where one party acts out of goodwill. Examples of unilateral contracts include gift (*hibah*), set-off debt (*ibra'*), will (*wasiyyah*), endowment (waqf), and loan (*qard*). On the other hand, bilateral contracts involve agreements made by two parties, with the requirement of consent from both sides. Bilateral contracts are commonly found in various Islamic commercial transactions. Examples of bilateral contracts include partnership (*shirkah*), exchange contracts (*'uqud al-mu'awadat*), security contracts (*'uqud al-tawthiqat*), and others. In these contracts, both parties willingly enter into the agreement and assume certain rights and obligations. Overall, the concept of "'*aqd*" encompasses a wide range of contracts in Islamic law, reflecting the different types of agreements and transactions that can occur between parties.

In order to ensure clarity and easy reference, the Shari'ah encourages the occurrence of contracts in writing form, especially in cases where disputes may arise. This written documentation plays a crucial role in enforcing the contract according to its terms and conditions. Verse no. 2: 282 of the Qur'an emphasises the importance of recording transactions involving future obligations within a specified timeframe and highlights the responsibility of parties to honour their commitments as agreed upon in the contract.

The primary contract of exchange in Islamic commercial law is the sale contract. It typically involves the exchange of commodities, the exchange of a commodity for money, or the exchange of money for money. These types of contracts are susceptible to risks such as *riba* (usury), *gharar* (uncertainty), exploitation, fraud, and risk. Islamic principles of law governing these transactions prioritise the principles of equality between the exchanged items and the immediate and simultaneous delivery or transfer of the items. This focus on equality and prompt transfer aims to mitigate the presence of *riba*.

In trading, contracts must not contain elements of *gharar* (uncertainty) or *jahalah* (lack of clarity). Contracts with such elements are considered void or voidable based on the degree of *gharar* or *jahalah* present. However, certain contracts in Islamic law are exempt from the requirement of precise specification and identification of the property being transferred. These contracts fall under the category of gratuity contracts (*'uqud al-tabarru'at*), which include gifts (*hadiah*), donations (*hibah*), and wills (*wasiyyat*), among others.

The key element shared by all exchange contracts is the transfer of ownership and possession from one party to another. If this transfer is absent or lacking in a contract, it can no longer be classified as a contract of exchange.

4.4 Types of Sale Contracts

Islamic finance encompasses a variety of sales contracts, each with distinct characteristics and legal implications concerning ownership transfer, risk assumption, and profit distribution. These contracts differ in their requirements and conditions, which must be fulfilled to be considered valid according to Islamic law. Sales contracts can be classified based on the nature of the goods exchanged, the method of payment, and other factors like profit disclosure and legal aspects. A sale contract, in terms of its validity, can be categorised into valid (*sahih*) or void (*batil*), though the Hanafi school of thought recognises three categories: *sahih* (valid), *batil* (void), and *fasid* (defective).

4.4.1 **Sahih** *or Valid Sale Contract*

A contract is considered valid and enforceable when it meets all the terms, necessary elements, and conditions under Shari'ah principles that include fairness, honesty, and avoiding prohibited practices such as interest-based transactions or unethical business practices. According to the Hanafi school, a *sahih* contract fulfils all the essential requirements, such as the legality of the parties, clear consent (*sighah*), certainty regarding the subject matter, and freedom from coercion or undue influence. An example of a *sahih* sale contract would be a fair and regular transaction between a seller and a buyer for the sale of a product. That sale contract includes details, such as the description of the product, the agreed-upon price, and the payment terms. Both parties must fully understand and agree to the terms of the contract, and the transaction must not involve any prohibited practices such as *riba* (interest), *gharar* (uncertainty), or deception. Furthermore, the transaction must be conducted fairly and transparently, with both parties fulfilling their obligations in a timely and honest manner.

4.4.2 **Batil** *or Invalid Sale Contract*

In Islamic finance, a contract is considered invalid or *'batil'* if it goes against the Shari'ah principles, such as involvement in *riba* (usury), gambling, unethical or harmful activities, uncertainty, or coercion. In a void sale, neither the buyer possesses title to the subject matter nor does the seller possess title to the price. However, a contract of sale will be void if it lacks any one of the conditions of the offer and acceptance, elements of valid sale like the buyer and seller and good or the service for sale or subject matter is not complied with. An instance of such a sale contract, suppose two parties agree to enter into a loan agreement, where one party will lend money to the other at an agreed-upon rate of interest. This contract would be considered void or '*batil*' in Islamic finance because it involves the element of interest, which is prohibited under the principle of *riba* (usury or interest). Another example would be if two parties enter into a contract where they agree to bet on the outcome of a sporting event. This contract would be considered void because it involves gambling, which is prohibited due to meeting the principle of *maysir* (gambling), or one party offers a Shari'ah-compliant product to a buyer, but the buyer rejects the offer. Other examples include the sale of items that are incapable or impossible to deliver, such as the sun, the moon, or stars, or the sale of goods by someone who is mentally unsound. In all these examples, the contracts do not comply with the principles of Islamic law and are therefore considered void.

A void contract holds no legal effect and cannot be enforced by the parties involved. From a Shari'ah perspective, a void contract is automatically terminated. If the parties intend to continue their contractual relationship, they must enter into a new contract.

4.4.3 *Defective or* **Fasid** *Sale Contract*

In Islamic finance, a *fasid* sale contract refers to a sale transaction that lacks condition(s) which is set by the Shari'ah and due to such lack, the contract does not reach the level of an invalid or *batil* contract. In addition, a defective contract refers to a contract that possesses all the necessary elements but is associated with a quality prohibited by the Lawgiver. A sale contract can also be *fasid* due to containing conditions in a contract that are considered unfair or unjust. For instance, a sale of an unknown subject matter or contracts involving uncertainty in terms of delivery, price, or the types of subject matter fall under this category. This is crucial to guarantee that all sale contracts in Islamic finance are in accordance with the principles of Shari'ah that protect the contract from any issues or disputes related to their validity. In other words, a defective or *fasid* sale contract is a situation where the conditions specified in the contract, i.e. subject matter or price, are not set accurately, the sale may technically exist, but it will be considered defective due to misappropriation in fulfilling certain condition(s). In the case of a *fasid* sale, the buyer is discouraged from taking possession of the subject matter. If he does so, he will become the owner as per the agreement but is also discouraged from using the item; instead returns it to the seller. A defective contract may become valid and enforceable once the irregularities or defects in the contract are rectified.

4.4.4 **Makruh** *or Reprehensible Sale Contract*

A sale is considered valid once the transaction is finished and the goods are in the buyer's possession, but it is considered *makruh*, or disliked, if it occurs after the call to prayer on Friday or if a third party intervenes to buy something that was being negotiated for sale between other parties.

4.4.5 **Mukhtalaf Fih** *or Disagreed Sale Contract*

A controversial sale contract in Islamic finance is a sale agreement that is not universally accepted in line with Islamic principles. These types of sales may have differing opinions and interpretations among Islamic scholars and can lead to debates and disagreements within the Muslim community. Examples of controversial sale contracts in IBF include sales involving ambiguity, uncertainty, exploitation, or sales that involve speculative practices such as futures and options trading. The determination of the permissibility of these types of contracts often depends on the interpretation of Islamic law and the relevant religious texts and consensus.

4.5 Types of Sale Contracts in Terms of Goods Exchanged

A sale contract, which is a contract for the exchange of goods, is a legally binding agreement between two parties. It involves one party agreeing to sell specific goods while the other party agrees to buy them. The contract delineates the terms and conditions of the sale, encompassing aspects such as the price, quantity, quality, and delivery date of the goods. Additionally, any warranties or guarantees provided by the seller concerning the goods are included in the contract. The purpose of the contract is to establish a clear understanding of the rights and responsibilities of both parties, ensuring a smooth and dispute-free transaction. The various types of contracts for the exchange of goods are as follows.

*4.5.1 Barter Trade (***Bay' al-Muqayadah***)*

Barter trading, also known as *bay' al-muqayadah*, involves the exchange of one commodity for another. This form of sale was prevalent in early human history. While it is permissible according to Shari'ah, it is not encouraged as it may lead to unfairness in the exchange of goods.

*4.5.2 Exchange Sale (***Bay' al-Sarf***)*

In this type of sale, known as the exchange of monetary forms, one form of currency is exchanged for another within the same or different category. This includes transactions involving gold, silver, or currency of the same or different types. The general requirement for such a sale is that the values of both currencies must be equal in amount when exchanged within the same category. Additionally, both parties involved in the transaction should take possession of the respective currencies before parting ways.

4.5.3 *General Sale (*Bay' al-Mutlaq*)*

Due to limitations in the barter trading system, the general sale has become the most widely employed and preferred mode of sale. This method was developed as a solution to address the challenges inherent in bartering. The general sale allows for a fair and straightforward determination of the price of goods, which is why it is highly encouraged by Shari'ah.

4.6 Classifications of Contract Based on Mode of Payment

The mode of payment in a contract refers to the method by which the buyer will pay the seller for the goods or services being exchanged. This can include various forms of payment, such as cash, check, credit card, bank transfer, or a combination of methods. The mode of payment is an important aspect of the contract as it determines the process by which the payment will be made, the timeframe for payment, and any additional fees or charges that may be associated with the payment. It is important to clearly specify the mode of payment in the contract to avoid confusion or misunderstandings between the parties. Following are the basic types of contracts based on the mode of payment.

4.6.1 *Spot Sale*

A spot sale is a type of transaction in which the payment is made, and the goods or services are delivered immediately or within a very short time. It is called a "spot sale" because the payment and delivery occur "on the spot". This type of sale is common in various industries, including the sale of commodities, foreign currencies, and financial instruments.

4.6.2 *Deferred Payment Sale (*Bay' Bithaman Ajil*)*

Bay' bithaman 'ajil (BBA) is a financing mode commonly utilised in Islamic banking and finance. It operates as a deferred payment sale, where the buyer provides an initial payment and commits to paying the remaining balance over an agreed-upon period. Typically, a profit is incorporated into the payment structure. BBA adheres to the principles of Islamic finance, which strictly prohibits the charging and receiving of interest (*riba*). Instead, all financial transactions must be based on mutual consent and fair treatment of all parties involved. The profit gained through BBA is considered a return on investment, distinguishing it from interest and rendering it permissible under Islamic law. The BBA contract will also be discussed comprehensively in Chapter 7.

4.6.3 Bay' al-Salam

This type of sale involves making full payment in advance while the delivery of the commodity takes place at a later date. It is an exceptional sale in Shari'ah and primarily utilised for agricultural financing to meet the requirements of underprivileged farmers. One crucial condition for this type of sale is to accurately determine the subject matter or commodity in order to avoid any potential disputes between the parties during the delivery process in the future.

4.7 Other Modes of Sale Contracts

There are modes of sales that are not included in either of the above-mentioned types of sale contracts. The following are to be considered among them.

4.7.1 Bargaining Sale

In this type of sale, the price is established through the mutual agreement without the requirement for the seller to disclose their cost price or profit margin. The sale relies entirely on the agreement reached between the buyer and seller, independent of any reference to the seller's cost price or profit.

*4.7.2 Trust Sale (*Bay' al-Amanah*)*

Bay' al-amanah is a type of sale that requires the seller to disclose both the cost price and intended profit to the buyer. This transaction is built upon trust between the parties involved. *Bay' al-amanah* can be further categorised into three forms:

1. ***Murabahah***: in which the commodity is sold at a price that includes an agreed-upon profit margin.
2. ***Tawliyyah***: in which the selling price equals the original acquisition cost without any additional profit.
3. ***Wadhi'ah***: in which the seller offers the commodity below its cost or at a discounted price. These distinctions provide various options for conducting sales while ensuring transparency and fair treatment between the buyer and seller (Blossom, 2020).

4.8 Prohibited Sale Contracts in Islamic Financial Transactions

The following sale transactions involve elements that are prohibited by Shari'ah, such as *riba* (usury), *gharar* (uncertainty), *maysir* (gambling), *darar* (harm), and *ghasb* (unlawful appropriation). These elements can result in the unjust apprehension of others' properties, leading to disputes, conflicts, and legal arguments. Hence, these transactions have been prohibited according to Shari'ah rulings.

4.8.1 Bay' al-Hasat

In pre-Islamic times, a unique type of transaction was conducted through the use of stones. The process involved the vendor and the buyer coming to a mutual agreement that the outcome of a stone being thrown into the air would determine the commodity to be sold. For instance, if the stone landed on a certain cloth, sheep, or camel, the buyer would be obligated to purchase that specific item. This type of transaction was characterised by its uncertain nature, as it relied on chance to determine the item to be sold, leading to a lack of clarity and unpredictability in the transaction.

4.8.2 Bay' al-Mulamasah

Bay' al-mulamasah refers to a sale transaction in which a piece of cloth that has already been folded is bought and sold simply by touching it. In this process, the parties involved would give up their right to examine or unfold the cloth before the transaction. The buyer would touch the garment but would not be permitted to unfold it or inspect it in any way. This type of sale placed significant trust in the seller, as the buyer was unable to fully assess the quality or condition of the item he was purchasing.

4.8.3 Bay' al-Munabadhah

Bay' al-munabadhah refers to a type of sale transaction concluded through the act of throwing an item, such as cloth, article, or stone, between two parties to signify the sale agreement. The parties involved would not inspect the item being sold and would simply exchange it by throwing it from one person to the other. The transaction would be completed with each party saying, "This is for that", to indicate the exchange. This type of sale was based on trust and relied on the parties to have a clear understanding of the item being sold, as no examination or inspection was allowed.

4.8.4 Bay' al-Muwasafah

Bay' al-muwasafah refers to a sales transaction where the goods being sold have not been physically seen or examined by the buyer prior to their purchase. The goods are only described, and their delivery is arranged for a later time.

4.8.5 Bay' al-Muzabanah

Muzabanah is a type of sale transaction in which a bulk amount of one type of fruit, such as green dates, is exchanged for a specified weight, measure, or a number of another type of fruit, such as ripe dates. The exact amount of the first type of fruit being sold is unknown, but the exchange is made for a definite amount of the second type of fruit.

4.8.6 Bay' al-Mukhadarah

In pre-Islamic times, farmers would often sell their crops, such as fruits, vegetables, and grain, before they were fully ripe. This practice was known to cause frequent disputes and arguments due to changes in the quantity and quality of the crops or other losses that may occur. To address this issue, the Prophet (SAW) has prohibited this type of sale, stating, "Do not purchase fruits until their quality is evident". This was meant to prevent conflicts arising from the sale of crops that were not fully mature or fully developed.

4.8.7 *Bay' al-Haml*

Bay' al-haml is a transaction where a fetus or an animal that is yet to be born is sold. This type of sale typically involved a contract where a she-camel was expected to give birth, and the offspring would eventually grow up and reproduce. The buyer would pay for a she-camel that had not yet been born but would be born from the immediate offspring of an existing she-camel. However, the Prophet Muhammad (SAW) prohibited such contracts. He explicitly forbade the practice of selling camels based on *Habal-al-Habala*, which was a term used to describe delivering the camel to the buyer after the she-camel had given birth.

4.9 Types of *Mukhtalaf Fih* or Disagreed Sale Contracts

Controversial sales refer to sales transactions that are subject to differing opinions among Muslim jurists and different schools of *fiqh*. These sales are considered contentious because of the lack of consensus on whether they are permitted or prohibited. This section will delve into four forms of such sales, examining the arguments presented by different jurists both in favour of and against their permissibility.

4.9.1 *Deposit or Earnest Money (*Bay' al- 'Urbun*)*

Bay' al- 'urbun refers to a sales agreement where a buyer intends to purchase a specific property making an initial payment to the seller as an indication of commitment. This payment, known as earnest money, is given with the understanding that if the sale is successfully concluded, the advance payment will be deducted from the total purchase price. Nonetheless, if the sale does not proceed, the down payment is considered a gift bestowed by the buyer upon the seller. Critics of *bay' al- 'urbun* argue that this type of transaction is characterised by uncertainties (*gharar*) and involves unjustly acquiring someone's money without proper compensation. They deem it a prohibited and invalid (*batil*) contract. In the Hanafi school of thought, it is considered a voidable

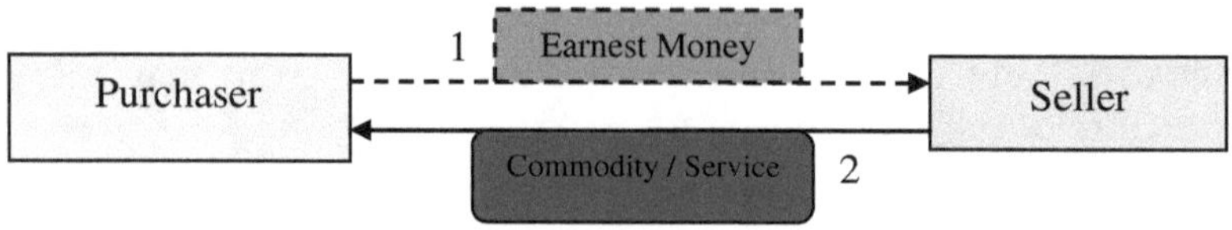

Fig. 4.2 Mechanism of *bay' al- 'urban* (*Source* Authors' own)

(*fasid*) contract. On the other hand, Imam Ahmad ibn Hanbal argues for its permissibility based on another hadith, despite the weak status of the hadith related to *bay' al- 'urbun*. Some Hanbali jurists also argue for the permissibility of *bay' al- 'urbun* in lease contracts, although the hadith they cited has also been deemed weak.

Figure 4.2 explains the mechanism of *bay' al- 'urban*:

*4.9.2 Debt Sale (*Bay' al-Dayn*)*

Dayn refers to "debt", and *bay' al-dayn* refers to the "sale of debt". This type of contract involves a creditor selling their receivable debt to a third party at a price lower than the actual debt amount. Without exception, classical Muslim scholars unanimously declared the prohibition of selling debt (*bay' al-dayn*) to a third party at a discounted price. This ruling remains widely accepted among contemporary Muslim scholars and is supported by the International Islamic Fiqh Academy (IIFA) of the Organisation of Islamic Cooperation (OIC), which considers *bay' al-dayn* to be a restricted transaction. On the other hand, it is permissible to sell the debt to the debtor at a discount price or to sell it to a third party at its original value. Another option for a creditor is to transfer the debt to a third party who has provided goods to the creditor through a "*hawalah*" transfer contract at the face value of the debt (Saleem, 2003). Scholars have identified four reasons for considering the sale of debt (*bay' al-dayn*) as prohibited. These reasons include the presence of *riba* (interest), *gharar* (uncertainty), lack of ownership on the part of the buyer, and potential risks associated with acquiring the debt. Conversely, some scholars argue that selling the debt corresponds to the price of the underlying commodity. Therefore, if a creditor sells the debt at a discount, it can be viewed as the sale of money for less money, which violates the requirement of equality and impulsiveness in the exchange of *ribawi* commodities, as indicated in the hadith on *riba al-fadl*. Furthermore,

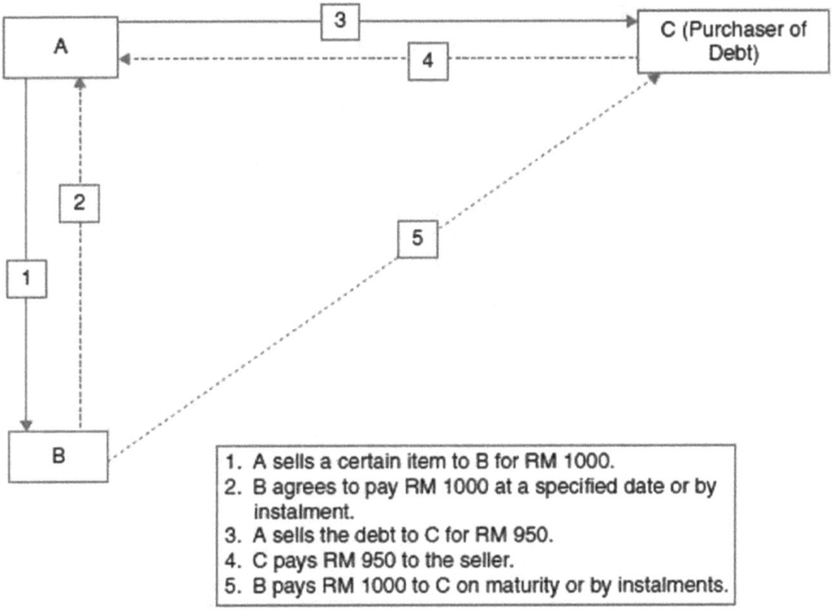

Fig. 4.3 Structure of *bay' al-dayn* (*Source* Saleem, 2003)

the purchaser of the debt, who buys it at a discount, later demands the full amount from the debtor, which may be considered *riba al-nasiyyah* (Saleem, 2003). The structure of *bay' al-dayn* is presented in Fig. 4.3.

*4.9.3 Buy Back Sale (*Bay' al- 'Inah*)*

A repurchase sale, known as *bay' al- 'inah*, is a type of agreement where a person or entity sells specific commodities to another party at a deferred price and immediately repurchases them at a discounted price. Typically, a sale contract is entered into to meet the mutual needs of both parties for the item being sold and its price. However, in a repurchase transaction (*bay' al- 'inah*), one party sells the asset with deferred payment and later buys it back at a lower cash price. The purpose of these two sales is not to acquire the asset, as it ultimately returns to the original owner, but rather to provide immediate cash to one party who will have to pay a higher deferred price in the future.

Despite the unlawful intention or purpose behind the second contract, the pillars and conditions of the agreement, such as offer, acceptance, contracting parties, and subject matter, are fulfilled. Muslim jurists have held different opinions regarding the presence of an unlawful hidden intention or purpose in the *bay' al- 'inah* contract. One group focuses on the expressed purpose of the parties as stated in the contract, while another group emphasises the hidden purpose that is not explicitly mentioned but can be inferred from the context.

The Hanafi and Shafi'i schools of thought primarily consider the agreement itself and the expressed purpose of the parties in determining the validity of *bay' al- 'inah*. The majority of Hanafi and Shafi'i jurists view it as a valid (*sahih*) contract. On the other hand, the Maliki and Hanbali schools of thought hold that *bay' al- 'inah* is prohibited. They take into account not only the contractual requirements but also the hidden intention or substance of the parties when deciding on the validity of *bay' al- 'inah*. This group of jurists considers the purpose or motive of the parties, even if not explicitly mentioned in the agreement, as long as one party is aware of the other party's unlawful intention or has the means to discover it through indications and circumstances surrounding the contract.

*4.9.4 Tripartite Sale (*Bay' al-Tawarruq*)*

Bay' al-tawarruq, also known as commodity *murabahah*, is a contract where a person purchases goods or commodities at a higher deferred price with the intention of selling them to a third party for a lower cash price. This definition refers to the traditional form of *tawarruq*, which is considered acceptable if it adheres to the rules and conditions of a sales contract. In this classical form, there is no prior agreement between the parties; the buyer acquires the item and subsequently sells it to a third party in the market. For example, Party A sells the item to Party B, who then sells it in the market to Party C. This simple *tawarruq* is based on real transactions occurring in the market. However, according to the views of scholars such as Ibn Taymiyya and Ibn Qayyim Al-Jawziyyah, the contract is regarded as ethically undesirable or reprehensible (*makruh*). Ibn Taymiyya specifically referred to *tawarruq* as a "sibling of *riba*" in terms of its resemblance to prohibited interest-based transactions. Nevertheless, *tawarruq* is only permissible in cases of necessity or

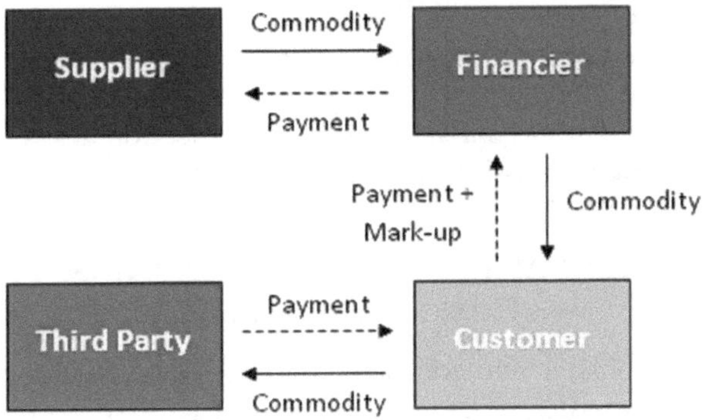

Fig. 4.4 Structure of the *tawarruq* sale (*Source* Mohamed et al., n.d.)

emergencies when an individual is in dire need of immediate cash and is unable to obtain it through other permissible means (Saleem, 2003).

The modern application of *tawarruq* by Islamic banks has sparked debates regarding its legitimacy. In its structured form, the transaction may lack genuineness and exist only on paper. The process involves a client borrowing money from the bank and agreeing to repay it with the added amount in instalments. The bank purchases a commodity using its own funds and then sells it to the customer at a higher deferred price. The customer, however, is not aware of the bank's ownership of the commodity and does not have any real involvement with it. Subsequently, the bank sells the commodity on behalf of the customer and deposits the proceeds into their account. These series of transactions are not physically observed and can be executed for multiple customers within a single day, with the customer primarily signing the necessary documents. Figure 4.4 explain the structure of the *tawarruq* sale.

4.10 Essential Elements for Sale Contracts

In Islamic law, the principles and rules governing contracts are derived from the divine sources of the Qur'an and Sunnah. Three essential conditions must be fulfilled in a contract:

- Offer and acceptance (*ijab* and *qabul*): both parties must express their consent and acceptance clearly and unequivocally.

- Contracting parties (*al-ʿaqidayn*): the individuals or entities entering into the contract must have the legal capacity and authority to do so.
- The subject matter (*mahal al-aqd*): the object or subject of the contract must be permissible and lawful according to Islamic principles.

4.11 Essential Elements and Conditions for Sale Contract in HPSM

In order to establish a sale contract, the initial two parties involved are the buyer and the seller. These two parties must adhere to the same conditions as the lessor and lessee do in an *ijarah* contract, as well as the partners in a *shirkah* contract. The reason for this requirement is that the buyer and seller in a sales contract, the lessor and lessee in an *ijarah* contract, and the partners in a *shirkah* contract all represent the same individual or entity in the whole process. The only variation lies in their roles within the respective contracts, which shift sequentially according to the contractual intervals.

Another essential element of a sales contract is the asset or item being sold, which shares the same necessary conditions as the contracts of *shirkah* and *ijarah*. Additionally, the price of the sold item is a crucial aspect of the sales contract, and its determination and currency at the time of contract formation are essential conditions.

The final element of a sales contract is the formal agreement itself, which encompasses conditions similar to those found in the *ijarah* and *shirkah* contracts that have been mentioned previously.

4.12 Application of the Above Using an Example Case Study

Ahmed owns a residential property and wishes to sell it to Aisha, who is interested in purchasing the property for personal use. They want to ensure that the sale contract adheres to Shari'ah principles and fulfils the essential conditions of a valid Islamic contract.

- Elements of the Sale Contract:
  - Offer and Acceptance: Ahmed expresses his intention to sell the residential property to Aisha by offering a specific price and

terms. Aisha accepts the offer and agrees to purchase the property at the specified price. Their consent and acceptance are clear and unambiguous.

- Contracting Parties: Ahmed and Aisha are both adults, mentally sound, and legally competent individuals. They possess the necessary legal capacity to enter into a contract. They have the authority to buy and sell property, and there are no legal restrictions that prohibit their participation in this transaction.
- Subject Matter: The subject matter of the contract is the residential property owned by Ahmed. The property is free from any encumbrances or legal disputes that may affect its transfer of ownership. It is important to ensure that the property is permissible and lawful, according to Shari'ah principles, without any involvement in prohibited activities or industries.
- Purchase Price and Payment Terms: Ahmed and Aisha agree on a purchase price for the property. They may negotiate and reach a fair and mutually acceptable price that reflects the market value of the property. The payment terms can be discussed, including the method and schedule of payments, to ensure compliance with Shari'ah principles and avoid any element of riba.
- Conditions and Representations: Both parties should disclose any relevant information or conditions that may affect the property's value or future use. For example, Ahmed must inform Aisha of any known defects or structural issues in the property. Aisha should also clarify her requirements or any specific conditions she expects the property to fulfil.
- Shari'ah-Compliant Contract: To ensure compliance with Shari'ah principles, Ahmed and Aisha should consult with an Islamic scholar or legal expert well-versed in Islamic commercial law. The contract should be drafted to incorporate the essential conditions of a valid Islamic contract, including clear terms, mutual consent, lawful subject matter, and obligations of both parties.

4.13 Problems and Solutions for the Example Case Study

- *Riba* (Usury) Issue:
  Problem: There is a risk of including interest-based financing or payment terms in the sale contract, which is prohibited in Shari'ah.
  Solution: Both Ahmed and Aisha should agree on a payment structure that avoids any form of interest or usury. They can explore alternative financing methods such as deferred payment, instalment plans, or utilising Shari'ah-compliant financial institutions that offer financing options without interest.
- *Gharar* (Uncertainty) Issue:
  Problem: If there is ambiguity or uncertainty in the terms of the contract, it may lead to a violation of Shari'ah principles.
  Solution: The contract should clearly specify the subject matter, price, payment terms, and any other relevant conditions to eliminate any uncertainty or ambiguity. Both parties should have a clear understanding of their rights, obligations, and expectations regarding the property and the transaction.
- Full Disclosure and Representations:
  Problem: If either party fails to disclose relevant information about the property, it may lead to disputes or misrepresentation.
  Solution: Ahmed must disclose any known defects or issues related to the property. Aisha should also communicate her specific requirements and expectations regarding the property. Both parties should engage in open and honest communication to ensure transparency and avoid any misrepresentation.
- Shari'ah Compliance:
  Problem: Without proper guidance, the contract may inadvertently include provisions or terms that are not compliant with Shari'ah principles.
  Solution: Ahmed and Aisha should consult with a qualified Islamic scholar or legal expert specialising in Islamic commercial law. The expert can review the contract and ensure its compliance with Shari'ah principles, providing guidance on necessary amendments or adjustments to ensure Shari'ah compliance.

Chapter Review Questions

1. What is the definition of sale (*bay'*) according to the Hanafi school?
   (a) Exchange of property for money
   (b) Exchange of an owned commodity for another in a specified manner
   (c) Exchange of corporeal property for a corresponding liability
   (d) Exchange of liability for another liability
2. How is sale defined in the Shafi'i school?
   (a) Exchange of property between the seller and buyer
   (b) Exchange of an owned commodity for another with the exchange of ownership and possession
   (c) Exchange of two corporeal properties
   (d) Exchange of money for money
3. What are the four basic elements of a sale contract?
   (a) Seller, purchaser, price, commodity
   (b) Money, property, offer, acceptance
   (c) Seller, buyer, liability, possession
   (d) Commodity, ownership, contract, payment
4. What does Qurtubi describe as the nature of the sale?
   (a) Exchange of corporeal property for a corresponding liability
   (b) Exchange of liability for another liability
   (c) Exchange of two corporeal properties or exchange of corporeal property for a corresponding liability or exchange of liability for another liability
   (d) Exchange of property between the seller and buyer
5. Which statement accurately describes the sale contract?
   (a) It is an exchange of a commodity for another commodity
   (b) It is an exchange of money for money
   (c) It is an exchange of property between the seller and buyer
   (d) It is an exchange of ownership and possession between the seller and buyer
6. What are the three fundamental conditions that must be met in an Islamic contract?
   (a) Offer and acceptance, contracting parties, and subject matter
   (b) Offer and acceptance, consideration, and subject matter
   (c) Offer and acceptance, intention to create legal relations and subject matter
   (d) Offer and acceptance, capacity to contract, and consideration

7. According to the Hanafi school of thought, how many categories of contracts are recognised?
   (a) One: valid (*sahih*)
   (b) Two: valid (*sahih*) and void (*batil*)
   (c) Two: valid (*sahih*) and voidable (*fasid*)
   (d) Three: valid (*sahih*), voidable (*fasid*), and void (*batil*)
8. What characterises a *sahih* contract according to the Hanafi school?
   (a) It fulfils all essential requirements and has clear consent
   (b) It is associated with a quality prohibited by the Lawgiver
   (c) It is missing an essential element or unfulfilled condition
   (d) It involves uncertainty in terms of delivery, price, or subject matter
9. What is the status of a void contract in Islamic law?
   (a) It can be enforced by the parties involved
   (b) It is automatically terminated and has no legal effect
   (c) It becomes valid and enforceable once defects are rectified
   (d) It can only be continued through the execution of a new contract
10. Which of the following is an example of a void contract?
   (a) Sale of an unknown subject matter
   (b) Sale with uncertain delivery terms
   (c) Sale of goods by a mentally incompetent person
   (d) All of the above

Answers

1. b
2. b
3. a
4. c
5. a
6. a
7. d
8. a
9. b
10. d

References

Abadi, A. A. a.-R. S. a.-H. (2001). *Awn al-Ma'bud Sharh Sunan Abi Dawud* (Vol. 9). Dar 'Ihya al-Turath al-Arabi.

Abdullah, N. I. (2005). *Islamic hire-purchase in Malaysian Financial Institutions: A comparative analytical book*. Loughborough University.

Al-Zuhayli, W. (2003). *Financial transactions in Islamic jurisprudence* (M. A. El-Gamal, Trans.). Dar al-Fikr al-Mu'asir.

Blossom. (2020). *Classifications of sale contract*. https://blossomfinance.com/posts/classifications-of-sale-contracts. Accessed 25 June 2023.

Daruqutni, A. a.-H. D. (1966). *Sunan Aa-Daruqutni* (Vol. 3). Dar Al-Ma'rifah.

Hasan, A. A. H. (2007). *Sales and contracts in early Islamic commercial law*. Islamic Research Institute.

Ibn Majah. (n.d.). *Sunan Ibu Majah* (Vol. 2). Dar al-Fikr.

Mohamed, B. F., Abdi, S. M., Siad, S. A., & Adawe, F. N. (n.d.). *Tawarruq*. https://slideplayer.com/slide/17072900/. Accessed 12 July 2023.

Moustafa, S. Q. (2001). *The sale of debt as implemented by Islamic financial institutions in Malaysia*. International Islamic University Malaysia.

Mubarakpuri, A. A. M. (2001). *Tuhfah al-Ahwazi Sharh Jami' al-Tirmizi* (Vol. 4). Dar al-Kutub al-'Ilmiyyah.

Saleem, M. Y. (2003). *Islamic commercial law*. Wiley.

CHAPTER 5

Operational Procedure of HPSM

Abstract This chapter addresses the challenge of consolidating diverse HPSM procedures across global banks by focusing on the illustrative example of Islami Bank Bangladesh Limited (IBBL) and the Malaysian Hire Purchase Act 1967. By examining these practical implementations, the chapter aims to enhance transparency, strengthen stakeholder confidence, and mitigate deficiencies in contract execution procedures that may impact customer satisfaction. The core objective is to illuminate the practical application of HPSM in Islamic banking and finance, unravelling its key aspects and procedures. The chapter explores the operational dynamics of HPSM, elucidating the contractual framework and roles of stakeholders such as buyers, sellers, and financial institutions. Emphasising mutual consent, transparency, and risk-sharing, it underscores the significance of these principles in HPSM transactions. The chapter systematically guides through the execution of Shari'ah-compliant HPSM contracts, encompassing procedures and documentation from application to ownership transfer. It underscores the necessity of due diligence and contractual obligations. Finally, this chapter equips readers with valuable insights to navigate HPSM transactions in the Islamic banking and finance context. Catering to individuals, professionals, and researchers, it provides a comprehensive understanding of real-world implications of HPSM.

Keyword HP · Hire Purchase · HPSM · HPSM contract

M. K. Hassan et al., *Hire Purchase Under Shirkah al-Milk (HPSM) in Islamic Banking and Finance*, https://doi.org/10.1007/978-3-031-50105-0_5

Preview

Implementing HPSM contracts involves following specific procedures, which can vary among banks globally. Consequently, consolidating all these procedures into a single book presents a challenge. In order to address this, the current chapter focuses on observing the procedures of Islami Bank Bangladesh Limited (IBBL) as an illustrative example of HPSM. However, the Malaysian Hire Purchase Act 1967 would also be a strong literature of this chapter as a supporting one to demonstrate the practical application of HPSM. These procedures and acts ensure transparency and enhance stakeholders' confidence. Any deficiencies or overlaps in contract execution procedures can adversely affect customer satisfaction.

The core objective of this chapter is to explore the practical application of HPSM, shedding light on its implementation and associated procedures in Islamic banking and finance. By examining the key aspects of HPSM contracts, readers will develop a comprehensive understanding of how this financing arrangement operates in real-world scenarios.

The chapter delves into the modus operandi of HPSM, providing an overview of the contractual framework and the key stakeholders involved. It explores the roles and responsibilities of the buyer, seller, and financial institution, emphasising the importance of mutual consent, transparency, and risk-sharing in HPSM transactions.

Executing HPSM contracts in a manner that adheres to Shari'ah principles requires a systematic approach. Hence, the chapter explores the requisite procedures and documentation involved in executing an HPSM contract. It covers the steps ranging from application and evaluation to fund disbursement and ownership transfer, underscoring the significance of conducting due diligence and fulfilling contractual obligations.

By providing a comprehensive overview of the practical application of HPSM, this chapter, moreover, aims to equip readers with the knowledge and insights necessary to navigate HPSM transactions in the Islamic banking and finance industry. It serves as a valuable resource for individuals, professionals, and researchers seeking a deeper understanding of the implementation and implications of HPSM contracts in real-world settings.

5.1 Initial Stage of Entering into the Contract

During the initial stage of implementing HPSM (Hire Purchase under *Shirkah al-Milk*), the lessor (bank) and lessee (client) engage in discussions regarding specific matters. These discussions primarily revolve around the client's investment needs, their past business track records, the feasibility of the proposed business project, its compliance with Shari'ah principles, and the intended purpose of the asset or good. At this stage, the client is typically made aware of the features of HPSM, including its commonly practised rules, regulations, terms, and conditions. Additionally, the client's capital contribution to become a partner in the *shirkah* (partnership)—the initial contract of HPSM—is determined. The bank then evaluates the proposal by examining the previous records of HPSM transactions of the particular branch in collaboration with the head office. After reviewing the proposal, the bank advises the client to submit his official application. In this case, if the proposal is exempted from any Shari'ah issues, it goes for further consideration, in case otherwise, the proposal gets rejected with a professional approach. However, after an affirmative decision to carry on the HPSM contract, the client is advised to open an *al-wadi'ah* current account and is required to maintain the account agreeably for a reasonable period of six months.

According to the Malaysian Hire Purchase Act 1967, section 4 (1) *(a)*, to enter the parties in the HPSM contract—reads hire purchase—"in a case where negotiations leading to the making of the hire-purchase agreement is carried out by any person who would be the owner under the hire-purchase agreement to be entered into, or by any person, other than the dealer, acting on his behalf, such person shall serve on the intending hirer a written statement duly completed and signed by him in accordance with the form set out in Part I of the Second Schedule".

However, the act in section 36 and its sub-sections a & b explains the matters related to a fake declaration by dealers, etc., in proposals, it states "that a dealer, an agent or a person on behalf of an owner prepares or causes to be prepared a hire-purchase agreement or offer in writing that, if accepted, will constitute a hire-purchase agreement with the intention of bringing about a contractual relationship between an owner and a hirer" and "the agreement or offer contains to the knowledge of the dealer, agent or person acting on behalf of the owner, as the case may be, a false statement or representation that is false in any material particular".

The act, on the other hand, in its section no. 4_A, 4_B, 4_C, and 4_D provide several conditions for the agreement to get approved, which are:

1. A written document is required for a hire-purchase agreement concerning any goods mentioned in the First Schedule.
2. The hire-purchase agreement ought to comply with either the national language or the English language.
3. All parties involved in the agreement, or their representatives, must sign the hire-purchase agreement.
4. "No owner, dealer, agent or person acting on behalf of the owner shall require or cause any intending hirer or his agent to sign a hire-purchase agreement or any other form or document relating to a hire-purchase agreement unless such hire-purchase agreement, form or document has been duly completed".
5. "No owner shall deliver or cause to be delivered to any dealer, agent or person acting on behalf of the owner a hire-purchase agreement or any other form or document relating to a hire-purchase agreement which has not been duly completed".
6. Every hire-purchase agreement should "specify a date on which the hiring shall be deemed to have commenced; specify the number of instalments to be paid under the agreement by the hirer; specify the amounts of each of these instalments and the person to whom and the place at which the payments of these instalments are to be made; specify the time for the payment of each of those instalments; contain a description of the goods sufficient to identify them; specify the address where the goods under the hire-purchase agreement are".
7. This section pertains to the complete amount paid or provided as a deposit, referred to as "deposit" both in this Act and in the agreement. It is important to explicitly state the amount paid in cash as well as the amount provided through non-cash methods. Furthermore, any costs related to the delivery of the goods, whether in full or in part, or any expenses owed to the hirer, must be encompassed within the overall sum, referred to as "freight" in this Act and in the agreement.
8. Each individual item of goods acquired under this Act must be accompanied by a separate hire-purchase agreement.

5.2 Process of Proposal Classification

The HPSM is classified into various types based on the proposals from clients, considering the different interests and investment requirements of clients. As a result, HPSM is typically divided into five distinct modes that take into account the customer's investment goals and purposes, which are:

5.2.1 *Hire Purchase Under* Shirkah al-Milk *Commercial*

Entrepreneurs who meet the eligibility criteria for forming a business and enterprise can participate in this particular category of HPSM investment. This category is open to individuals, business farms, groups, companies, or societies. The investment within this category is exclusively allocated for Shari'ah-compliant commercial purposes. This specific category of investment is referred to as "Hire Purchase under *Shirkah al-Milk* Commercial".

5.2.2 *Hire Purchase Under* Shirkah al-Milk *Industrial*

The purpose of this HPSM investment category is to provide financing for clients engaged in various sectors such as land, buildings, machinery, equipment, and transportation, among others. It is specifically referred to as "hire purchase under *shirkah al-milk* industrial" in this category, emphasising its focus on industrial activities.

5.2.3 *Hire Purchase Under* Shirkah al-Milk *Agriculture*

The investment category known as "hire purchase under *shirkah al-milk* agriculture" specifically caters to the agriculture sector. Under this category, the bank offers financing for agricultural equipment, machinery, shallow machines, tube and deep tube wells, tractors commonly utilised in cultivation, as well as agricultural-related transportation. This category is designed to support agricultural activities in a *Shari'ah*-compliant manner.

5.2.4 *Hire Purchase Under* Shirkah al-Milk *for Transport or Motor Vehicles*

Transportation financing, whether personal or commercial, is an essential sector of HPSM in every jurisdiction. Almost every Islamic bank in the world finances any type of transportation, including the bus, truck, car, taxi, launch, steamer, cargo vessel, and air transport under the HPSM or hire-purchase agreement. In the case of motor vehicles, the Malaysian Hire Purchase Act 1967, in its sections $4_{E,}$ $4_{F,}$ and $4_{G,}$ highlights the following as conditions:

1. "Where the goods comprised in a hire-purchase agreement is a motor vehicle, a hirer may make a request in writing to an owner to keep the registration certificate of the motor vehicle".
2. "A hire-purchase agreement shall not be entered into where the goods comprised in the hire-purchase agreement is a motor vehicle which has been altered or modified in its construction and structure".
3. "Where goods to be comprised in a hire-purchase agreement are a second-hand motor vehicle, the person who intends to enter into the hire-purchase agreement in respect of such second-hand motor vehicle shall declare in writing any defects of the second-hand motor vehicle in accordance with the inspection report by the relevant authority determined by the Controller".

5.2.5 *Hire Purchase Under* Shirkah al-Milk *Real Estate*

In recent times, investing in the real estate sector has presented a new avenue for banks and financial institutions. Surprisingly, there has been a significant rise in customer interest within the banking sector regarding the hire purchase under *shirkah al-milk* real estate products. IBBL facilitates financing through this product, allowing customers to acquire land, buildings, markets, and apartments for both personal use and commercial purposes.

5.2.6 *Hire Purchase Under* Shirkah al-Milk *Scheme*

The hire purchase under the *shirkah al-milk* investment category offers transactions in the form of assets intended for personal use or rental based on schemes that align with the preferences of both the bank and the customer. However, any scheme formulated must adhere to the principles of Shari'ah. This categorisation is referred to as hire purchase under the *shirkah al-milk* scheme.

5.3 Eligibility of Client for Finance

The client's eligibility for bank financing requires a clean track record. The client must not have any previous or current involvement in fraud, failures, bankruptcies, or unresolved issues with other financial institutions, including banks, local financial entities, credit institutions, and leasing institutions within the country, as well as all other branches of the financing bank. To ensure transparency, the financing bank seeks confidential reports from other banks regarding the client's past dealings, if any, and the client's proposal remains on hold until these reports are obtained. In the case of IBBL, it also contacts the Credit Information Bureau (CIB) of the country's central bank through the head office investment division of IBBL to obtain periodic reports on the client.

Additionally, the client is required to disclose any existing liabilities with other banks, financial institutions, and leasing companies, including any branches of the financing bank. Furthermore, as part of the process, the financing bank requests the client to provide their financial statements or balance sheets for the last three consecutive accounting years (the specific duration may vary from country to country). This requirement applies specifically to proposals involving a minimum amount of five million or more in the local currency, such as the Bangladeshi Taka (BDT). It is important to note that this regulation applies to all types of applicants, regardless of whether they are individuals, proprietorships, partnerships, private or public limited companies, or any other trust entities.

In order to secure the bank's financing, a mortgage indenture will be executed by the client, serving as security or deposit. Consequently, the bank will conduct an inspection of the proposed mortgaged property, be it a building, land, or any other asset, to thoroughly examine the authenticity and accuracy of the associated documents. The evaluation of the primary market and forced sale value of the property being mortgaged will be conducted accordingly. The bank's legal advisor or designated lawyer will carefully examine the documents pertaining to the mortgaged property to assess their legal aspects. The lawyer's decision plays a crucial role in determining the final acceptance or rejection of the proposal. The client's capacity to manage liabilities must be scrutinized and analyzed, considering whether they possess the ability to effectively handle such obligations. This assessment should be clearly outlined in the appraisal form, along with an analysis of the client's liquid assets, including cash and book debts, to ensure the necessary cash flow.

5.4 Determination of the Leasing Rate and the Selling Price of the Asset

The determination of the selling price for the bank's share in the asset follows established guidelines and takes into account the cost price, Expected Rate of Return (ERR) for the entire investment period (including the gestation period), and other relevant factors. Based on this calculation, the rental amount for the asset is determined, considering the cost price, usage, and the bank's expected rate of return. The rent continues to accumulate until the bank's ownership of the asset(s) reaches zero, at which point the lessee has the option to purchase the bank's share. The lessee, as a co-owner, then pays a fixed rent for the bank's share or portion of the asset, typically on a specified timeframe (daily, weekly, fortnightly, monthly, quarterly, semi-annually, or annually) or per unit of work or service (such as per trip or mile).

Moreover, the payment of the asset's selling price will be divided into multiple shares to align with the rent payments based on the agreed-upon rental agreement. The client partner will make rent payments according to the agreement starting from the date of receiving the property in orderly form or upon completion of the specific work or service. Simultaneously, the client partner will gradually acquire the shares of the bank's assets by purchasing them in parts. This will be done by making scheduled payments as specified in the contract for the specified part of the bank's share in the asset.

Once the lessee completes the payment for the bank's share of the asset, ownership of the asset is immediately transferred to the lessee. At this point, the bank will cease charging rent proportionally to the portion that has been sold. Consequently, upon receiving the full payment and transferring the ownership of the asset as per the agreement or undertaking, the bank will no longer have any ownership rights over the asset. Once the price of the asset is determined and agreed upon in the contract, it cannot be escalated unless the hirer or purchaser fails to fulfil the terms of the contract, leading to the asset being sold to a third party. In such situations, the bank reserves the right to levy compensation for the outstanding rent based on the Expected Rate of Return (ERR) as specified in the *ijarah* agreement.

5.5 Documentation Stage for Security Options

Before the bank purchases the property on behalf of the client, appropriate documentation for the required securities must be prepared meticulously. However, the specific documentation requirements vary depending on the business category and the status of the individual or entity involved. For instance, the property can be acquired by the bank for the client without requiring a mortgage from the client. Alternatively, a mortgage can be arranged on behalf of the client, securing the property to be purchased by the bank. It is also possible for the property to be secured solely by the client's oath or pledge. Consequently, different categories of transactions necessitate distinct documentation procedures.

5.6 Categorisation of the Businesses to Finance

Banks worldwide consider various investment sectors based on market demand in specific jurisdictions when implementing the HPSM contract. These sectors are typically determined initially, and their documentation must be maintained with transparency. Examples of common investment categories under HPSM include joint business farms, private or public limited companies, trust organisations, and cooperative societies.

5.7 Rent Payment Schedule and Proposed Selling Price

The rent payment method for the bank's share or portion of the asset is determined by calculating the rent per unit of time (such as daily, weekly, or monthly) as specified in the accepted Sanction Advice by the hirer partners. This payment method becomes effective from the date the asset is handed over to the hirer partners in usable condition.

Subsequently, the schedule for payment of the bank's share or portion of the asset's sale price is established, either in instalments or as a lump sum, based on the guidelines outlined in the agreement, applicable state acts, resolutions, or standards provided in the sanction advice. It is essential to mention the total number of instalments, account for each instalment, and specify the last payment date for each instalment. The number of instalments should correspond to the number of shares into which the asset (i.e., the bank's share) is divided. Finally, to execute the HPSM agreement, the Pro-forma must be completed and signed by both parties, appropriately witnessed, and stamped accordingly. According to the practice of IBBL, the agreement, among others, must contain the following clauses:

(a) The client undertakes to purchase the property, while the bank commits to sell it during the estimated hire period or before its expiry. The purchase and sale can occur either in parts or as a whole.

(b) The agreement includes an indemnity clause, which stipulates that in the event the client fails to make timely payments of accrued rent or the agreed-upon sale/purchase price within the hire period, the client is obligated to compensate the bank for any losses incurred as a result of disposing of the asset as determined by the bank. The rent on the bank's portion of the asset will keep accumulating at the agreed-upon rate until the client, who is the hirer, completes full payment of the purchase consideration or sale price. Afterwards, the bank will utilise its right to recoup any income loss from the security provided, which means the client will be required to provide sufficient securities for this purpose.

(c) The registration clause specifies the terms for shared ownership of the property between the bank and the client. The property can be registered exclusively in the bank's or client's name or in the name of a mutually agreed-upon third party.

Once all these requirements are fulfilled according to the regulations, the client will commence acquiring ownership of the bank's share of the specific asset gradually, following the predetermined payment schedule outlined in the HPSM agreement. As the lessee, the client bears the responsibility of ensuring proper maintenance and protection of the asset at their own expense. Moreover, the client is obligated to grant the owner (i.e., the bank) access to the asset for necessary inspections when required.

5.8 Progression Phase

The development period encompasses the time between the initial payment, signifying the acquisition of ownership of the property, and the date when the lessee receives the property in a functional and suitable state, allowing it to generate the anticipated services or benefits for the lessee. This entire preparatory phase is referred to as the "gestation or interim period", during which the asset is made, constructed, or installed to reach a usable and observable condition.

During the gestation period, the asset is still undergoing construction, installation, or manufacturing processes. As the asset cannot generate the expected services or benefits during this period, the lessor does not impose any rental charges on the lessee. However, if there are additional costs, such as utility expenses, value addition, or market demand costs associated with the property, the financer (such as a bank) is permitted to agree upon a higher price than the prevailing market rate. This higher price allows the financer to recover the underlying costs and capitalise on the advantages of the gestation period.

Therefore, throughout the investment's gestation period, the bank is prohibited from collecting any rent. Instead, the bank will calculate the sale price of the asset at a higher amount to accommodate for its Expected Rate of Return (ERR) over the complete lease period, including the gestation period. As a result, the bank may determine the value of its portion of the asset by combining the cost price and factoring in the gestation period as a time value, which is then documented in its financial records.

The Malaysian hire-purchase act, in its section no 6_A, $6_{B,}$ and $6_{C,}$ discusses the option to the hirer for the term charges of lease tenure, which are, for example, as follows:

1. The asset owner must provide the hirer with the option to select either a fixed rate or a variable rate for the charges in a hire-purchase agreement.
2. If the hirer chooses a variable rate for the charges, it will be calculated by adding a specified percentage margin to the base lending rate.

The act also entitles rights to the owner to revise the base lending rate, which are:

1. In a hire-purchase agreement where the terms charges are subject to a variable rate, the owner has the right to modify the base lending rate at any point during the agreement's duration.
2. In the event that the owner adjusts the base lending rate, the rate and overall amount of the terms charges, as well as the instalment amount or the number of instalments, will be revised accordingly in the hire-purchase agreement.
3. In the event of the owner revising the base lending rate, it is required for them to provide a notice to the hirer containing the following information:
   (a) The updated base lending rate.
   (b) The adjusted rate of terms charges.

(c) The revised total amount of terms charges.
(d) The modified amount of instalments or the updated number of instalments, depending on the circumstances.

4. Where the owner has revised the base lending rate, the hirer may opt whether:

(a) To retain the existing number of instalments and vary the amount of instalments.
(b) To retain the existing amount of instalments and vary the number of instalments.

5.9 Insurance or Takaful in HPSM Contract

Any financed asset must have adequate insurance coverage to mitigate losses and damages that may arise during the financing period. A comprehensive "all risk" takaful policy should be obtained from a reputable and licensed insurance company that is recognised or approved by the financing bank. This policy serves to protect the financier's rights and interests as the beneficiary in the event of losses or damages. However, if the customer is unable to obtain the insurance coverage recommended by the financier, the financier may allow the customer to select an insurer that meets the requirements set by the financier.

Furthermore, in the case of selecting a conventional insurance company, the premium paid cannot be included as a component of the property's purchase price. The initial sum insured should be based on either the asset's valuation or its purchase price. In subsequent years, the estimated sum may be reduced but should still be adequate to cover the remaining financing amount. However, it is the responsibility of the customer to bear the cost of the insurance contribution.

In the context of IBBL, the client is required to obtain a comprehensive insurance policy that covers all typical risks for an amount equal to the asset's price plus an additional 10%. This insurance policy should include a bank mortgage clause and can be obtained from an Islamic insurance company, Sadharan Bima Corporation (a state-owned non-life insurer and reinsurer in Bangladesh) or any insurance company approved by the bank.

If the client takes possession of the asset, they must obtain comprehensive contract insurance coverage with a bank mortgage clause. The client is responsible for providing the insurance policy or cover note, along with the premium payment receipt, to the bank for record-keeping purposes. The bank reviews the payment receipt to ensure that it reflects the desired amount and warranties as specified by the bank and also verifies that the policy has been appropriately stamped.

The insurance policy will be recorded in the insurance policy register (B-39) and securely stored in a fireproof safe or locker, jointly supervised by the branch manager and the investment department officer. In the event of an accident, the client will be instructed to file a claim with the relevant insurance company through the bank, following all necessary procedures within the specified timeframe.

If the client is unable or fails to secure insurance coverage, the bank will arrange the insurance on behalf of the client. The bank will inform the client about the amount that will be recovered from them through a debt to their investment account. However, if the asset is stored in the bank's warehouse as collateral, the premium will be recovered proportionally from the client. It is important to note that sections 26 and 28 of the Malaysian Hire Purchase Act 1967 encompass the following insurance provisions for a hire-purchase agreement, which are:

1. An owner shall cause to be insured in the name of the hirer—
   - Motor vehicles included in a hire-purchase agreement are required to be insured for the first year only.
   - All other goods included in a hire-purchase agreement must be insured for the entire duration of the hire-purchase period.
2. In the case where the goods involved in a hire-purchase agreement are motor vehicles, the hirer is responsible for ensuring that the vehicle is insured for the second year and all subsequent years while it remains under hire-purchase.
3. The owner is not permitted to mandate that the hirer obtains insurance coverage from a specific registered insurer.
4. If the hirer fails to renew the insurance policy or obtain a new one, the owner has the option to arrange insurance for the motor vehicle, and any resulting costs will be the responsibility of the hirer.
5. Except for insurance amounts related to motor vehicles for the second and subsequent years, all payments due for insurance shall be included in the hire-purchase price.
6. In the context of insuring goods included in a hire-purchase agreement, if the insurer provides any commission or rebate, such as a no-claim rebate or a similar form of rebate (excluding legitimate agency commission), to an owner who is also a genuine agent of

the insurer and arranges the insurance on behalf of the hirer, the hirer has the entitlement to receive the commission and rebate. Any person who knowingly facilitates such payments or allows such commission or rebate to be given to an owner, as well as any owner who accepts such commission or rebate, will be held accountable for an offence under this Act.

The following conditions are to be observed in terms of the content of contracts of insurance:

(a) identify the goods or the part of the goods to be insured.
(b) contain a statement of the amount and period for which the goods are insured or are to be insured.
(c) if the amount for which the goods are or are to be insured will vary during the period of the agreement contain a statement showing the varying amounts.

In order to mitigate the insurance disputes, the following measures are to be taken.

(a) requiring differences or disputes arising out of a contract of insurance to be referred to arbitration.
(b) providing that no action or suit shall be maintainable upon such a contract or against the insurer in respect of any claim under, or difference or dispute arising out of, such a contract unless the claim, difference, or dispute has been referred to arbitration or an award pursuant to arbitration proceedings has been first obtained;
(c) providing that arbitration or an award pursuant to arbitration proceedings is a condition precedent to any right of action or suit upon such a contract; or
(d) otherwise imposing by reference to arbitration or to an award made in arbitration proceedings any limitation on the right of the person to bring or maintain any action or suit upon such a contract.

5.10 Guarantor in HPSM Contract

Malaysian Hire Purchase Act 1967, in its section $20_{A,}$ exposes that "an owner may require a hirer to furnish a guarantor or such number of guarantors acceptable to the owner to guarantee the performance of the hirer's obligations under the hire-purchase Agreement". Concerning the booking fee of the intended property, the Malaysian Hire Purchase Act 1967 in its section 30_A that there might be a booking fee for the hire purchase contract, and the amount of the booking fee "shall not exceed one per cent of the cash price of the goods". "Notwithstanding anything under this act, the booking fee shall form part of the deposit". However, "an owner, dealer, agent or person acting on behalf of the owner shall refund ninety per cent of the booking fee to the intending hirer upon the withdrawal of the booking of the goods comprised in a hire-purchase agreement".

Despite in a few cases, the amount of the security deposit or mortgage is undescribed; however, the Malaysian Hire Purchase Act 1967 clearly mentions the approximate amount of deposit in a hire-purchase agreement which is described in act no. 31.

- "Where the minimum amount of the deposit in respect of any goods or class of goods is not prescribed, an owner who enters into a hire-purchase agreement without having first obtained from the proposed hirer thereunder a deposit in cash or in goods, or partly in cash and partly in goods, to a value not less than one-tenth of the cash price of the goods comprised in the agreement, shall be guilty of an offence under this Act".
- "An owner shall collect the deposit upon the signing of the hire-purchase agreement".
- "If any owner, dealer, agent or person acting on behalf of the owner fails to deliver the goods intended for the hire-purchase agreement to the intending hirer, the owner, dealer, agent or person acting on behalf of the owner shall refund the full amount of the deposit to the intending hirer".

In section 21, the provisions of guarantors are discussed such as:

1. Unless otherwise stipulated in this Act, a guarantor's liability under their guarantee is not relieved due to the implementation of this Act.
2. The liability of the guarantor remains valid even if the owner has lawfully taken possession of the goods included in a hire-purchase agreement as outlined in the agreement's terms, regardless of whether the goods have been subsequently returned to the hirer

under the provisions of this Act. However, it is important to clarify that this provision does not uphold the guarantor's responsibility if the owner and the hirer have entered into a new agreement specifically addressing the goods covered by any hire-purchase agreement.

3. The liability of a guarantor shall not surpass that of the hirer whose obligations they have guaranteed. However, it is important to note that this Act does not nullify any agreement in which the guarantor assumes responsibilities that are not included in the obligations imposed on the hirer under the particular hire-purchase agreement for which the guarantee is being provided.
4. In the event that goods are delivered to the hirer pursuant to a hire-purchase agreement and subsequently repossessed by the owner, any guarantor who has made payments to the owner in line with their guarantee possesses the same entitlement to recover that money as if they were the hirer of the goods. However, during the calculation of the amount received by the owner, all payments made and the value of any other consideration provided by or on behalf of the hirer will be regarded as if it had been paid or provided by the guarantor. It is important to emphasise that the guarantor cannot claim an amount exceeding the actual money they have paid.

Section 22 explains the issues where the guarantor is not bound, which says: When a guarantor agrees to be bound by a contract that guarantees the fulfilment of the hirer's obligations under a hire-purchase agreement:

(a) To pay to the owner an aggregate sum which is larger than the balance originally payable under the agreement or
(b) To perform an obligation in respect of goods other than the goods comprised in the hire-purchase agreement, the agreement so entered shall be void unless the agreement is executed by the guarantor in the presence of a Magistrate, a Commissioner for Oaths or a Notary Public.

Section 23 discusses the rights of the guarantor against the owner, which are:

1. At any point, the guarantor under this section has the option to obtain a release by settling the outstanding amount owed to the owner by the hirer.

2. After making such payment, he is entitled to—
   (a) The guarantor is empowered to take legal action against the hirer, acting on behalf of the owner, in order to address any breach of the hirer's obligations specified in the hire-purchase agreement. This authority is granted on the condition that the guarantor provides the owner with suitable indemnification for any costs incurred. Alternatively, if the guarantor obtains a legal assignment of the hire-purchase debt, they have the option to file a lawsuit in their own name;
   (b) The guarantor is entitled to demand the transfer of all securities held by the owner from the hirer, serving as a measure to guarantee the fulfilment of the hirer's obligations.
3. In case the owner makes a claim against the guarantor based on the guarantee, the guarantor has the right to assert any setoff or counter-claim that the hirer may have against the owner.

Section 24 ensures the rights of the guarantor against the hirer, for example:

1. The guarantor has the right to receive compensation from the hirer for any claim brought by the owner based on the guarantee.
2. The guarantor has the authority to enforce timely payment of the instalments related to the hire-purchase agreement from the hirer, and to do so, they can seek an order from a Magistrate's court.

Hire purchase under *shirkah al-milk* is a contract which is being practised by many conventional and Islamic banks globally. Except for a few differences in procedures and stipulations, the practice of HPSM both in conventional and Islamic banks seems not dissimilar in large comportment. As to be a financing contract, HPSM in Islamic banks plays a significant role in the home, vehicle, agricultural, and industrial types of equipment financing, albeit; it has other purposes to finance too. In order to execute this investment approach, the bank provides financing or provisions for the necessary equipment or goods on a rental basis, incorporating a customary practice aligned with Shari'ah principles. This practice involves the transfer of ownership of the specific property or equipment to the client at the final stage of the contract, once the client has fulfilled the complete payment as per the agreement, enabling them to become the owner of the bank's portion.

Chapter Review Questions

1. What is discussed between the lessor (bank) and lessee (client) in the initial stage of implementing HPSM?
   (a) Feathers of HPSM
   (b) Feasibility of the proposed business project
   (c) Client's need for investment
   (d) All of the above
2. What is the purpose of determining the client's capital contribution in the *shirkah* contract?
   (a) To evaluate the client's financial stability
   (b) To determine the profit-sharing ratio
   (c) To ensure compliance with Shari'ah principles
   (d) To assess the client's commitment to the contract
3. What does the bank evaluate when reviewing the proposal for the HPSM contract?
   (a) Previous history of the HPSM transaction
   (b) Compliance with Shari'ah principles
   (c) Feasibility of the proposed business project
   (d) All of the above
4. According to the Malaysian Hire Purchase Act 1967, what should be included in a hire-purchase agreement?
   (a) Description of the goods
   (b) Specified number of instalments and payment details
   (c) Address where the goods are located
   (d) All of the above
5. In the case of motor vehicles, what conditions are highlighted by the Malaysian Hire Purchase Act 1967?
   (a) Keeping the registration certificate upon request
   (b) Prohibition of entering into hire-purchase agreements for modified vehicles
   (c) Declaration of defects for second-hand motor vehicles
   (d) All of the above
6. According to the Malaysian Hire Purchase Act 1967, what is the minimum value of the deposit required in a hire-purchase agreement?
   (a) One-fifth of the cash price
   (b) One-tenth of the cash price
   (c) Half of the cash price
   (d) Equal to the cash price

7. Which of the following statements is true regarding the liability of a guarantor under the Malaysian Hire Purchase Act 1967?
   (a) A guarantor is discharged from liability under his guarantee.
   (b) The liability of a guarantor ends when the owner takes possession of the goods.
   (c) A guarantor's liability is the same as that of the hirer.
   (d) A guarantor's liability is preserved even if a new agreement is made between the owner and hirer.
8. What rights does a guarantor have against the owner under the Malaysian Hire Purchase Act 1967?
   (a) The right to transfer ownership of the goods to the guarantor.
   (b) The right to sue the owner in the name of the hirer.
   (c) The right to receive compensation from the owner.
   (d) The right to request an extension of the hire-purchase agreement.
9. According to the Malaysian Hire Purchase Act 1967, what can a guarantor do if the owner makes a claim against him on the guarantee?
   (a) Seek reimbursement from the hirer for the amount claimed by the owner.
   (b) File a counter-claim against the owner for breach of contract.
   (c) Demand immediate repayment of the hire-purchase debt from the owner.
   (d) Settle the claim directly with the owner without involving the hirer.
10. What can a guarantor do if the hirer fails to pay the instalments as per the hire-purchase agreement?
   (a) File a lawsuit against the hirer and the owner jointly.
   (b) Apply to a court of a Magistrate for an order to compel the hirer to pay the instalments.
   (c) Request a refund of the deposit from the owner.
   (d) Transfer the hire-purchase agreement to another guarantor.

Answers

1. d
2. b
3. d

4. d
5. d
6. b
7. d
8. b
9. a
10. b

CHAPTER 6

Accounting Treatment in HPSM Contract

Abstract This chapter provides an inclusive analysis of the accounting treatment of HPSM contract, drawing a comprehensive comparison between the accounting treatment of Islamic and conventional hire purchase investments. The focus is on elucidating the various stages and approaches employed in managing hire purchase accounts, shedding light on several essential methods. It is crucial to acknowledge that these methods might not have universal applicability across all jurisdictions, as different regions often utilise distinct approaches. Since the chapter offers a comparative accounting entry of hire purchase, through this in-depth exploration, readers will be equipped with valuable insights into the accounting entries associated with both Islamic and conventional hire purchase transactions, thereby enhancing the overall value of this study.

Keyword Accounting · HPSM · Islamic · Conventional

Preview

This chapter aims to improve comprehension of the hire purchase sale model (HPSM) by comparing the accounting treatment between Islamic and conventional hire purchase investments. It will delve into various stages and approaches used for hire purchase account management, shedding light on several key methods. Nonetheless, it is important to

M. K. Hassan et al., *Hire Purchase Under Shirkah al-Milk (HPSM) in Islamic Banking and Finance*,
https://doi.org/10.1007/978-3-031-50105-0_6

note that these methods may not be universally applicable across all jurisdictions, as different regions may employ distinct approaches. Therefore, the chapter will offer a general overview of hire purchase accounting treatments.

6.1 Accounting Entries Stages of Investment on Islamic HPSM

The following stages are considered for the accounting entries for Islamic Hire purchase, which are as follows:

1.1

Event: while receiving equity from the client for purchasing of asset/property.

Debit: Dr. cash/*al-wadi'ah* current account of the client.

Credit: Cr. HPSM equity of the client.

1.2

Event: while making payment for purchase/procurement/making the asset/property.

Debit:

(a) Dr. Hire purchase under shirkah al-milk account (bank's equity)
(b) Dr. HPSM equity of the client

Credit: Cr. payment order account/current A/C (favouring seller/ maker/ buying agent of the HPSM asset/property as per purchase contract/contract with the seller/maker/buying agent).

1.3

Event: while taking various costs of purchase/procurement/making/ maintenance of the HPSM asset/property into account:

Debit: hire purchase under the shirkah al-milk account of the client.

Credit: payment order/ account of the recipient etc.

1.4

Event: while booking the amount of value addition (on completion of procurement /building /making of the asset and handing over of the same to the client).

Debit: Dr. Hire purchase under the shirkah al-milk account of the client.

Credit: Cr. unearned income account on HPSM asset/property A/C.

(Amount of value added over the cost price as a result of fresh valuation, now transferred to Unearned Income Account).

1.5

Event: while rent will accrue at the end of each month after the asset/property is handed over to the client in usable form:

Debit: Dr. Hire purchase under the shirkah al-milk account of the client.

Credit: Cr. investment income account (rent on HPSM).

1.6

Event: As per agreement, storage, insurance, and maintenance costs, if any, incurred after delivery of the HPSM asset/property to the client, the cost shall be paid by the client from his own source. In case, the client fails to pay the same charges/expenses in cash in time, the bank will pay the same to the debit of the HPSM investment account of the client by passing the following entries:

Debit: Dr. Hire purchase under the shirkah al-milk account of the client.

Credit: Cr. payment order/account of the recipient.

1.7

Event: at the time of recovery/reimbursement of the expenses incurred by the bank for storage, insurance, and maintenance of the asset/property after delivery to the client:

Debit: Dr. cash/*al-wadi 'ah* current A/C of the client.

Credit: Cr. hire purchase account of the client. it may be noted that any amount paid by the client shall first be credited towards adjustment of "other charges", and then "rent and principal" proportionately as per its outstanding position.

1.8

Event: while the instalment is recovered/realised, the following entries shall be passed:

Debit: Dr. cash/current A/C of the client.

Credit:

(a) Cr. HPSM account of the client (principal amount)

(b) Cr. Investment income (rent on HPSM)

1.9

Event: while reversing the proportionate amount of profit from the unearned income account:

Debit: Dr. unearned income account

Credit: Cr. investment income account (HPSM).

1.10

Event: if any hire purchase under the shirkah al-milk account becomes classified below B/L status, the following entries shall be passed for transferring rent accrued from the beginning of the year to date from the investment income account to rent suspense A/C:

Debit: Dr. investment income account (HPSM).

Credit: Cr. rent suspense account (HPSM).

1.11

Event: While charging rent on the HPSM account as long as the classification status remains below B/L:

Debit: Dr. HPSM account (rent).

Credit: Cr. rent suspense A/C (HPSM).

If it is classified as Bad/Loss, the charging of rent shall be stopped as per Bangladesh Bank classification (in the case of the practice of Bangladesh perspective) rules.

1.12

Event: If the amount of rent is paid by the Client, despite the Investment A/C is classified.

Debit: Dr. cash/client's *al-wadi'ah* current A/C.

Credit: Cr. HPSM account (rent).

After declassification:

Debit: Dr. rent suspense A/C

Credit: Cr. investment income A/C.

Rent suspended earlier owing to classification, transferred to investment income (A/C).

1.13

Event: at the time of waiver of principal/rent & charges (if any, by the corporate office:

Debit:

(a) Dr. rent suspense A/C (HPSM) (for the amount of rent suspended earlier and kept with the branch)
(b) Dr. unearned income A/C (value addition for the gestation period)

Credit: Cr. HPSM account (principal, rent, and other charges should be shown separately).

6.2 Accounting Entries Methods of Investment in Conventional Hire Purchase

From an accounting perspective, both the hire purchase and the instalment payment system are treated similarly. To properly account for them, the following key considerations should be considered (Accounting Education University, n.d):

(a) The cash price represents the amount that one would pay when purchasing an asset outright without any instalment payments.
(b) Hire price = cash price + interest for the risk of giving asset on instalment.
(c) Down payment: a down payment refers to the initial payment made at the commencement of a hire-purchase agreement. There are four distinct methods for accounting for hire purchase.

6.2.1 1st: Cash Price Method

In the cash price method, hire purchase transactions are treated like any other regular transactions. When transactions or events occur, they are documented and recorded accordingly.

1.1. Journal Entries in the Books of Purchaser

1.1.1

Event: while buying assets on hire purchase

Debit: asset on hire purchase account Dr.

Credit: vendor account Cr.

1.1.2

Event: while paying the down payment to the vendor.

Debit: vendor account Dr.

Cash/bank.

1.1.3

Event: when Interest is due on unpaid instalments

Debit: interest on hire purchase account Dr.

Credit: vendor account Cr.

1.1.4

Event: while instalment payment (interest payment will be also included in it).

Debit: vendor account Dr.

Credit: cash/bank account Cr.

1.1.5

Event: while transferring interest to the profit and loss account.

Debit: profit and loss account Dr.

Credit: interest on hire purchase account Cr.

1.1.6

Event: depreciation charge.

Debit:

(a) Depreciation account Dr.
(b) Assets on hire purchase account Dr.

1.1.7

Event: if the asset is returned.

Debit: hire vendor account Dr.

Credit: asset on hire purchase account Cr.

In the books of Hire Vendor

1.2.1

Event: while giving assets on hire.

Debit: hire purchaser account Dr.

Credit: HP sale Cr.

1.2.2

Event: while the down payment received.

Debit: bank account Dr.

Credit: HP sales Cr.

1.2.3

Event: for interest receivable.

Debit: hire purchaser account Dr.

Credit: interest account Cr.

1.2.4

Event: for instalment due.

Debit: instalment due account Dr.

Credit: HP sales Cr.

1.2.5

Event: for instalment received.

Debit: bank account Dr.

Credit: hire purchaser account Cr.
1.2.6
Event: for instalment not due at the year.
Debit: hire purchase stock account Dr.
Credit: trading account Cr.

(a) **1.2.6**
Event: for stock reserve
Debit: stock Reserve account Dr.
Credit: hire purchase stock account Cr.
(b) **Disclosure in the balance sheet**
(a) Current assets
(b) Hire purchase debtor

6.2.2 2nd: Interest Suspense Method

Under this method, banks open an interest suspense account. Any interest that remains unpaid on the hire purchase asset is allocated to the interest suspense account. When the interest becomes due, the interest account is debited, and the interest suspense account is credited.

1.2.The following entries will pass in the books of the hire buyer:
1.2.1
Event: for transferring total interest payable on the hire purchase deal.
Debit: interest suspense account Dr.
Credit: purchase account Cr.
1.2.2
Event: when interest is due.
Debit: interest account Dr.
Credit: interest suspense account Cr.
All other entries will be the same as the first method.
1.3. In the books of hire vendor
1.3.1
Event: for transferring total interest payable to the interest suspense account.
Debit: hire purchaser account Dr.
Credit: interest suspense account Cr.

1.3.4
Event: stock reserve account on opening stock.
Debit: stock reserve account Dr.
Credit: hire purchase adjustment account Cr.
1.3.5
Event: stock reserve on closing stock.
Debit: hire purchase adjustment account Dr.
Credit: stock reserve account C.

6.3 Conclusion

The fundamental distinction in hire purchase lies in the ownership structure. In conventional Banks, the loan itself is owned by the bank, not the underlying asset, whereas Islamic Banks hold proportional ownership of the asset. In the context of conventional banking, interest is typically charged quarterly (with variations based on specific jurisdictions) and can be capitalised in case of nonpayment, resulting in compounding interest. Conversely, Islamic Banking charges rent on a monthly basis, without any compounding effect.

Chapter Review Question

1. While receiving equity from the client for purchasing of asset/ property in Islamic hire purchase, the following answer is correct:
   a. Cr. cash/*al-wadi'ah* current account of the client and Cr. HPSM equity of the client.
   b. Cr. cash/ *al-wadi'ah* current account of the client
   c. Cr. HPSM equity of the client.
   d. None of the above
2. While taking various costs of purchase/procurement/making/ maintenance of the HPSM asset/property into account, the status of debit would be:
   a. Payment order/account of the recipient
   b. Hire purchase under the shirkah al-milk account of the client
   c. HPSM equity of the client
   d. All above
3. While rent will accrue at the end of each month after the asset/ property is handed over to the client in usable form in Islamic hire purchase, the status of credit would be:
   a. Hire purchase under the shirkah al-milk account of the client

b. Investment income account (rent on HPSM)
c. Hire purchase under the shirkah al-milk account of the client
d. Payment order/account of the recipient

4. While reversing the proportionate amount of profit from the unearned income account, the status of debit would be:
a. Cr. investment income account (HPSM)
b. Investment income account (rent on HPSM)
c. HPSM equity of the client
d. Unearned income account

5. While charging rent on the HPSM account as long as the classification status remains below B/L, the status of credit would be:
a. HPSM account (rent)
b. Payment order/ account of the recipient
c. Rent suspense account (HPSM)
d. All above

6. In the cash price method of conventional hire purchase, while buying assets on hire purchase, the debit side is:
a. Vendor account
b. Asset on hire purchase account Dr
c. a & b
d. None of the above

7. When interest is due on unpaid instalments in conventional hire purchase, the credit side is:
a. Vendor account
b. Client account
c. Rent suspense account
d. All the above

8. When goods are sold on hire purchase in conventional banks, the debit would be on the side of:
a. Vendor account
b. Asset on hire purchase account
c. Rent suspense account
d. Hire purchase stock account

9. When instalments become due for payment in conventional hire purchase, the debit side is:
a. Hire purchase debtors account
b. Hire purchase stock account
c. Rent suspense account
d. All the above

10. When cash is received in a conventional hire purchase, the credit side would be:
    a. Cash account
    b. Hire purchase debtor account
    c. Unearned income account
    d. None of the above

Answers

1. a
2. b
3. b
4. d
5. c
6. b
7. a
8. d
9. a
10. b

CHAPTER 7

Ownership Transfer and Shari'ah Issues in HPSM

Abstract This chapter extensively examines the Shari'ah considerations that arise during the application of HPSM. It is structured into distinct sections, each addressing specific Shari'ah issues. These sections encompass topics such as the transfer of ownership within HPSM, the implications of conditional sales within Shari'ah, the legal status of *wa'd* (promise) in HPSM, the presence of dual contracts within HPSM applications, and the Shari'ah aspects of dual contracts in a single transaction. By delineating these comprehensive sections, the chapter aims to offer readers an in-depth comprehension of the diverse Shari'ah intricacies that are interconnected with the practical implementation of HPSM. It serves as a valuable resource for fostering a profound understanding of the nuanced Shari'ah dimensions that underlie the execution of HPSM transactions.

Keyword *Wa'd* · *Ijarah* · Ownership Transfer · Lease · Sale

Preview

This chapter focuses on the Shari'ah issues related to the application and execution of HPSM. These issues have been divided into several sections, i.e. Shari'ah issues related to the transfer of ownership in the application of HPSM; issues of sale with condition(s) in Shari'ah; issues related to

M. K. Hassan et al., *Hire Purchase Under Shirkah al-Milk (HPSM) in Islamic Banking and Finance*,
https://doi.org/10.1007/978-3-031-50105-0_7

the legal status of *wa'd* (promise) in HPSM; Shari'ah issues related to having two contracts in one contact in the application of HPSM and Shari'ah issues of two contracts in one (*bay'atan fi bay'*). It is anticipated that this chapter will provide readers with a deeper understanding of the various Shari'ah issues associated with the practical application and execution of HPSM.

7.1 Procedures for Transferring the Ownership After *Ijarah* Tenure in HPSM

There are several methods available for transferring the legal title to the lessee in HPSM. The transfer of ownership takes place once the tenure of the *ijarah* contract is completed. The following are the different types of ownership transfer options in the HPSM contract:

7.1.1 Transferring the Ownership Through a Gradual Sale

In this particular type of sale, the property is acquired jointly by two parties, namely the bank and the client, based on an agreed *shirkah* agreement. Both parties have shared ownership of the property. The bank then leases its share or portion to another party, referred to as the lessee or client partner, for a fixed period and a predetermined fixed rent. As part of the agreement, the bank commits to gradually selling or transferring ownership of its portion to the lessee in proportion to their agreed consideration of payment. At the end of the rental period, upon the lessee completing the full payment of the property price, he/she becomes entitled to acquire the legal title of the leased portion from the bank. In this particular type of sale under HPSM, the total price of the property being leased is determined in advance and divided over the lease contract period, allowing the lessee to make gradual payments of the proportionate fixed rent towards the total price. This gradual payment structure enables the lessee to acquire ownership of the property gradually, with the eventual purpose of becoming the full owner by the end of the lease period. For each portion of the property sold (or unit of time as per the agreement), a separate sale contract must be executed between the lessor and the lessee. The rent amount is proportionally deducted from the payment, leading to a decrease in the lessor's ownership and an increase in the lessee's ownership share of the property.

If, for any reason, the lease contract is terminated before the full legal title is transferred to the lessee, the lessee will retain the ownership share corresponding to the payments made, while the remaining portion will be retained by the bank (IBBL, n.d (b)).

*7.1.2 Transferring the Ownership Through a Gift (*Hibah*) Contract*

In this type of practice, the lessor enters into a lease agreement with the lessee, with a prior commitment to transfer the legal title of the property to the lessee through a gift (*hibah*) contract upon fulfilling certain conditions. These conditions typically include the completion of all rental payments without any additional consideration. Once the lease period expires and all rental instalments are settled, the legal title of the property can be transferred. This transfer can be done through a separate gift deed executed by the lessor or by issuing a conditional gift deed that specifies the transfer is contingent upon the settlement of all rental instalments. As a result, the legal title is automatically transferred when the lease period ends and all fixed rent instalments are paid. It is important to note that the entire gift contract process is treated as having no consideration, as it is solely a separate gift contract.

In this mode, the rental payments agreed upon are fixed and sufficient not only to cover the capital cost but also to generate a reasonable profit for the lessor. Importantly, the agreed-upon rentals are not considered as the price or part of the price of the asset. The full ownership of the asset remains with the lessor until the final settlement of all rental instalments is made (IBBL, n.d (b)).

7.1.2.1 Shari'ah *Issues in a Gift (*Hibah*) Contract with Stipulations*

Jurists are with different positive and negative opinions on the conditional gift contract (*hibah*). They have widely discussed the issue as per their own opinions and understanding based on Shari'ah texts, which are as below:

1. Aqil (1978) and Al-Shadhili (2014) elucidate that according to the majority of Muslim jurists, including Hanafi, Shafi'i, Hanbali, Zaydi, and Imami, the gift (*hibah*) contract with a condition is an invalid one. To them, an effective ownership contract must be realised on the spot without any delay at the same contractual session.

If a contract is stipulated with a condition (*hibah*), the immediate transfer of the ownership will not occur, and this is against the requirement of a gift (*hibah*), where an immediate transfer of ownership must occur and not based on any assumption or conjecture. Any contract based on an assumption which may or may not happen may lead to uncertainty.

2. The consensus among scholars from various schools of jurisprudence is that a gift contract with a compensatory condition is considered valid, and the condition itself is also deemed valid (Al-Zuhayli, 2002). Despite concurring on the legality of the contract, there are variations among those who affirm its validity regarding the specific characteristics of the contract, like:

   a. According to some Hanafi scholars, the initial contract is considered a valid gift (*hibah*) contract, but it eventually transforms into a sale contract. The legal ruling pertaining to gift contracts applies before the transfer of ownership takes place. Therefore, the gift and its compensation, such as rentals or instalments, can be retained prior to the actual exchange. Subsequently, after the exchange occurs, the contract is treated as a sale. In cases where a defect is found in the property, the return of the property to its original owner is only necessary. In most cases, the contract can be revoked, but if the compensation is related to real estate, the right of preemption (*shufa'ah*) is required. This perspective is advocated by certain Hanafi scholars (Al-Zuhayli, 2002).
   b. According to the Zufar of the Hanafi school, the gift (*hibah*) contract is regarded as a sale contract from its inception until its conclusion. All the conditions applicable to sale contracts are therefore required to be applied to the gift (*hibah*) contract accordingly. However, many Hanafi scholars maintain their stance that the gift (*hibah*) contract is a hybrid form, as it is technically considered a gift but possesses the substance of a sale. Consequently, the contract incorporates certain elements from both the gift and sale contracts (Al-Zuhayli, 2002) and the contract is considered valid when the condition is appropriately and clearly defined (al-Shadhili, 2014).
   c. According to the Maliki school of thought, the contract is predominantly regarded as a sale, but there are situations where it can be treated as a gift. The occasional differentiation between

gift and sale contracts arises when a gift is given with an uncertain or unknown reimbursement or compensation, along with an indefinite deferral period. In such cases, the donor (lessor in the HPSM contract) must accept the reimbursement and is not allowed to delay it in the event of any defect being identified. However, there is an exception that permits the return of the reimbursement only when an extreme defect is detected (Al-Zuhayli, 2002).

d. According to the majority of Shafi'i and Hanbali scholars, the gift (*hibah*) contract is essentially treated as a sale contract. In this view, the recipient (lessee in HPSM) is obligated to pay the specified amount and is bound by all the regulations governing a sale contract. This interpretation is primarily influenced by the condition of compensation, which deviates from the nature of a traditional gift. As a result, the gift contract is transformed into a sale contract and should be treated accordingly (Al-Zuhayli, 2002). AAOIFI Shari'ah Standard No. (9) supports the permissibility of a gift contract that includes a condition upon the completion of the *ijarah* contract. Al-Shadhili (2014) explains that the rationale behind the validity of a gift contract with a condition lies in the concept of *tabarru'*, where someone who contributes voluntarily is esteemed and commended. Therefore, the person who is esteemed and praised can allocate their *tabarru'* as they desire, as long as it does not involve engaging in prohibited (*haram*) actions or impeding permissible (*halal*) matters.

AAOIFI Shari'ah Standard No. (9) and Shadhili (2014) bring a hadith that strengthens their opinion in which it is mentioned that the Prophet (SAW) sent a gift to Negus (The former emperor of Ethiopia) on the condition that he should be alive at the time of the arrival of the Prophet (SAW). The hadith has been narrated from Umm Kalthum Binti Abi Salamah: when Prophet (SAW) married Umm Salamah, he said to her, "I sent a gift to the emperor of Najjashi (Ethiopia) a necklace and musk. Prophet (SAW) said, I did not hear except he is dead, and I did not see, except my gift will be returned to me if it is returned to me, I will give it to you". So, Umm Salamah replied: "like what had been said by the Prophet (SAW) and the gift was returned, he (SAW) gave every one of his wives the musk, and he (SAW) gave Umm Salamah the remaining of necklace and musk". Imam Ahmad narrated that this hadith is considered no less than a *hasan* level, in which the narrators are reliable (Shadili, 2014). Another narration of hadith, in which it was comprehended that the Prophet (SAW) has halted giving the gift to Umm Salamah until the condition is attained; he (SAW) only gifted the necklace to her when it was returned after King Najjashi's death (Shadili, 2014).

7.1.3 Transferring the Ownership in Exchange for a Token Amount

In this contract, the transfer of ownership of the property to the lessee occurs after the predetermined lease tenure, which is associated with a specific rent amount. The legal title of the property is then transferred to the lessee through a separate sale contract, wherein an agreed token payment is made. This token payment can be determined based on mutual agreement, and it may correspond to the value of the property (IBBL n.d, (b)). The transformation of the contract, as mentioned earlier, consists of three different contracts:

1. The *shirkah* contract is at the initial stage.
2. The lease contract is at the second stage.
3. The final stage of the sales contract occurs when the leasing tenure reaches maturity. At this point, the contract can either transition into the sale stage or be terminated if the lessee refuses to pay the agreed-upon instalments. If the lessee wishes to purchase the leased property, the sale contract will be executed at the end of the lease tenure by making a payment of the agreed token price (al-Shadili, 2014). It is important to note that this sale contract is contingent upon the lessee settling all agreed rentals within the specified tenure and paying the property's price in the form of a token price. From a Shari'ah perspective, the matter of ending a contract with such a condition should be comprehensively discussed.

7.1.4 Transferring the Ownership by Paying a Specified Amount

This arrangement is implemented by leasing a specific property and establishing a fixed rental amount for a predetermined period. A condition is stipulated that upon completion of the lease, a fixed and agreed-upon amount must be paid in order to transfer the legal title of the property, effectively constituting a sale contract. Initially, the *ijarah* contract takes effect, while the sale contract becomes effective only after the lease contract expires (IBBL, n.d(b)). To illustrate, a lessor offers a lessee the opportunity to lease a particular good or property for a specified payment within a certain period. The condition is that if the lessee settles all the instalments within this duration, the lessor agrees to sell the property to the lessee at a predetermined price. The lessee then accepts the leasing arrangement based on these terms (al-Shadili, 2014).

According to al-Shadili (2014), the sale contract in this context involves determining the price of the property in advance based on its actual value. This price is to be settled by the lessee after the lease period concludes. As a result, the subject matter of the lease contract transforms into the subject matter of the sale contract, while the lessee gains both the benefits and physical ownership of the property. These changes are carried out through the contractual consequences and compliance with Shari'ah principles (al-Shadili, 2014).

Furthermore, this type of sale does not necessitate a new wording (*sigah*) as it is already encompassed within the previous offer made by the lessor stating "I sell", and the acceptance of the offer by the lessee saying, "I accept" (al-Shadili, 2014).

7.1.5 Transferring the Ownership by Paying an Equivalent Amount of Remaining Rental Instalment Before Ending the Lease Contract

The contract described is primarily a promise-based agreement between the lessor and the lessee. In this arrangement, the lessor promises the lessee that the legal title of the leased property will be transferred to him at any point during the lease period if he fulfils his obligation of paying all the remaining rental instalments. Therefore, the *ijarah* contract remains in effect until the legal title is transferred to the lessee. Once the legal title of the property is transferred, the *ijarah* contract closes down for the remaining duration, as both the benefits and the property itself become the lessee's ownership. It is important to note that this type of sale requires a separate sale contract to be executed at the time of the sale (IBBL, n.d (b)).

7.2 Issues Related to Sale with Condition(s) in *Shari'ah*

Undoubtedly, until the transfer of ownership in HPSM, the contract remains an effective leasing contract because of its exact wording (*sigah*) for a leasing transaction with no uncertainty; however, the sale contract with conditions after maturity of the lease tenure requires a rigorous investigation in the eyes of Shari'ah, whether any condition in a sale contract is valid or not? If the condition is valid, then its time and position must be acquired, and, in case of invalidity, the contract is deemed to be void.

Abdullah (1988) elucidates a fatwa of *Majallah al-Ahkam al-Adliyyah* when a contract is subject to a specific condition; its validity is subject to the fulfilment of that particular condition. For instance, if the agreement stipulates that the contract will become invalid if the lessee fails to make the full payment of the agreed-upon instalments, this is referred to as an "abolishing" (*fiskh*) condition in civil law and *"khiyar al-naqd"* in Islamic jurisprudence. However, there are varying opinions among scholars regarding leases with conditions. After examining the statements of jurists, these conditions can be classified into different categories. The schools of *fiqh* (Islamic jurisprudence) concur that certain conditions can be incorporated into contracts if they align with the principles of Shari'ah. Generally, these conditions can be categorised into four types (Al-Funaysan, 2000).

(a) Terms and conditions are the principal elements of the contract, i.e. conditions on the seller to hand over the goods and on the buyer to make the payment, and the seller's freedom to halt the good until its price is paid in full (Al-Zuhayli, 2003) or partially based on their mutual agreement. Naturally, a contract cannot happen unless it attains its core and attributed conditions. Thus, "such conditions articulate the requirements of the contract since the establishment of ownership, exchange of possession, and withholding of the object prior to the delivery of the price are among the requirements of commutative contracts" (Al-Kasani, 2005).

(b) Terms and conditions play a crucial role in securing and strengthening a contract. In the context of a long-term loan agreement, for instance, it is common to require the borrower to furnish a guarantor or pawn as a means to safeguard the loan amount. This practice serves as an alternative to traditional documentation and acts as a guarantee for payment, thereby fulfilling the obligations outlined in the sales contract and ensuring eligibility for delivery. Consequently, the inclusion of a guarantor or collateral serves to fortify the contract's integrity (Al-Zuhayli, 2003). Hence, it is imperative to thoroughly discuss and address such conditions comprehensively (Al-Kasani, 2005):

1. If the pawned asset and the guarantor are unknown, the sale will be deemed defective (*fasid*). This is because, for instance, if the seller says: "I would like to sell this good for you on a condition that you would pledge with me an objective of equal price", but this wording has been done without identifying the object to be pledged or making a condition for a guarantor and does not specify a particular person. Hence, the uncertainty of the condition leads the contract to ignorance (*jahalah*) which causes the contract to be defective. However, if both parties agree to sell a specific pawned object throughout the sale period, then it should be permissible as the obstacle of ignorance to the object to be pawned is already removed (Al-Zuhayli, 2003).
2. When the two parties do not agree on an object to be pawned, the buyer pays the price in cash within the sale contract tenure; then, the sale would be valid. This is because the actual objective of the contract is to acquire the price for the buyer, and the object of pawning is to secure the price, too, which meanwhile the seller has gained. So, once the main objective is achieved, which is the price without pawning, then the contractual aspect of pawning is irrelevant.
3. According to Al-Zuhayli (2003), Imam Zufar states that an inappropriate condition that does not align with the contractual requirements would render the contract defective. However, when it comes to the condition of pledging or requiring a guarantor, there is a conflict in the contract if such a condition is considered defective. Nevertheless, the majority of Hanafi scholars hold the view that the presence of such a condition does not invalidate the contract. Despite contradicting the form of the contract, the inclusion of a pledge or guarantor is permissible and serves as a means to secure the payment of the price from the lessee to the lessor or from the buyer to the seller. Consequently, the seller's rights are safeguarded through the act of pledging or providing a guarantor.

(c) According to al-Taskhiri (2014) and Al-Zuhayli (2003), terms and conditions that do not contradict the fundamental characteristics of a contract can be validly stipulated and legally permitted. However, it is essential to avoid incorporating any element of uncertain (*gharar*) condition into the contract (al-Taskhiri, 2014). However, certain conditions do not directly strengthen the contract; but they may still bring benefits to one of the contracting parties. For instance, a buyer may purchase cloth with the condition that the seller will sew it into a shirt (Al-Funaysan, 2000). Nevertheless, according to Zufar, such sale contracts with additional conditions are not considered valid under Shari'ah law because they do not pertain to the essential requirements of the contract, and the benefits derived from these conditions are one-sided rather than mutually beneficial. Consequently, these conditions are deemed defective. Therefore, buying cloth with the condition that the seller will sew it into a shirt would be considered a defective condition (Al-Zuhayli, 2003) as it only benefits the customer rather than both parties. In contemporary times, such conditions are prevalent in long-term sales agreements that resemble manufacturing contracts ("*istisna*"). Consequently, Al-Zuhayli (2003) argues that the condition in a sale contract is overruled similarly to how it is overruled in "*istisna*" contracts.

(d) If the terms and conditions of a contract directly contradict the purpose of the agreement and impose unreasonable requirements, they are considered invalid within a Shari'ah-compliant sale contract. An example of such a condition would be stipulating that the buyer cannot possess or utilise the sold item's benefits or that the lessee is prohibited from using the leased asset. These conditions are contradictory to the substance of a typical Shari'ah-compliant sale contract. Consequently, despite the conditions being invalid (Niazi, 1991), the contract itself may still remain valid.

Scholars engage in a debate regarding the legal status of contracts that contain conditions and the validity of conditions that contradict the contract's objective. However, the Hanafi school summarises the types of conditions which are valid (*sahih*), defective *(fasid),* and invalid *(batil)* (Al-Kasani, 2005; Al-Sarakhsi, 2013):

The valid conditions are those which meet all necessary requirements of a valid contract that are simply stipulated to facilitate the extra opportunity or to protect the rights of both parties and are not contrary to the objective of the contract. On the other hand, defective (*fasid*) conditions are simply stipulated to obtain extra facilities for either party. In such cases, the contract is deemed defective, but it still retains its validity with defective condition(s). Examples of contracts with defective (*fasid*) conditions include purchasing wheat with the condition that the seller grinds it, buying cloth with the condition that the seller sews it into a shirt, or selling with the condition that the buyer provides a loan to the seller. According to the Hanafi school of thought, these conditions are considered defective because they provide an additional benefit to one party without an equivalent counter value, which is deemed usury. Hence, these conditions are categorised as defective (Al-Zuhayli, 2003).

Invalid (*laghw* or *al-batil*) conditions are those that explicitly harm one of the contracting parties. An instance of such a condition is a sale with the stipulation that the buyer is prohibited from reselling or gifting the item to others. According to the majority of Hanafi scholars, this type of sale is permissible, but the condition itself is invalid. This is because the condition does not provide any advantage or benefit to either party and therefore, it does not render the contract invalid, too, based on the prohibition of usury, which entails an additional benefit for one of the parties.

Maliki and Shafi'i jurists believe that the second and third categories of conditions of the Hanafi should be classified as void, which invalidates the contract. Yet, the Maliki and Shafi'i scholars consider that there are conditions inherently deemed to be invalid, but they do not invalidate the contract itself. Likewise, some conditions in a sale contract to them are inherently valid and do not invalidate the contract, such as the stipulation of riding on the sold animal or living in the sold house for a known short period. Despite this, Shafi'i school considers these conditions invalid (Kharofah, 1997). Each school of *fiqh* classifies certain conditions in a sale contract to be valid or not; the views of Shafi'i school concerning the conditions in a sale contract are as follows:

a. If a condition is necessary as a prerequisite for a contract, such as a requirement that the sold object be delivered in accordance with the agreement and that the buyer can return the purchased asset if any defects are discovered, then such a condition in the sale contract is considered valid (Al-Zuhayli, 2003; Al-Shirbini, 1994).
b. A contract remains valid when a valid condition is associated with it, such as opting for deferment, including a pledge or providing a guarantor, even if the condition benefits one of the contracting parties and is not a fundamental requirement of the contract. The validity or invalidity of a condition depends on its legal characteristics (Al-Shirbini, 1994).

c. When conditions directly contradict the purpose and substance of a contract, both the conditions and the contract itself are considered invalid. For example, a condition that restricts the buyer from reselling the purchased goods or giving them as gifts would be deemed invalid. Such conditions render the sale contract invalid, as stated in the hadith of the Prophet (SAW), where he prohibited transactions with conditions (*bay' wa shart*) (Al-Shirbini, 1994).

Hanbali scholars embrace a different opinion saying that a sale contract is rendered invalid if it is executed based on two conditions. This legal ruling of Hanbali school has been ascertained due to a hadith where Prophet (SAW) prohibited two conditions in a single sale transaction; he (SAW) says, "the following are not permissible: a loan and a sale in one transaction, two conditions in one sale, or selling that which is not in your possession" (Abadi, 2001). Nevertheless, Hanbali scholars categorised the conditions of a sale contract into four, and they are as follows:

a. Conditions that are included as prerequisites of a contract, such as delivery conditions, options during the sale session, and immediate exchange, are considered redundant and do not alter the status or nature of the contract (Al-Zuhayli, 2003).
b. There are conditions, such as deferment, options, pledging, guaranty, certification, or the description of specific characteristics of the sale object that result in additional advantages for either or both parties involved in the contract, are allowed and must be attained in the contract in order to make the contract valid (Al-Zuhayli, 2003).
c. Within this category, certain conditions exist that are not fundamental prerequisites for achieving the primary objective of the contract but can yield reasonable advantages for either party. These conditions can be classified into two types. The first type encompasses conditions associated with the sale object, which benefit the seller. For instance, in a contract for selling a house, the seller may include a provision stating their intention to stay in the old house for a short period. Similarly, in an animal sale contract, the seller might specify that he will ride the animal to a particular location (Al-Zuhayli, 2003) or cover a specific distance. This condition holds validity based on a hadith narrated by Jabir, where the Prophet (SAW) purchased a camel and included a condition that the seller would transport him on that camel to his house in

Madinah (Al-Sundi, 1998). Additionally, there are instances where two conditions are combined within a single contract. For example, selling a good to someone with the condition that they will sell another good to the seller. However, this type of condition is considered defective and renders the sale itself defective due to the prohibition of combining two sales in one contract (Al-Zuhayli, 2003).

d. In certain cases, some conditions contradict the purpose of a contract and are deemed rationally unacceptable. An instance of such a condition is when a seller includes a provision in the contract stating that the buyer is forbidden from reselling the item. While other schools of thought consider this type of contract null and void, Imam Ahmad holds the belief that the contract itself is valid, and it is the condition within the contract that is deemed invalid.

The Maliki scholars have paid attention to the conditions embedded in the contract (Al-Zuhayli, 2003), and they are:

a. If the seller includes a condition in the contract that restricts the buyer from engaging in any private or public transactions with the purchased goods, such as reselling them or giving them as gifts, the contract will be considered invalid.
b. Based on the mentioned hadith of Jabir, if the seller includes a condition in the sale that would benefit him, the sale with that specific condition is considered valid. For instance, selling a car with the condition that the buyer must allow the seller to ride in it to a specific place or cover a certain distance.
c. In such a scenario, the sale itself would be considered valid, while the condition attached to it would be deemed invalid. For example, if the seller includes a condition in the contract stating that the sale becomes void if the price is not delivered within three days, the condition would be invalid, but the sale would still be valid. However, if the seller states, "Whenever I return the price of the sold item to you, you must return the sold item to me", this is known as *bay' al-wafa* (redemptive sale) according to the Hanafi school of thought, in this case, the sale would not be permissible.

Ibn Taymiyyah outlines a distinct perspective that diverges from the viewpoints that are discussed earlier by various schools of *fiqh* regarding sales with conditions. According to him, if a condition does not contradict the principles of Shari'ah, it is considered permissible. This stance is rooted in Qur'anic verses and Prophetic sayings that emphasise the importance of fulfilling commitments, promises, and pledges, thereby encouraging their observance. Prophet (SAW) said, "People are bound by their condition as long as it does not make prohibited permissible and permissible prohibited of Shari'ah" (Ibn Taymiyyah, 2011). He further emphasises that both the contract and conditions are acceptable principally, as he says, "and this notion is proved by al-Qur'an and Sunnah, and it's the prioritised opinion of the school of Hanbalis. So, there is no scope to accept anything which is prohibited by Allah and vice-verse (no scope to reject anything permissible), but the stipulator is free to assert something was not obligatory before". "Stipulating a qualitative article or a mortgage in the sale contract, and extra dowry in marriage over the normal case, can require obligations or deprive what was allowed before" too. Moreover, asserting obligations in a contract by mutual consent in favour of the imposer is to protect his rights (Hama, 2007).

To summarise the discussion of conditions in the sale contract, this is to clarify that the hadith which prohibits a sale with condition(s) is the most frequently referred evidence for those who invalidate the conditions in a sale contract. However, this hadith is not authentic (*sahih*) as it does not fall under the criteria of being an authentic hadith. Hence, the statement of Ibn Taymiyyah is the strongest and most preferable one, which is also the opinion of many contemporary Muslim scholars. Rationally, a valid condition does not contradict the Shari'ah principles and the objective of the sale contract; rather protects the rights of both contracting parties. Especially in modern-day transactions, a sale without conditions raises several risks against both parties, while a transaction deals with a massive amount of money. Along with the view of Ibn Taymiyyah, the other schools of thought are also not reluctant to agree with the need for a condition in the sale contract. Therefore, those schools of thought precisely exhibit their view on which ground the condition can be accepted in the sale contract and on which ground it cannot.

7.3 Issues with the Legal Status of *Wa'd* in a Sale Contract

Certainly, the promise holds significant importance in various future-oriented financial agreements, such as hire purchases under *shirkah al-milk*, as well as options and forward contracts. In the context of a hire purchase under the *shirkah al-milk* contract, the lessor (usually a bank) assures the lessee that they will transfer the legal ownership of the leased asset once the specified term is completed and all relevant instalments or conditions are fulfiled. Presently, numerous contracts in modern economic activities incorporate the element of promise as a fundamental component, including future, option, and forward contracts. Classical and modern Muslim scholars debate the issue of promise and exhibit several opinions on whether it is to be binding or not:

(a) According to the views of most Hanafi, Shafi'i, Hanbali, and Zahiri jurists, as well as many of their successors like Sabaki and Asqalani, the binding nature of a promise is not primarily based on its legal aspect but rather on its religious significance (Asqalani, 1999). This perspective stems from the belief that fulfilling a promise is a widespread practice in Islam (Al Shadhili, 2014) as Allah (SWT) in verse no. 34 of Surah al-Isra says:

إِنَّ الْعَهْدَ كَانَ مَسْئُولًا وَأَوْفُوا بِالْعَهْدِ ۖ

And fulfil [every] commitment. Verily, the commitment is ever [that about which one will be] questioned.

So, the promising parties are bound to fulfil their promise so that the contract can be executed following the Shari'ah requirement, but from the legal perception, the contracting parties are not forced to attain the promise. Contrarily, the Hanafi school of thought holds the belief that if a promise includes specific conditions, then it becomes obligatory to fulfil the promise from a legal standpoint (Al-Zuhayli, 2002). This perspective is exemplified in the context of a hire purchase transaction, where a promise to transfer the legal ownership of a leased property is made after the completion of the instalment payments.

Kharofa (1997) asserts that a contract should encompass both legal and moral (religious) foundations, whereas a promise within a contract holds primarily moral value. He further cites that honouring a promise is not solely an obligation but also a commendable virtue and responsibility. However, both Kharofa (1997) and Usmani (1998) acknowledge that there are certain circumstances under which a promise can be legally enforced by a court of law, thus validating its enforceability from a legal standpoint. Usmani (1998) further goes on to argue that, considering the demands of the modern economy, a promise within the Islamic financial spectrum can be deemed legally binding. In the modern Islamic financial industry, numerous products cannot be effectively implemented without the inclusion of a promise due to the presence of excessive risk and uncertainty. Examples of such products include *bay' as sarf*, HPSM, forward *ijarah*, and others.

(b) According to the Maliki school of thought, there are specific perspectives regarding the binding nature of a promise within a contract. In their view, the promise becomes enforceable if the promisee (lessee) fulfils the conditions outlined in the contract, such as completing the payment of instalments in a hire-purchase agreement. This means that the promise of the promisor (lessor), who pledged to transfer the ownership of the property upon the lessee's completion of the instalments, becomes binding (Alish, 1958). Another factor that contributes to the binding nature of the promise, particularly in a hire purchase contract, is the consideration that the paid rental amount exceeds the ordinary market price, thereby enabling the lessee to obtain the legal title of the property in accordance with the lessor's promise (Al-Zuhayli, 2002). The resolution of the International Islamic Fiqh Academy (IIFA, 2021) in its fifth session that took place in Kuwait on the issue of promise in contact holds the same view of Malikis where stated:

> Promise is unilaterally given by one of the parties. The promisor is religiously bound even if there is no reason to make the promise legally binding on him. However, he is legally bound if the promise is suspended on something or promised party spends some money because of the promise. The promisor either should honour his promise or compensate the promised party for any loss incurred because of the promise.

The second viewpoint of the Maliki school suggests that a promise should be upheld if it has been made for a specific purpose, even if the promise itself does not directly affect the main objective. However, if there are valid reasons for not fulfilling the promise, this is not obligatory to fulfil it (Al-Shadili, 2014).

(c) The notion that a promise should be honoured based on religious grounds rather than legal obligations is not only supported by the majority of Hanafi, Shafi'i, Hanbali, and Zahiri scholars but has also been advocated by certain successors of the Maliki school also (Al-Shadili, 2014).

(d) In contrast, certain Malikis, along with Ibn Shubramah, Samurah Ibn Jundub, and Sa'id Ibn Ashwa al-Kufi, hold the notion that a promise is legally binding within a contract (Al-Shadili, 2014). This viewpoint aligns with the resolutions of the First Conference of Islamic Banks in 1399H and the Second Conference in 1403H, which have accepted and acknowledged the enforceability of promises within contracts (Al-Zuhayli, 2002).

Considering the discussion over a promise in a contract, reasonably, the argument that holds greater precedence is the statement of those who argue that the promise becomes legally binding when the promisee (lessee) assumes the obligation to fulfil the rental instalments, which grants him ownership of the leased asset as per the promisor's (lessor's) promise. Thus, a promise can be binding both from legal and religious aspects based on the discussed pieces of evidence of the Qana'nic verses and the Prophetic narrations, which have also been exhibited in the earlier discussion on "sale with a condition".

7.4 Issues with Two Contracts in One in HPSM

The implementation of HPSM has introduced complex legal and religious considerations within the Islamic banking and finance sphere. One significant area of debate and controversy revolves around the question of whether HPSM, which comprises three distinct contracts executed sequentially, can be regarded as a single composite contract or as a combination of separate contracts. Specifically, the focus is on the potential implications of having "two contracts in one" within the HPSM framework, as it raises concerns about compliance with Shari'ah principles and Prophetic (SAW) sayings.

This is crucial to delve into the Shari'ah issues associated with the concept of having two contracts in one in the context of HPSM. It explores the various arguments and perspectives presented by scholars and jurists, examining the underlying hadiths that guide the matter. The primary objective is to gain a comprehensive understanding of the different interpretations and scholarly opinions surrounding the permissibility or prohibition of combining multiple contracts within the HPSM arrangement.

Through an extensive analysis of relevant sources, including scholarly works, Shari'ah standards, and legal texts, this chapter aims to shed light on the intricacies and implications of this contentious issue. It addresses questions such as whether the combination of *shirkah*, hire, and sale contracts in HPSM can be considered as one integrated contract and the extent to which it adheres to the principles of Islamic finance. By exploring the divergent viewpoints, evaluating the chains of narrations, and examining the authenticity of relevant hadiths, this section aims to contribute to the ongoing discourse and provide valuable insights into the complex nature of HPSM and its compliance with Shari'ah requirements.

7.4.1 *Hadiths About the Issue of Two Contracts in One*

Despite HPSM being a combination of three different contracts that come one after another, which are *shirkah,* hire, and sale however, all three contracts are to be executed separately, yet, they all render the same objective, and that is achieving the ownership of the contract by the lessee and making a profit by the lessor. In this regard, there is room to assume that the HPSM contract is made by three contracts in one which are widely debated and argued among scholars based on the prohibitions of the Prophet (SAW). Hence, this is inevitable to investigate this controversial issue of "two contracts in one" in modern hybrid contracts of IBF. The controversy has been envisaged based on some hadiths where the Prophet (SAW) prohibits two contracts in one. Al-Qaradaghi (2009), in his book *Buhuth fi Fiqh al-Muamalat al-Maliyyah al-Mu'asarah,* studied those different hadiths according to their chain *(sanad),* sources, authenticity, narrations, and scholar's opinion on.

There are mainly three hadiths that discuss the issue of two contracts in one; one of them is cited by Imam Ahmad, Ibn Hibban, al-Bayhaqi, Ibn Abi Shu'ayb, and Ibn Nasr (Hama, 2007):

"نهى رسول الله صلي الله عليه و سلم عن صفقتين في صفقة"

The Prophet (SAW) prohibited two transactions combined in one bargain.

The other hadith is reported by al-Hakim, al-Nasa'i, Imam Ahmad, al-Darami, Imam Malik, al-Haithami, al-Tirmidhi (Surah, 1999), Abu Da'ud, Ibn Khuzayma, al-Daraqutni, Ibn Jarud, Imam Abu Hanifah, and Ibn Hazm (Hama, 2007):

"لا يحل بيع و سلف و لا شرطان في بيع و لا ربح ما لم يضمن و لا بيع ما ليس عندك"

Advance loan and sale are not lawful, and two conditions in one sale are not lawful, and no profit till it comes in possession and no sale what is not in your possession. (Abadi, 2001)

Another hadith is narrated by al-Hakim, al-Nasa'i, Imam Ahmad, Imam Malik, al-Tirmidhi, Ibn Jarud, al-Bayhaqi, Ibn Hibban, Abu Da'ud (Al-Farisi, 1993), Ibn Abi Shaybah, and al-Tabrani (Hama, 2007):

"نهى رسول الله صلي الله عليه و سلم عن بيعتان في بيعة"

The Prophet (SAW) forbade two sales in one sale.

Regarding the authenticity of the first hadith, it is worth mentioning that several other hadiths bear a salient resemblance to the initial one. For example, the first hadith, "the Prophet (SAW) prohibited two transactions combined in one bargain", is identical to the hadiths "combination of two transactions in one is *riba*". Both hadiths are mentioned in the same context though the second hadith lacks authenticity. The hadith is narrated by Imam Ahmad and some others. Albani (1985), through his investigation of this hadith, retrieves that the hadith of Imam Ahmad seems to be weak in its source. However, if a hadith is narrated in several ways but established as weak in sources, it still is qualified to be a piece of evidence (Hama, 2007).

To Imam al-Tirmidhi and Ibn Hazm, the second hadith, "Advance loan and sale are not lawful, and two conditions in one sale are not lawful, and no profit till it comes in possession and no sale what is not in your possession" is an authentic hadith. Hakim (1987), in his book *al-Mustadrak,* also apprehends that "this is an authentic hadith according to the many scholar's judgment", and this proclamation is also carried out by Imam al-Dhahabi. When such judgements on this hadith are attainable, Al-Qaradaghi (2000) believes that the hadith should be referred to as strong evidence in the financial spheres.

The third hadith, "the Prophet (SAW) forbade two sales in one sale", is narrated by Abu Hurayrah, Abu Saeed Khudri, and Abdullah Ibn Umar. Since the hadith has been narrated by recognised companions of the Prophet (SAW), there should not be any issue with its authenticity, and it can be a standard in the financial realm (Hama, 2007).

7.4.2 Jurist's Dispute over the Interpretation of Those Hadiths

In order to properly analyse the legal status of the two contracts combined into one, it is vital to scrutinise the interpretations, intentions, and explanations provided by Muslim scholars regarding the specific terms used in three hadiths that address the issue of conducting two contracts within a single transaction or two sales within one transaction.

The term "*safaqah*" mentioned in the first hadith signifies the act of "shaking hands" after concluding a contract. However, scholars argue that the underlying intention behind this handshake is the agreement of a transaction (*bay'*), which complements the concept conveyed in the second hadith (Ibn Mandhur, n.d). Thus, many scholars interpret both hadiths as conveying the same concept. Ibn Masud, sketching from these hadiths, holds the notion that combining two contracts within one transaction is not permissible. For instance, if someone states, "I have sold this item to you for a specific price in cash. However, if you wish to pay in instalments, the price will be higher", the contract includes two prices within a single offer without any clear distinction between them (Al-Qaradaghi, 2009). As a result, the contract incorporates two prices within the same transaction, rendering it void. This perspective is shared by numerous other scholars, including Sammak, Abd al Wahhab bin Ata, Abu Ubay, Ibn Sirin, Nasa'i, and Ibn Hibban.

Despite scholars agreeing with the interpretation of the prohibition of two contracts in one, some scholars, in contrast, disagree with that interpretation and comprehend that two contracts in one are valid if the seller can only be entitled to a lower price in case of deferred transaction. Al-Qaradaghi (2009) elucidates the statement of Ta'wus, where he ascertains if you said to a buyer, "I sold this good to you in the form of cash payment for this specific price and for deferred payment of that price and the contract executed on that offer" the seller is entitled to the lower price for the longer period. Imam Awza'i, one of those scholars, stands in favour of the opinion of Ta'wus.

The other hadith, "advance loan and sale are not lawful, and two conditions in one sale are not lawful, and no profit till it comes in possession and no sale what is not in your possession", obtains three different financial rulings. The hadith prohibits the combination of two contracts (one for debt and one for sale) within a single transaction or under certain conditions. This hadith is also understood to convey a similar idea as two other hadiths. However, there are three alternative interpretations put forth by other scholars:

To begin with, Ibn Rif'ah explains that the term condition in this hadith refers to the inclusion of a clause related to the price, specifying the distinction between immediate cash payment and deferred payment within a single wording (*sigah*) that constitutes the offer and acceptance process. For instance, if someone offers to sell a good with a cash payment price and a deferred payment price, and the buyer accepts the offer without specifying either price, this interpretation is accepted by the majority of jurists from the Hanafi, Maliki, and Shafi'i, schools of thought. This understanding complements the interpretation of the third hadith, where the Prophet (SAW) prohibited combining two sales in one contract (Al-Shadhili, 2014). This observation is also shared by Albani (1985), who notes that both hadiths are narrated from the same source, but only their wording (*matan*) is exhibited differently.

Furthermore, the meaning of the hadith "stipulation of one contract in another" refers to a situation where a seller includes a condition in the contract that involves the buyer selling back the goods at a specified price or where someone sells goods with the condition that the buyer sells another good at a particular price to the seller (Shadili, 2014). This type of contract creates a situation where both parties become applicants for each other's goods, and they have stipulated a sale contract on each other. This interpretation is supported by some jurists from the Zaydi and Ibadi schools of thought (Shadili, 2014). However, it is important to note that this interpretation deviates from the actual meaning of the hadith. In the scenario where a sale is made jointly with the condition that the seller sells a product to the buyer at an agreed price, there is only one contract and one condition. The first *sigah* signifies the requirements of the contract itself, while the second *sigah* signifies the requirements of the condition. Therefore, this is not a case of having two conditions within one contract (Shadili, 2014).

In addition, the third interpretation of the hadith involves the stipulation of two void conditions in one contract, as upheld by the Hanbali school of thought. According to their view, if two void conditions are stipulated in a contract, the contract becomes void. However, they argue that stipulating two or more valid conditions in a contract is allowed, and such contracts remain valid (Shadili, 2014). Ibn Qudamah adheres that a sale is void if there are two conditions on it, but only one condition will not invalidate it too. Imam Ahmad likewise, opines that one condition is permissible, what is prohibited is two conditions in one contract whose argument complements the hadith in which the Prophet (SAW) warns that "Advance loan and sale are not lawful, and two conditions in one sale are not lawful, and no profit till it comes in possession and no sale what is not in your possession". A statement of Abu Abdullah has been elucidated by Shadhili (2014), who said that there are scholars who do not prefer to put even one condition in a sale contract; however, they further tainted their view by saying that one condition is permissible in a sale contract and what is restricted by the Prophet (SAW) is stipulating two conditions in one sale. The hadith had practically shown a condition in a valid sale contract when Jabir sold his camel and stipulated to take him to Madinah.

Moreover, the explanation of another hadith where "the Prophet (SAW) forbade two sales in one sale" aligns with the first hadith. This means that having two prices within one offer or sale is not permissible. However, if the buyer and seller engage in negotiations and agree upon a single price, the contract will then be valid (Al-Qaradaghi, 2009).

7.4.3 Mitigating Dispute over Combination of Multiple Contracts in One

While a comprehensive discussion has already been provided regarding the authenticity and actual meaning of the mentioned hadiths, the main focus of the discussion now shifts towards determining the legal status of combining two contracts into one, especially in HPSM. Notably, each hadith begins with a negative approach towards certain aspects of a contract. However, Scholars have shown their aptitude to carry out equitable conclusions on the issue, which are as follows:

> Many scholars state that the prohibitions in these hadiths are subject to certain natures of the contract to nullify it. However, Hanafis ascertain that the contract is not subjective to be nullified by the prohibition "do not do" unless there are attributed issues that have been realised. Thus, according to the majority of jurists, the legal implication of these hadiths is the prohibition of adhering to two different prices within the same contract. This refers to situations where one price is offered for immediate cash payment at the market price while another price is set for deferred payment, which is typically higher. An instance of such an offer is when a person states, "If you sell me this product, I will sell you that one". The underlying reason behind the prohibition of combining two contracts into one is to prevent the presence of *riba* in the first contract and to avoid uncertainty or ambiguity in the second contract. (al-Shawkani, 1984; al-Qaradaghi, 2009)

Undeniably, some scholars do not agree with the applicability of contracts in Islamic law in which a condition or two contracts in one are enacted. However, if those scholars have precisely investigated the actual substance of the hadiths, they would ideally not restrict the applicability of contracts and not hold the view that conditions are fundamentally disallowed within a contract (Al-Qaradaghi, 2009).

Accordingly, due to the frequent reluctance of some scholars to validate a contract in which one or more conditions are injected, or more than one contract in one is practised, the nature of the conditions in contracts is ignored unjustifiedly. In these hindrances, some scholars go to the extent of not considering a contract valid even if it contains only one condition, except if the permissibility of that particular condition is explicitly supported by the Shari'ah sources. On the other hand, some scholars believe that a contract with two invalid conditions would render it void, but if there is only one invalid condition, it will not invalidate the entire contract. However, it is worth mentioning that the aforementioned views on this issue have been expressed without a precise investigation into the nature and characteristics of the conditions mentioned in the hadiths. In these hadiths, there is no specific indication of the exact nature and characteristics of the conditions or contracts being referred to (al-Qaradaghi, 2009).

After a comprehensive examination of all three hadiths and considering the interpretations of Muslim scholars, including their narrators, it can be concluded that the phrases "*safaqataini fi safaqah*" (two transactions combined in one), "*bay 'atan fi bay'*" (two sales in one contract), and "*shartan fi bay'*" (two conditions in one sale) essentially convey the same meaning. For example, if someone sells a product to another person with an offer that includes both a cash payment of USD 80 and a deferred payment of USD 100 within a single contract, it would be considered invalid. However, if the contract separates the options of cash payment or deferred payment, regardless of the price, it would be valid. To the view of Ibn Taymiyyah and Ibn Qayyim, the prohibitions mentioned in these hadiths are specifically applicable to the practice of "*bay ' al- 'inah*",[1] a specific type of transaction, and should not be generalised to other contracts that are in line with Shari'ah principles.

According to the framework of HPSM, the contract comprises three distinct contracts: *shirkah* (partnership), *ijarah* (leasing), and sale. However, there is a lack of specific literature among jurists addressing whether these three contracts are combined into one or if each contract is executed

[1] *Bay ' al- 'ina* is a contract where a person sells his property to another at cash for less than the market price and buys back the property for deferred higher price due to entertain a need for cash.

separately within the HPSM framework. While there may be no explicit scholarly works of literature on this matter precisely, there are indications in the "Stage of HPSM" (IBBL, n.d(b)) document that suggest the separate execution of all three contracts, one after another. Furthermore, the Malaysian Hire Purchase Act 1967 also provides similar guidelines and regulations regarding the execution of hire purchase contract.

Similarly, within the context of HPSM, which involves lease and sale contracts, many scholars assert that Islamic hire purchase does not constitute two contracts combined into one. This ensures that the contract does not encompass the simultaneous existence of both lease and sale contracts in one entity. Hence, this type of contract, particularly HPSM, should not be treated as prohibited based on the Prophetic sayings that were thoroughly discussed earlier. The reason for this is that the formation of the *shirkah*, *ijarah*, and sale contracts within HPSM is not simultaneous but sequential. The first contract is the *shirkah* contract, which must adhere to the requirements of a *musharakah* contract. A second contract is an *ijarah* contract, which must comply with the requirements of an *ijarah* contract, regardless of whether the rent remains at the current market value or is set higher. Finally, the third contract is the sale contract, which is executed by transferring ownership of the property upon completion of all payments, whether through a nominal price or no consideration mode, as the lessee has already made the payment, and the lessor is prepared to transfer the legal title, thereby avoiding any Shari'ah-related issues.

Furthermore, the transfer of legal title in the context of HPSM is also a result of the contractual promise undertaken by the lessor (Hama, 2007). Al-Dasuqi, in his book *Sharh al-Kabir*, argues that a lease contract is not rendered void if it is combined with a sale contract in a single transaction. Similarly, a sale contract remains valid when enacted alongside a lease contract. According to al-Dasuqi, such contracts do not contradict each other, even if they involve leasing and selling the same goods (al-Shadhili, 2014). Maliki jurists maintain the view that stipulating one contract within another is permissible as long as it serves the purpose of the contract and is in accordance with Shari'ah. Ibn Taymiyyah holds a similar perception in this regard. Additionally, Malikis, Shafi'is, and Hanbalis permit the combination of sale and lease contracts. This is because both sale and lease contracts, particularly in the context of hire purchase, often share similar aspects of conditions and pillars in their structure (al-shadhili, 2014).

Chapter Review Question

1. Which type of ownership transfer in hire purchase under *shirkah al-milk* involves the gradual transfer of legal title of the leased property?
   a. Hire purchase through the transfer of legal title by gift (*hibah*)
   b. Hire purchase through the transfer of legal title at the end of the lease period for token consideration
   c. Hire purchase through the gradual transfer of legal title
   d. Hire purchase through the transfer of legal title by paying a specified amount
2. According to Aqil and Al-Shadhili, what is their opinion on the gift (*hibah*) contract with a condition?
   a. The contract is considered valid.
   b. The contract is considered invalid.
   c. The contract is considered valid but with certain characteristics.
   d. The contract is considered valid only in specific cases.
3. Which school of jurisprudence treats the gift (*hibah*) contract as a sale from the beginning to the end?
   a. Hanafi
   b. Maliki
   c. Shafi'i
   d. Hanbali
4. In Hire Purchase under *shirkah al-milk*, when is the legal title of the property transferred to the lessee?
   a. At the beginning of the lease period
   b. At the end of the lease period by paying a specified amount
   c. Gradually, during the lease period
   d. It depends on the type of contract chosen
5. Which type of hire purchase under *shirkah al-milk* involves the transfer of legal title before the ending of the lease period for an equivalent price to the remaining rental instalments?
   a. Hire purchase through transfer of legal title by gift (*hibah*)
   b. Hire purchase through the transfer of legal title at the end of the lease period for token consideration
   c. Hire purchase through the gradual transfer of legal title
   d. Hire purchase through transfer of legal title before the ending of the lease period

6. Based on which verse of the Qur'an some scholars say that promise is binding?
   a. Surah al-Isra verse no. 34
   b. Surah al-Baqarah, verse no. 34
   c. Surah Ibrahim, verse no. 34
   d. Surah al-Imran, verse no. 34
7. What is the main emphasis of the discussion regarding the legal status of two contracts in one?
   a. Prohibition of offering two different prices in the same contract
   b. Validity of contracts with conditions in Islamic law
   c. Applicability of contracts with two contracts in one
   d. Avoidance of usury and uncertainty in contracts
8. According to the majority of Hanafi, Shafi'i, Hanbali, and Zahiri jurists, the promise in contracts is:
   a. Legally binding
   b. Religiously binding
   c. Not binding legally but religiously
   d. None of the Above
9. The Hanafi school of thought believes that a promise in a contract must be honoured legally if:
   a. The promise is made by the lessor
   b. The promise stipulates any condition
   c. The promise is made by the lessee
   d. The promise is not mentioned in the text
10. What does the Malaysian Hire Purchase Act 1967 indicate about the execution of all contracts?
    a. They are applied together in the same agreement
    b. They are applied separately based on sequences
    c. The matter depends on the wish of the financial institution
    d. None of the above

Answers

1. c
2. b
3. a
4. d
5. d

6. a
7. a
8. c
9. b
10. b

References

Aqil, Jamal al-Din T. (1978). *Aqd al-Hibah bayna al-Fiqh al-Islami wa al-Qanun al-Muduni*. Dar al-Huda.

Abdullah M. A. (1988). Al-ta'jir al-muntaha bi al-tamlik wa al-Suwar al-Mashru'iyyah fih. *Majallah Majma' al-Fiqh al-Islami, 4*(5).

Al-Shadhili, H. A. (2014). Leasing Ending with Ownership. In *Leasing Ending with Ownership and Leasing Bond (al-Ijarah al-Muntahiyah bi al-Tamlik) Its Ruling and Contemporary Application* (pp. 21–81). Islamic Banking and Financial Institute Malaysia (IBFIM).

Al-Zuhayli, W. (2002). *Al-Mumalat al-Maliyyah al- Muasarah: Buhuth wa Fatawa wa Hulul*. Dar al-Fikr.

Al-Funaysan, S. (2000). Al-'ijar al-muntahi bi al-tamlik. *Majallah al-Buhuth al-Fiqhiyyah al-Mu'asirah, 48*.

Al-Sarakhsi, M. Ibn Ahmad. (2013). *Al-Mabsut* (Vol. 5). Dar al-Nawadir.

Al-Taskhiri, M. A. (2014). Leasing Ending with Ownership and Concept of Promise. In *Leasing Ending with Ownership and Leasing Bond (al-Ijarah al-Muntahiyah bi al-Tamlik) Its Ruling and Contemporary Application* (pp. 103–115). Islamic Banking and Financial Institute Malaysia (IBFIM).

Al-Zuhayli, W. (2003). *Financial Transactions in Islamic Jurisprudence* (M. A. El-Gamal, Trans.). Dar al-Fikr al-Mu'asir. Beirut.

Al-Kasani, A. B. Ibn Muhammad. (2005). *Bada'i al-Sana'i' fi al-Tartib al-Shara'i'* (Vol. 5). Dar al-Hadith.

Al-Sharbini, M. Ibn Muhammad al-Khatib. (1994). *Mughni al-Muhtaj* (Vol. 2). Matba'at al-Babi al-Halabi.

Abadi, Abu Abd al-Rahman. Sharf al-Haq. (2001). *Awn al-Ma'bud Sharh Sunan Abi Dawud* (Vol. 9). Dar 'Ihya al-Turath al-Arabi.

Al-Sundi, Nur al-Din. Abdul Hadi. (1998). *Sahih Al-Bukhari bi Hashiah al-Imam al- Sundi* (Vol. 2). Dar al-Kutub al-Ilmiyyah.

Asqalani, Ibn Hajr. (1999). *Fath al-Bar* (1st ed., Vol. 5). Dar al-Manar li al-Tab wa al-Nashr wa al-Tawji'.

Alish, M. A. (1958). *Fath al-Ali al-Malik fi al-Fatawa ala Madhhab Malik* (Vol. 1). Maktabah wa Matba'a Mustafa al-Babi al-Halbi wa Awladuhu.

Al-Qaradaghi, A. M. (2009). *Buhuth fi Fiqh al-Muamalat al-Maliyyah al-Mu'asarah* (1st ed.). Dar al-Basha'ir al- Islsmiyyah.

Al-Farisi, Ala al-Din. (1993). *Sahih Ibn Hibban bi Tartib Ibn Bilban* (2nd ed., Vol. 11). Mu'assasah al-Risslah.

Albani, M. Nasir al-Din. (1985). *Irwa al-Jalil fi Takhrij Ahadith Manar al-Sabil* (2nd ed., Vol. 5). Al-Maktabah al-Islami.

Al-Qaradaghi, A. M. (2000). Al ijarah al-muntahyyah bi al-tamlik. *Majalat al-Majma' al-Fiqh al-Islami, 1*(1).

Al-Shawkani, M. Ibn Ali. (1984). *Nayl al-Awtar Sharh Muntaqa al-Akhbar* (Vol. 3). Maktabah al-Kulliyyat al-Azhariyyah.

Hama, A. O. (2007). *Islamic Hire-Purchase Transaction.* International Islamic University Malaysia.

Hakim, M. Ibn Abdullah. (1987). *Al-Mustadrak ala al-Sahihayn fi al-Hadith* (Vol. 2). Dar al-Fikr.

Ibn Taymiyyah, Ahmad Ibn Abd al-Halim. (2011). *Al-Qawa'id al-Nuraniyyah al-Fiqhiyyah* (Vol. 2). Maktab al-Rashid.

IIFA. (2021). *Resolutions and Recommendations of the International Islamic Fiqh Academy of Organization of Islamic Cooperation.* International Islamic Fiqh Academy.

Kharofah, Ala al-Din (1997). *Transactions in Islamic Law*. A.S Noordeen.

Niazi, L. A. K. (1991). *Islamic Law of Contract.* Doyal Sing Trust Library.

Surah, M. Ibn 'Isha (1999). *Sunan al-Turmidhi* (Vol. 3). Dar al-Hadith.

Utsmani, S. M. (1998). *Al-Mu'amalat al-Maliyyah al-Mu'asarah fi al-Fiqh al-Islami* (2nd ed.). Dar al-Nafa'is.

CHAPTER 8

Ijarah and *Shirkah* Contracts In Islamic Finance

Abstract Islamic home financing serves as a means of financial support for those seeking to purchase their home. *Bay' bithaman ajil* (BBA), *musharakah mutanaqisah* partnership (MMP), and *ijarah mawsufah fi al dimmah* (IMD) are designed to serve for the necessity of infrastructures. Typically, MMP is a form of diminishing partnership in which both the customer and the bank enter into a joint ownership agreement, while BBA is a deferred payment sale model where the bank purchases the house at an agreed price and subsequently sells it back to the customer at a higher price, including a profit margin, over a financing period and the IMD is a sale of future usufruct in exchange of immediate cash. In addition, in the present day, *sukuk* has become widely utilised by both Islamic corporations and government entities. It has gradually captured a growing portion of the global fixed-income market. Unlike traditional bonds, *sukuk* investors do not hold a debt obligation from the issuer. Instead, they own a proportionate share of the underlying asset linked to the investment. Among many types of *sukuk*, *ijarah* and *musharakah sukuk* are two of them. This chapter will discuss the above-mentioned financial products and their underlying issues.

Keywords *Musharakah mutanaqisah* · MMP · BBA · *Ijarah Sukuk* · *Musharakah Sukuk*

M. K. Hassan et al., *Hire Purchase Under Shirkah al-Milk (HPSM) in Islamic Banking and Finance*,
https://doi.org/10.1007/978-3-031-50105-0_8

Preview

Over the years, Islamic home financing has experienced remarkable growth, as evidenced by the Malaysian market. In Malaysia, the value of Islamic home financing transactions surged from RM29.8 billion in 2010 to RM131.1 billion by the close of 2017. This substantial increase accounted for 27.1 per cent of the total financing provided by Islamic banking institutions (Rashid et al., 2020). Islamic banking and finance provide ethical and efficient alternatives, particularly for Muslims, by eliminating the concept of interest (*riba*). Islamic home financing serves as a means of financial support for Muslims, particularly those seeking to purchase their long-cherished home. *Bay' bithaman ajil* (BBA), *musharakah mutanaqisah* partnership (MMP), and *ijarah mawsufah fi al dimmah* (IMD) are designed to serve for the necessity of infrastructures. They operate on Shari'ah principles, with contracts based on sales and purchase transactions between two or more parties. In Islamic home financing contracts, the inclusion of elements such as usury (*riba*) and uncertainty (*gharar*) is strictly prohibited in accordance with Islamic principles. Financial institutions offer various Islamic home financing options, including *bay' bithaman ajil* (BBA), *musharakah mutanaqisah* partnership (MMP), and *ijarah mawsufah fi al dimmah* (IMD) or (forward *ijarah*) in many jurisdictions.

Typically, MMP is a form of diminishing partnership in which both the customer and the bank enter into a joint ownership agreement. On the other hand, BBA is a deferred payment sale model where the bank purchases the house at an agreed price and subsequently sells it back to the customer at a higher price, including a profit margin, over a financing period, while the IMD is a sale of future usufruct in exchange of immediate cash.

In addition, since the emergence of Islamic finance, *sukuk* has also gained significant esteem in many Muslim and non-Muslim countries. In the present day, *sukuk* has become widely utilised by both Islamic corporations and government entities worldwide. It has gradually captured a growing portion of the global fixed-income market.

Sukuk is a financial instrument that represents a collective ownership stake in a tangible asset, typically associated with a specific project or investment activity. Unlike traditional bonds, *sukuk* investors do not hold a debt obligation from the issuer. Instead, they own a proportionate share of the underlying asset linked to the investment. Consequently, *sukuk* holders are entitled to a portion of the earnings generated by the asset, distinguishing them from bondholders. Many types of ***sukuk*** have been developed in several jurisdictions; ***ijarah*** and ***musharakah sukuk*** are two of them. In this chapter, the above-mentioned financial products and their underlying issues will be discussed.

8.1 *Musharakah Mutanaqiasah* Partnership (MMP)

Musharaka Mutanaqisah Partnership (MMP), also known as diminishing ***musharakah***, is a type of partnership where one partner gradually acquires the equity share of the other partner. This acquisition takes place over time, either at the market value or at a predetermined price agreed upon during the sale. The transfer of ownership is completed when the buying partner obtains full title to the equity. The process begins with the establishment of the partnership, and subsequent buying and selling of equity occur between the partners. To ensure Shari'ah compliance, the buying and selling arrangement must not be explicitly mentioned in the partnership contract. Instead, the buying partner can provide a promise to buy, and this separate agreement for buying and selling should be independent of the partnership contract. It is not permissible to link one contract as a condition for finalising the other. Under this arrangement, both parties share the ownership risk in the property in proportion to their capital contributions. To generate profit, an Islamic bank leases its share in the property to the customer at a predetermined rental rate. This rental amount is adjusted with each cycle of the bank's sale and purchase of its share in the property to the customer (Ali & Falahi, 2016).

The MMP seems identical to the *hire purchase under shirkah al-milk* (HPSM), which involves three distinct contracts like HPSM, which are: *musharakah* (partnership), *ijarah* (lease), and *bay'* (sale). To begin with the contract, the customer and the bank enter into a ***musharakah*** agreement, which establishes a joint ownership arrangement (***shirkah al-milk***) for the asset being financed. Both parties become co-owners of the asset. Further, the bank leases its share of ownership in the asset to the customer through an *ijarah* contract. For instance, the customer contributes an initial share of 30% towards owning the asset, while the bank provides the remaining 70%. In the subsequent stage, the customer gradually purchases the bank's 70% share in agreed-upon portions over time until they fully own the asset. As the customer makes periodic payments, the rental amounts are shared between the customer and the bank based on their respective percentage of ownership, which changes as the customer acquires the bank's share. With each rental payment, the customer's share ratio increases due to the periodic redemption, ultimately leading to full ownership (Mydin Meera & Abdul Razak, 2009).

8.1.1 *The Implementation Process of the MMP Contract*

The MMP, being a hybrid contract, is one of the leveraging contracts, especially in Malaysia. Many Malaysian banks are currently applying this contract for financing proposes. The following are the execution stages of an MMP contract:

1. When a customer requires financing to purchase a house, he approaches an Islamic Bank and applies for finance through the MMP contract. Upon receiving the customer's financing requirement, the Islamic Bank evaluates the customer's creditworthiness and grants approval for the request if it complies with the bank's policy.
2. In accordance with the approved Finance to Value (FTV), the Islamic bank and the customer jointly acquire the property in their respective proportions and make the corresponding payment for the purchase. The bank requests an undertaking from the customer, wherein he commits to gradually purchasing the entire share held by the bank in the property over the financing period. This undertaking serves as a means for the bank to enforce the immediate purchase of the bank's current share in the property if the customer defaults or breaches the terms of the agreement.
3. As per the customer's commitment, he continues to acquire the bank's share at regular intervals during the finance period. Each time the customer purchases the bank's share, a distinct sale and purchase agreement is executed between both parties. Simultaneously, the customer enters into a lease contract with the bank, where they lease the bank's portion of the property and make specified rent payments for a designated duration.
4. As per the lease agreement terms, the customer pays the rental amount to the bank on the specified due dates, which aligns with the bank's regular sale of its specific portion to the customer. The rental amount for each rental period is adjusted to reflect the decrease in the bank's share of the leased property. Through a

separate agency agreement, the customer is appointed as the bank's agent to handle major maintenance tasks and arrange for *takaful* for the bank's share in the property. The bank covers all the costs and expenses incurred by the customer under this agency agreement. Additionally, the bank provides a fixed agency fee to the customer, which is generally a nominal amount, for their services.

5. To secure its financing, the bank has the option to place a mortgage on the entire property or request alternative forms of collateral. On the other hand, to ensure the customer's right to settle the finance early, he may request an undertaking from the bank. This undertaking would involve the bank committing to sell its entire portion to the customer at any given point during the finance period.

8.1.2 Acceptability of MMP

While there are varying opinions among Islamic jurists, the majority concurs that MMP is permissible and compliant with Shari'ah principles. Shari'ah scholars widely acknowledge the validity of a combined sale and lease contract. Furthermore, there is no explicit prohibition in Shari'ah texts against MMP. Taking into account the public interests (*maslahah*) and benefits (*manfa'ah*) associated with MMP in investments, it is deemed permissible within the bounds of Shari'ah (Smolo, 2007).

Nevertheless, some scholars hold different views regarding the validity of the MMP contract. According to their perspective, the contract should be deemed invalid due to the presence of certain doubtful elements. They argue that MMP resembles interest-based transactions, as its main objective is to provide loans to clients and generate additional funds from the loan amount (Al-Kawamelah, 2008).

In addition, the International *Fiqh* Academy (IIFA) of the Organisation of Islamic Cooperation (OIC) declared in its 15th session 1998 that MMP is a valid contract in accordance with Shari'ah principles. Furthermore, the Shari'ah Advisory Council of Bank Negara Malaysia, in its 56th meeting, affirmed that MMP is a recognised contract in Shari'ah and that the current practice of the contract is permissible (BNM, 2007).

8.1.3 *Advantages of an MMP Contract*

The application of MMP is unique for many reasons. Mydin Meera and Abdul Razak (2009), like many other scholars, outlined the following dynamics of MMP:

(a) The MMP is widely acknowledged as being Shari'ah compliant on a global scale, unlike other similar products such as the *bay' bi thaman ajil* (BBA), which is primarily recognised in South-East Asian countries like Malaysia, Indonesia, Brunei, and others. But, the MMP has been successfully adapted for contractual use across different nations.
(b) Under the MMP, the value of the house consistently corresponds to the market price, and the rental amount is determined either by the prevailing market rental values or by an agreed-upon price at the time of acquisition.
(c) In the MMP, the financer is not obligated to maintain a fixed profit rate throughout the financing tenor. This flexibility arises from the ability to periodically adjust the rental rate in accordance with the prevailing market conditions. It is also possible to link the rental rate to economic variables such as the Rental Index or House Price Index.
(d) The financier's ability to effectively handle liquidity risks is enhanced under the MMP, as rental payments can be adjusted after each subcontract period. In contrast, such flexibility is not available in similar contracts like the BBA.
(e) The MMP offers greater flexibility in financing structure, as customers have the option to expedite the ownership of the property by repaying the financier's principal sum more quickly, without the requirement of calculating rebates.
(f) In the event of defaults under the MMP, the equity of the financier remains unaffected, allowing them to receive higher rental portions when delayed payments are eventually made.
(g) In the event of default and subsequent auction of the property, the bank, in the case of MMP, will ensure that the property is sold at a fair value. This is because a lower selling price would also impact the bank's own position.

8.1.4 *Disadvantages of an MMP Contract*

Osmani and Abdullah (2010) agreed with the advantages of the MMP; however, they identified the following disadvantages of MMP too, which are as follows:

(a) The fluctuation of rental prices in the housing market represents a significant challenge for the MMP. Typically, rental prices tend to increase over time, which can pose difficulties for customers. Another issue that arises with this contract is the question of tax payment. It is suggested that the tax should be paid using the profit added to the bank's equity rather than from the profit added to the customer's share.

(b) Another noteworthy feature is the client's promise (*wa'd*) to gradually purchase the bank's share until he becomes the sole owner of the property. Islamic jurists dispute the obligatory or recommended nature of fulfilling this promise. If it is deemed obligatory, the bank has the legal authority to impose a fine on the client for non-compliance. Conversely, if fulfilling the promise is considered recommended, the client retains the freedom to either proceed with the promise or terminate it at any time. In the latter case, the bank should not possess any legal right to impose fines on the customer.

8.2 *Bay' bi Thaman Ajil* (BBA) (Sale on Deferred Payment)

Historically the BBA was adopted into the Islamic financial spectrum in 1983, whose starting jurisdiction was the Malaysian market by the Bank Islam Malaysia; later, it became popular with other banks in the same jurisdiction and other jurisdictions like Indonesia and Brunei. In Pakistan and Bangladesh, it is termed *bay' muajjal.*

The BBA contract is a financing arrangement that enables sales to be conducted through deferred instalments. In this contract, the calculation of the mark-up or selling price is based on the predetermined annual rate of profit that the bank seeks to achieve from the transaction. BBA facilitates the acquisition of an asset through a deferred payment sale concept. In this arrangement, the bank purchases the specified asset and then sells it to the customer at an agreed price. The price includes the actual cost of the asset to the bank, along with the bank's profit margin. The customer is permitted to make instalment payments within the agreed period and according to the agreed terms.

In other words, BBA financing is available for the purchase of residential houses and commercial buildings and can also be utilised for additional operating or working capital requirements. BBA, also known as *bay' muajjal,* as said earlier, is a financing arrangement characterised by deferred payment. It is commonly referred to as a sale by instalment, wherein the asset is delivered immediately, and the payment is deferred to a later date.

8.2.1 The Implementation Process of the BBA Contract

In the process of BBA financing, the customer first selects a property and typically pays 30% of the selling price as a down payment. The customer then approaches the bank to finance the remaining 70%. Subsequently, an agreement is signed between the customer and the bank. Under the agreement, the bank purchases the property from the customer for an amount equivalent to the financing required. The bank then disburses the remaining 70% of the funds to the developer or seller. In turn, the customer agrees to repurchase the asset from the bank at a price that includes the financing amount and a profit margin determined by the bank. This repurchase amount is paid on deferred terms based on the agreed-upon tenor or financing period.

8.2.2 Acceptability of BBA Contract

According to certain scholars, the sale arrangement in BBA is permissible as long as the market price or selling price is determined and agreed upon by both parties at the inception of the contract. Hanafi, Shafi'i, Maliki, and Hanbali schools of thought consider for such a contract to be permissible, but it is essential that the price is fixed and the payment duration or period is clearly defined in the contract. Any discrepancies or variations in the price or duration would render the contract invalid. Al-Kasani stated that "the price may be increased based on deferment", while Al-Shirazi expressed that "sales in one transaction" are not permissible. However, BBA has been classified as one of the most controversial and disputed financing products in modern-day transactions for several reasons.

8.2.3 *The Major Issues Behind Dispute Over a BBA Contact*

a. In the case of a transaction of financing a house that is yet to be completed, BBA inherently includes elements of *gharar al-fahish* (excessive uncertainty), which are significant concerns for purchasers in housing projects. Hence, studies suggest altering the BBA and moving to MMP. For example, the ambiguity regarding whether the amount paid to the supplier is "*urbon*" (down payment) or "*hamish jiddiyyah*" (security deposit) is a source of uncertainty in the contract's inception. This lack of clarity creates a condition for *gharar*, which can render the contract invalid.
b. The fixed financing mode of BBA can result in liquidity management challenges. This is primarily due to the disparity in the cost of funds, which is based on a floating rate, while the income is generated from fixed-rate *murabahah* and *ijarah* contracts. The duration mismatch between these rates can pose significant concerns in terms of liquidity management.
c. BBA, being a debt-type home financing, can be considered somewhat similar to conventional financing, and customers may encounter higher financing costs in the event of early redemption or defaults.
d. Arbitraging activities have led to a convergence between the BBA mode and conventional financing. In this convergence, the computational formulas resemble those of conventional financing, and the profit rate is aligned with the market interest rate. Instead of charging interest, financiers apply a profit rate that is influenced by the prevailing market interest rate.
e. The BBA structure can potentially be deemed void based on the argument that it is unfair and inequitable to the general public. The perceived inequity arises from the profit margin being higher than the actual debt owed, which can be considered a form of *riba* (usury). Additionally, in the event of borrower default, the borrower is required to repay the entire debt amount along with the profit margin for the entire instalment period without being entitled to any fair or reasonable rebate.
f. In the unfortunate event of a housing project failure and subsequent abandonment, the purchaser under the BBA scheme is still obligated to continue making monthly instalments to the bank. Regrettably, the BBA contract does not include provisions that safeguard the interests of purchasers in case the construction of the houses is abandoned.

g. In the case of default payment, the ownership of the asset remains with the bank, acting as the financier. There is no proportional transfer of ownership based on the amount paid by the customer, which leads to the violation of justice.

8.3 *Ijarah Mawsufah Fi al-Dimmah* (IMD) (Forward *Ijarah*)

Despite the emergence of numerous financing modes within the Islamic finance industry, *ijarah mawsufah fi al-dhimmah* (IMD) stands out as one of the noteworthy and significant modern Islamic finance products. In classical *fiqh* works of literature, IMD has been traditionally discussed within the purview of leasing and forward sale contracts. However, in the modern practice of Islamic finance, Islamic banks and financial institutions have recognised and utilised IMD as a distinct and independent financial instrument.

The IMD is a hybrid contract that combines elements of a forward sale and a redeemable leasing agreement. It has been referred to by contemporary scholars as "forward leasing". Under this structure, the IMD contract allows for the purchase of an entire construction project or portions of it upon completion (Ahmad et al., 2020). The concept of IMD to Abu Ghuddah (2007) refers to a leasing agreement in which the lessor commits to provide the specified usufruct completely, as stipulated by the qualities of *salam*. This comprehensive provision of usufruct helps to eliminate potential conflicts regarding the usufruct itself, whether it pertains to the benefits of an object, such as leasing a specific car, or the services of a human, such as tailoring or teaching. The lessor does not need to possess the benefit at the time of the contract; rather, the usufruct is attached to the future, enabling the lessor to possess it by the agreed-upon time when the execution of the *ijarah* takes place. In other words, IMD is a sale of future usufruct in exchange for immediate cash based on a *salam* contract.

8.3.1 The Implementation Process of the IMD Contract

An IMD takes place to purchase a property that will be delivered in the future, such as a home, office, or plant, whose price is to be undertaken in cash by the financer, then moved to an *ijarah* contract, whose payment (rentals) comes within a specific period after completion of particular infrastructure or during its construction depending on the policy of particulars jurisdiction. In this case, the rental amount must be determined and known at the time of the contract. The rental rate must be fixed for the entire duration of the *ijarah* agreement. In some cases, the customer is required to provide a deposit of up to 20% of the property's value, which can be either the Open Market Value or the selling price determined by the property developer. However, considering the volatility of market conditions, it is permissible to use a floating rate that can change periodically. In such situations, the tenor of the *ijarah* can be divided into shorter intervals or phases, with each interval having a specific rate agreed upon by both parties at the time of the *ijarah* contract. Alternatively, the parties may opt for a short-term *ijarah* contract that can be renewed at future dates. This allows for adjustments to be made based on changes in market conditions. Additionally, during the IMD application, the customer—in certain jurisdictions—is entitled to an option to be covered by a *takaful* offered by the bank. At the end of the leasing period, the ownership will be transferred to the customer by sale, another financial arrangement (Dieng, 2019; Fincyclopedia, 2021).

8.3.2 Acceptability of the IMD Contract

The permissibility of IMD is derived from the broader principles of *ijarah* and *salam* contracts. However, there is disagreement among scholars regarding the legality of IMD. Scholars base their arguments on the conditions of *ijarah* and *salam*, offering their perspectives on the jurisprudential adaptation and specific conditions of IMD. On the other hand, to authenticate IMD, scholars draw upon the pieces of evidence from the Qur'an, the Sunnah, and *Ijma* (consensus) that maintain the overall permissibility of *ijarah* and *salam* contracts.

In contrast, IMD, as a particular hybrid contract, receives its permissibility from different purviews. The major schools of Islamic jurisprudence, i.e. Hanafi, Maliki, Shafi'i, and Hanbali, unanimously agree on the legality of IMD. However, there is a difference in the basis for their approval. Hanafi scholars permit it based on *istihsan* (juristic preference), while scholars of the other three schools allow it based on the general perception of the *ijarah* contract. Yet, the scholars who permit IMD do not provide specific evidence to justify its legality in specific. Instead, they refer to the legality of the original *ijarah* and *salam* contracts.

While they do not cite specific evidence, hence, differ in terms of the evidence they incorporate. For instance, some scholars consider IMD similar to *salam* in terms of its conditions. Therefore, they argue that the evidence supporting the legality of IMD is the same as that of *salam*. Conversely, others who find the attributes of *salam* satisfactory except for the requirement of advanced payment of recompense consider the evidence supporting the legality of original *ijarah* that applies to IMD as well. In addition, among contemporary scholars, al-Buti, Abu Ghuddah, al-Shubayli, Kamal, and Qurahdaghi are of the opinion of the permissibility of IMD (Ahmad et al., 2020). The Shari'ah Advisory Council of Bank Negara Malaysia has also approved the IMD based on the *salam* contract. It is worth mentioning that a Hanfi view was later identified that disapproves of the application of IMD based on the notion that they recognise property which has tangible attributes or substance, and for that reason, IMD is null because it involves property under construction that does not yet exist. However, this view was examined by Monawer and Aziz (2015), and they found otherwise.

8.3.3 Basic Standards for an IMD Contract

The fundamental condition that governs the rules and framework of IMD is the thorough consideration of all the attributes of the *salam* contract as specified in the obligation. This is essential because IMD is essentially a form of *salam* contract that pertains to usufruct. It is necessary to encompass all the characteristics stipulated in the *salam* contract's obligation when engaging in IMD. This is because the nature of the intended use varies depending on the qualities involved. Failing to precisely determine the usufruct can lead to disputes arising from ambiguity. By incorporating the *salam* contract's attributes into the framework of *ijarah*, potential disputes can be prevented, and the transaction can be conducted with greater clarity and certainty, thus reducing uncertainty (*gharar*).

8.3.4 Risks that Encounter the IMD Contract

In an IMD contract, the customer may encounter higher-than-expected rental amounts due to the use of a floating rate. The monthly rental payment fluctuates based on changes in the Base Rate determined by the financer or bank. If the declared rate is higher than the previous rate, the rental amount is required to be revised accordingly. It is worth noting that there is always a cap on the rental payment, such as—in the case of Kuwait Finance House—a maximum of 12%, while the minimum rate is set at 4%.

If a construction project is abandoned, the lessee is required to pay liquidated damages to the bank. Unfortunately, this eliminates the advantage of having a refund option in the event of project abandonment, which is a crucial aspect of IMD. As a result, the lessee not only experiences financial losses in terms of rental payments and deposits but also becomes liable for liquidated damages. This exposes ordinary homebuyers to significant risks since they have no control over the completion of the construction project.

8.4 Ijarah Sukuk

Sukuk, as Islamic financial certificates, serve as Shari'ah-compliant alternatives to Western bonds. These certificates adhere to the principles of the Islamic belief system and provide investors with a means of investment. Unlike traditional interest-paying bonds, which are not permissible in Shari'ah, *sukuk* operate differently. When issuing *sukuk*, the issuer sells certificates to a group of investors, who, in turn, contribute funds that are used to acquire specific assets. Consequently, the investors hold direct partial ownership of these assets. Additionally, the originator commits to repurchasing the *sukuk* at a future date at their original value (Ganti, 2022). *Sukuk* are best fit to be structured, being rooted almost in every Shari'ah-based and compliant product that is currently in practice on a global scale. *Ijarah* and *musharakah sukuk* are two of them.

An *ijarah sukuk* is a financial instrument that represents proportional ownership of the usufruct of a well-defined and existing asset such as real estate, aircraft, or ships from an originator, i.e. an Islamic financial institution or market player to an SPV (Special Purpose Vehicle), who then issues certificate to investors in accordance with Shari'ah principles. It is tied to an *ijarah* contract, as defined by Islamic law. This *sukuk* grants the owner the right to possess the underlying asset, receive rental income, and freely transfer or dispose of the *sukuk* without affecting the issuer's right to utilise the asset (al-Amine, 2001). This receivable, therefore, may be calculated by reference to a fixed rate or variable rate depending on the type of *sukuk* issued.

Upon issuance, the originator enters into a purchase undertaking, granting the SPV the authority to require the originator to buy back the assets in the event of *sukuk* dissolution or upon scheduled maturity. The exercise price for this repurchase is equivalent to the principal amount plus any accumulated but unpaid periodic distribution amounts. The funds received by the SPV are then utilised to fulfil the dissolution amount owed to the investors concerning the *sukuk*.

8.4.1 *Implementation Process of* Ijarah Sukuk

(a) In the context of an *ijarah sukuk* transaction, the originator purchases the asset from the seller and subsequently sells it to an SPV. Alternatively, the SPV directly acquires the asset from the seller based on the originator's requirements. In order to pay for the acquired asset, the SPV issues *sukuk* to *sukuk* holders.

(b) *Sukuk* holders transfer the *sukuk* proceeds to the SPV, which then disburses the received funds to the originator for asset acquisition. If the SPV directly purchases the asset from the seller, the proceeds are utilised to fulfil the payment to the asset seller. Subsequently, the SPV leases the asset back to the originator, who acts as the lessee.

(c) In the lease transaction, the originator pays regular rentals to the SPV in exchange for usufruct. The SPV then allocates these lease payments to *sukuk* holders, the lessor, as periodic distribution amounts, which are equivalent to the amount received from the originator or lessee.

(d) Upon the maturity of the *sukuk*, the originator, the lessee, repurchases the asset from the special purpose vehicle (SPV). The originator then makes the payment for the repurchase price to the SPV. Subsequently, the SPV distributes the repurchase price to the *sukuk* holders as a dissolution distribution amount.

An alternative variant of *ijarah sukuk* exists where there are SPV or financial intermediaries involved in issuing the instrument. In this scenario, the originator directly issues *ijarah sukuk* to acquire the asset. The ownership of the asset is then transferred to the *sukuk* holders, while the issuer or originator becomes the beneficiary of the *ijarah sukuk* or the user of the asset. In this arrangement, there is no premium paid to an Islamic intermediary, although the issuer may receive contractual compensation from the transaction.

The SPV is established solely as a neutral intermediary in the transaction. Therefore, if the lessor is involved in an SPV without substantial ownership of the underlying asset and without utilising it for financing purposes, the lessee, i.e. originator, assumes full responsibility for repair and insurance costs. As a result, the lessee covers these expenses through higher lease payments.

8.4.2 *Characteristics of an* Ijarah Sukuk

The *ijarah sukuk* is characterised by the following natures:

a) The trading of *ijarah sukuk* in the market is leveraged by various market forces, including general market conditions, economic factors, the overall financial market, opportunity cost, and the pricing of tangible investments. Moreover, *ijarah sukuk* is exposed to certain risks. These include the risk associated with the lessee's capacity and willingness to make rental payments, market risks associated with potential fluctuations in asset pricing, as well as costs related to maintenance and insurance and credit risk associated with the originator. An ownership risk in *ijarah sukuk* is also realised as owners are responsible for bearing all costs related to the fundamental characteristics of the assets, while the lessee assumes the responsibility for maintenance expenses (Rohmatunnisa, 2008).

b) The expected return on certain types of *ijarah sukuk* cannot be fully predetermined at the commencement of the contract due to the inclusion of maintenance and insurance costs, which may vary and cannot be precisely determined in advance.

c) *Ijarah sukuk* possesses complete negotiation and can be traded in the secondary market, providing a considerable level of flexibility. This flexibility arises from the approach taken in managing issuances and enhancing marketability. The rules governing flexibility in *ijarah* enable the securitisation of the *ijarah* contract, which plays a vital role in addressing liquidity management challenges.

8.4.3 *Issues that Hinder the* Ijarah Sukuk

To begin with, one of the major issues that hinder the *ijarah sukuk* is not having access to the necessary underlying asset for all prospective issuers. Moreover, *ijarah sukuk* entails significant transaction costs, including maintenance and insurance expenses. This is because Shari'ah principles mandate that the asset must remain in operational condition, and if it requires repairs, the lease may be suspended until the asset is restored in its orderly manner. Additionally, there are costs associated with Shari'ah fees and audits, which are not only expensive but also time-consuming. Furthermore, penalties may be imposed on the lessee or borrower in the event of late payment of lease instalments which is one of the controversial Shari'ah issues. A notable critique is directed towards the practice of using an interest rate as a benchmark concerning *ijarah sukuk*. In many cases, the return on *ijarah sukuk* is linked to the LIBOR (London Inter-Bank Offer Rate) on US dollar funds or a comparable local rate.

8.5 *Musharakah Sukuk*

According to the AAOIFI Shari'ah Standard No. 17, Para 3/6, the *musharakah sukuk:*

> are certificates of equal value issued with the aim of using the mobilised funds for establishing a new project, developing an existing project or financing a business activity on the basis of any of partnership contracts so that the certificate holders become the owners of the project or the assets of the activity as per their respective shares, with the Musharakah certificates being managed on the basis of participation or Mudarabah or an investment agency.

8.5.1 *Basics of a* Musharakah Sukuk

In a *musharakah* partnership, the profits are distributed among the partners based on predetermined ratios. If the profits exceed the amount needed to fulfil the issuer's obligations towards the *sukuk* holders, the excess is usually set aside in a cash reserve. This reserve is then used to provide payments to the *sukuk* holders if the profits in a given period are not sufficient to cover the regular distribution amount.

Under Shari'ah principles, partnerships are broadly classified into two categories: *shirkah al-'aqd* (contractual partnership) and *shirkah al-milk* (property partnership). When it comes to *sukuk* issuances, *shirkah al-'aqd* refers to an agreement between the originator and the trustee to pool their assets, labour, or liabilities. On the other hand, *shirkah al-milk* involves a transaction that leads to joint ownership of an asset by the originator and the trustee. When deciding on the structure of a ***sukuk***, it is important to determine the nature of the originator's business and assess the availability of assets that can support the ***sukuk*** issuance. If there are no tangible assets that can be contributed to the partnership in accordance with Shari'ah principles, opting for the ***shirkah al-'aqd*** structure may be more suitable (Latman & Watkins LLP, n.d).

According to the AAOIFI Shari'ah Standard No. 17, Para 5/16/6, the issuer of the certificates extends an invitation to engage in a partnership with them for a specific project or defined activity. The subscribers, who become partners in the ***musharakah*** contract, contribute the realised funds that form their share in the ***musharakah*** capital. As certificate holders, they possess ownership of the partnership's assets along with the associated profits and losses. They are also entitled to their portion of the profits, if any, generated by the partnership.

8.5.2 Issues with Musharakah Sukuk

The popularity of ***musharakah sukuk*** has declined as Shari'ah scholars now hold the belief that it is impermissible for the originator to provide a purchase undertaking to the trustee, committing to buy the ***musharakah*** assets for an amount other than the market value of the trustee's interest in those assets at the time of sale. This viewpoint stems from the principle that both partners should bear the risk of both profit and loss. Consequently, the diminished appeal of this structure is primarily due to the inability to ensure the return of the initial investment to ***sukuk*** holders through a redemption undertaking at face value (Latman & Watkins LLP, n.d).

Chapter Review Questions

1. *Musharakah Mutanaqisah* Partnership (MMP) is also known as
   a. Diminishing *musharakah*
   b. Diminishing *ijarah*
   c. *Musharakah sukuk*
   d. *Ijarah sukuk*
2. What is the legal opinion of IIFA-OIC regarding the permissibility of MMP?
   a. It is not permissible
   b. It keeps silent in this regard
   c. It is permissible
   d. None of above

3. One of the advantages of MMP is:
   a. It is widely acknowledged as being Shari'ah compliant on a global scale
   b. Under the MMP, the value of the house consistently corresponds to the market price
   c. The MMP offers greater flexibility in the financing structure
   d. All above
4. The BBA was initiated into the Islamic financial spectrum in:
   a. 1983 in Malaysia
   b. 1990 in Saudi Arabia
   c. 2001 in Bangladesh
   d. 2012 in Indonesia
5. *Ijarah Mawsufah Fi al-Dimmah* (IMD) has the qualities of:
   a. *Murabahah*
   b. *Salam*
   c. *Wakalah*
   d. *Hawalah*
6. *Ijarah Mawsufah Fi al-Dimmah* (IMD) is a:
   a. Hybrid contract
   b. Classical contract
   c. Shari'ah-compliant contract
   d. a & c
7. A financial *sukuk* that represents proportional ownership of the usufruct of a well-defined and existing asset. This is an:
   a. *Ijarah sukuk*
   b. *Musharakah sukuk*
   c. *Mudarabah sukuk*
   d. *Murabahah sukuk*
8. Which one is the TRUE statement?
   a. A *sukuk* can be formed with SPV
   b. A *sukuk* can be formed without SPV
   c. a & b
   d. None of the above
9. Which one of the following is one of the characteristics of *ijarah sukuk*?
   a. Tradable in the secondary market
   b. Tradable in the primary market
   c. Tradable in both primary and secondary market
   d. a, b, & c

10. One more sukuk is discussed in this chapter, what is that sukuk?
    a. *Musharakah sukuk*
    b. *Mudarabah sukuk*
    c. *Murabahah sukuk*
    d. None of them

Answers

1. a
2. c
3. d
4. a
5. b
6. d
7. a
8. c
9. d
10. a

References

Abu Ghuddah, Abd al-Sattar. (2007). Al-tatbiqat al-amaliyyah li al-ijarah al-mawsufah fi al- dhimmah. *Paper presented at the 28th al-Barakah Symposium on Islamic Economics.* Jeddah.

Ahmad, A. U. F., Monawer, A. T. M., & Ayinde, L. (2020, June). Takyif fiqhi on the permissibility of ijarah mawsufah fi al-dhimmah: A critical analysis. *International Journal of Islamic Thought, 17.*

Al-Amine, M. B. M. (2001). The Islamic bond market: Possibilities and challenges. *International Journal of Islamic Financial Services, 3*(1).

Ali, M. I., & Falahi, I. R. (2016). *Islamic Banking: Principles and Practices.* Hyderabad. Marifa Academy.

Al-Kawamelah, N. A. K. (2008). *Musharakah Mutanaqisah and its Contemporary Practice: Jordan Islamic Bank as an Example.* Dar al-Nafa'is. Jordan.

BNM. (2007). *Distinct Features of Islamic Financial Transactions: Perspective on Musharakah Mutanaqisah (Diminishing Partnership).* Bank Negara Malaysia. Kuala Lumpur.

Dieng, M. M. (2019). The applicability of ijarah al-mawsufah fi al-dhimmah in Malaysia. *International Journal of Management and Applied Research, 6*(4), 196–207.

Fincyclopedia. (2021). 'Forward ijarah', available at: https://fincyclopedia.net/islamic-finance/f/forward-ijarah (accessed 06 July 2023).

Ganti, A. (2022). What is a sukuk? Sharia-Compliant Bond-Like financial instruments. Available at: https://www.investopedia.com/terms/s/sukuk.asp (accessed 06 July 2023).

Monawer, M. A. T., & Aziz, A. A. (2015). Dispute over the legality of al-ijarah al-mawsufah fi al-dhimmah: A survey of fiqhi opinions. *ISRA International Journal of Islamic Finance, 7*(1), 49–74.

Mydin Meera, A. K., & Abdul Razak, D. (2009). Home financing through the musharakah mutanaqisah contracts: Some practical issues. *Journal of King Abdulaziz University: Islamic Economics, 22*(1).

Osmani, N. M., & Abdullah, M. F. (2010). Musharakah mutanaqisah home financing: A review of literatures and practices of Islamic banks in Malaysia. *International Review of Business Research Papers, 6*(2), 272–282.

Rashid, S. N. M., Abd Rahman, M., Hadi, A., Yahya, N. C., & Md Rasid, N. F. (2020). Bai bithaman ajil (BBA) and musharakah mutanaqisah (MM): Comparative analysis. *Advances in Business Research International Journal, 6*(2), 19–29.

Rohmatunnisa, D. (2008). *Design of Ijarah Sukuk*. University of Nottingham.

Smolo, E. (2007). *A Theoretical Comparison between al-Bay' Bithaman Ajil, Musharakah Mutanaqisah Partnership and Ijarah Sukuk*, Master's Dissertation. International Islamic University Malaysia.

CHAPTER 9

Hybrid Contracts and Issues in Islamic Finance

Abstract The rapid growth of the IBF industry inevitably requires constant product innovation in line with Shari'ah principles to fulfil the diverse demand of its multi-facet customers, taking into consideration technological advancement, digital inclusion, and electronic accessibility. As per the changing nature of the market and the customers, the Islamic financial system cannot solely rely on the core classical financial contracts; instead, it must introduce newly devised products in order to maintain steady progress and sustainability as well as to align with market dynamics and customer preferences. Hybrid contracts are the end solution in this regard. Over the decades since IFS's inception, it has shown the aptitude to devise many hybrid products, with some gaining wide acceptance while others stirring controversies. A hybrid contract evolves from a single contract into a versatile structure. It is grouped from several contracts or products. In the contemporary Islamic financial spectrum, there are a considerable number of hybrid products in practice in various jurisdictions. Since the HPSM, MMP, BBA, IMD, *ijarah sukuk,* and *musharakh sukuk* are hybrid products, this chapter will highlight the permissibility of a hybrid contract and its underlying issues.

Keywords Hybrid Contract · Islamic Finance

M. K. Hassan et al., *Hire Purchase Under Shirkah al-Milk (HPSM) in Islamic Banking and Finance,*
https://doi.org/10.1007/978-3-031-50105-0_9

Preview
The rapid growth of the Islamic finance and banking industry is inevitably required constant product innovation in line with Shari'ah principles to fulfil the diverse demands of its multi-faceted customers, taking into consideration technological advancement, digital inclusion, and electronic accessibility. As per the changing nature of the market and the customers, the Islamic financial system cannot solely rely on the core classical financial contracts; instead, it must introduce newly devised products in order to maintain steady progress and sustainability as well as to align with market dynamics and customer preferences. Hybrid contracts are the end solution in this regard. Over the decades since IFS's inception, it has shown the aptitude to devise many hybrid products, with some gaining wide acceptance while others stirring controversies. A hybrid contract evolves from a single contract into a versatile structure. It is grouped from several contracts or products. In the contemporary Islamic financial spectrum, there are a considerable number of hybrid products in practice in various jurisdictions.

The products that are discussed in this book, i.e. HPSM, MMP, BBA, IMD, *ijarah sukuk,* and *musharakh sukuk* are also classified as hybrid products. Although the several underlying issues of those products have comprehensively been studied in their respective sections, yet, there remains a need for a study on the structure of "hybrid product" in particular.

9.1 What Is a Hybrid Contract

Since the hybrid contract is a new terminology that is used only in the modern Islamic financial domain, hence, the classical *fiqh* works of literature lack a vibrant introduction to the definition of a "hybrid" contract in a specific manner. The hybrid contract can be understood through the Arabic term *'uqud al-murakkabah* that refers to the English term "combination of contracts".

A combination of contracts—that is, a hybrid contract—is defined by Hammad (2005) as.

> an agreement between the two parties or more to carry out a contract that contains two or more contracts with different features and legal consequences to achieve a desired viable transaction. All legal effects and consequences from of the hybrid contract agreement, as well as all rights and obligations thereof, is seen as an integral and undivided, as the legal effect of a contract.

According to AAOIFI Shari'ah Standard No. (25)—Combination of Contracts:

> Combination of contracts is a process that takes place between two parties or more, and entails the simultaneous conclusion of more than one contract. Hence, combination of contracts may take any of the following forms: 2/1/1 combining more than one contract without imposing any of them as a condition in the other, and without prior agreement (muwata'ah) to do so, (2/1/2) combining more than one contract while imposing some of them as conditions in the other, without prior agreement to do so, (2/1/3) combining more than one contract subject to prior agreement (muwata'ah), but without imposing any of them as a condition in the others, (2/1/4) agreement to conclude the deal through any of different contractual forms as will be finally decided in the future.

9.2 Legal Status of a Hybrid Contract

Many modern contracts have not existed previously in the earlier eras because of the lack of their necessity at that time. However, in recent decades, there are many modern contracts that have been introduced in the Islamic banking and finance sectors all over the world. Some of those contracts are claimed to be Shari'ah compliant, and some of them yet are applied with controversies. Hence, the question is here, what is the legal status of a hybrid contract to Muslim scholars? In response to this question, the scholars are divided into two opinions:

(a) Some Hanafi and Shafi'i scholars consider the impermissibility of a new contract (which has not been practised in the classical era) albeit, practically, the permissibility of a new contract is evident in the Shari'ah that is indicated through various sources of Islamic jurisprudence. The opinion of impermissibility has also been comprehended by Ibn Hazm, a few Malikis and Hanbalis too. They, concerning their opinion, employed the following hadith to strengthen the opinion:

In the story of A'isha (RAA), when she intended to buy a slave girl to free her, the owner of the slave agreed to the sale but stipulated that the *wala*[1] would remain under his custody. The atypical stipulation of the

[1] An old practice in buying and selling the slaves that the buyer/freer will keep the right of inheritance of the slave.

seller gives the right of the legal inheritance to the seller in which the customary nature of the contract moves to a new characteristic which has been opposed by the Prophet (SAW) when the issue raised before him:

> ما بال أقوام يشترطون شروطا ليس في كتاب الله تعالى, من اشترط شرطا ليس في كتاب الله له، و إن شرطه مائة مرة شرط الله أحق و أوثق
>
> Why do some people stipulate some conditions are not mentioned in the Qur'an? If anybody stipulates, any condition is not mentioned in the Qur'an considered void though there hundred of stipulations are made. The stipulation of Allah is more authentic and strongest.

So, the right of *wala* will belong to the person who frees the slave (al-Shawkani, 1984).

Despite the fact that the hadith clearly nullifies any condition which is not exhibited in the Qur'an, however, scholars refuted the hadith contending that the intention of the prohibition by the Prophet (SAW) was the essence of the condition, not the condition itself, particularly (al-Funaysan, 2000). However, there is another hadith of prohibition of the new act that was not commanded by the Prophet (SAW). The hadith has been narrated by 'A'isha (RAA) that Prophet (SAW) said:

> من عمل عملا ليس عليه أمرنا فهو رد
>
> Whoever does an action which does not have our command will have it rejected. (Khan, 1984)

The term "action" in the hadith includes the new contract, which is to be prohibited if it is not in line with Prophetic command. Albeit, the term "action is refuted, contending that the prohibition in the hadith is only for "worship" instead of the transaction" (Hama, 2007).

A story can be traced based on the above-mentioned hadiths, where an employee committed adultery with the wife of his employer. They agreed on something to mitigate the problem between themselves and went to Prophet (SAW) to consult with him and to get his approval on their agreed matter. But Prophet (SAW) dismissed the mutual agreement because of the absence of such an agreement in Shari'ah (Hama, 2007). There is another hadith where Prophet (SAW) said:

"نهي رسول الله صلى الله عليه و سلم من بيع و شر

Prophet (SAW) prohibited sale with a condition.

This hadith proves that there is no permissibility to change any existing contract by incorporating one or more conditions in it. However, this hadith being unauthentic contradicts other authentic hadiths (Ibrahim, 1987).

(b) Imam al-Shafi'i, Imam al-Zayla'i from Hanafi, Imam al-Shatibi from Maliki and Ibn Taymiyyah and Ibn Qayyim from Hanbali schools assume that the contracts are originally permitted unless there is explicit Shari'ah evidence prohibits it (Ibn Taymiyyah, 2011). They fetch pieces of evidence from the Qur'anic and the Prophetic texts. As to be the texts of the Qur'an, they bring verse no. 1 of Surah al-Ma'idah, where Allah (SWT) commanded people to maintain their promises; He (SWT) says:

يَا أَيُّهَا الَّذِينَ آمَنُوا أَوْفُوا بِالْعُقُودِ

O you who believe! Fulfil your (all) obligations.

In the verse no. 34 of Surah al-Isra, He (SWT) warned people to be concerned about their engagements, He (SWT) then says:

إِنَّ الْعَهْدَ كَانَ مَسْئُولاً وَ أَوْفُوا بِالْعَهْدِ

And fulfil every engagement, for every engagement will be inquired into.

The two words in both two verses, " *'aqd* and *'ahd*", refer to a holistic engagement in terms of the general perspective of any kind of transaction in people's daily life. The exception will only be applied in such transactions when any non-Shari'ah-compliant element is encountered that harms the contractual objective and requirements (Hama, 2007). Accordingly, there is a hadith in which the Prophet (SAW) stated:

المسلمون على شروطهم إلا شرطا أحل حراما أو حرم حلالا

Muslims are bound by the conditions they made except a condition that legalises impermissible act or invalidates permissible act. (Ibn Majah, 2007)

The hadith encourages people to fulfil their promises which indicates the permissibility to form a new contract based on required conditions that do not overrule the Shari'ah objective. In another hadith Prophet (SAW) says:

> اربع من كن فيه كان منافقا خالصا و من كان فيه خلة منهن كان فيه خلة من نفاق حتى يدعها: إذا حدث كذب و إذا عاهد غذر و إذا وعد أخلف و إذا خاصم فجر

> Whoever has the following four (characteristics) will be a pure hypocrite (*munafiq*), and whoever has one of the following four characteristics will have one characteristic of hypocrisy unless and until he gives it up: Whenever he is entrusted, he betrays, whenever he speaks, he tells a lie, whenever he makes a covenant, he proves treacherous, and whenever he quarrels, he behaves in a very imprudent, evil and insulting manner. (Khan, 1984)

Many texts in the Qur'an and Sunnah prohibit breaking promises and affirm the punishment for those who break them, as in the verse no. 27 of Surah al-Baqarah Allah (SWT) warns, "those who break Allah's covenant after it is ratified, and who sunder what Allah has ordered to be joined, and make mischief on earth: they cause loss (only) to themselves".

Based on the earlier discussed verses and hadiths, every contract is assumed to be an action generally and principally permissible to be practised if there is no harmful and non-Shari'ah element in that contract. As historically proven, before the time of the Prophet (SAW), the non-believers of Arab restricted some matters, including foodstuffs, on them, which Allah (SWT) later disclosed in the Qur'an and condemned accordingly. And those actions have not been approved by Allah (SWT). Ibn Taymiyyah (2011) said, "If we ban contracts and conditions between people, we are prohibiting something that Allah did not prohibit. Conversely, agreements or actions that are related to worshipping can be banned, except with Shari'ah approval. Moreover, contracts are ordinarily practised by Muslims and non-Muslims and do not need a statement from Shari'ah to approve them".

Characteristically, forming a (new) contract is subject to the consent of both parties, and any obligation in a contract is what they agree upon. Allah (SWT), in verse no. 29 of Surah al-Nisa thus, says, "But let there be a trade amongst you by mutual consent". Hence, the view of Imam

Ahmad and Imam Malik of the affirmative opinion of forming a new contract is associated with the required condition. Therefore, no contract is to be void unless there is an explicit Shari'ah text or analogy that prohibits it (Hama, 2007).

To summarise the current discussion on the legal status of the new contract, it can be said that the view of the jurists who opine in favour of forming a new contract is to be preferred based on the development of verses and hadiths if the contract does not contradict with the Shari'ah requirements. However, the current IBF industry requires frequently innovative products that fit people's modern needs in line with Shari'ah. If forming a new contract gets prohibited, the people's lives will be in hardships and difficulties, which Islam wants to remove. On the other hand, the IBF is to keep its growth competing with its conventional counterparts; in this hindrance, if innovation or forming a new contract is restricted, the long-cherished hope for the people who seek to transact according to Shari'ah concerning their holy faith would open the door for non-Shari'ah transactions. AAOIFI Shari'ah Standard No. (25), in Para 3, ascertains the permissibility of combined contracts, which is mentioned as:

> It is permissible in Shari'ah to combine more than one contract in one set, without imposing one contract as a condition in the other, and provided that each contract is permissible on its own. Combining contracts in this manner is acceptable unless it encounters a Shari'ah restriction that entails its prohibition on exceptional basis.

9.3 *Shari'ah* Obligations in a Hybrid Contract

Despite hybrid contracts being permissible, however, standards setters like AAOIFI and many scholars set strict conditions that must be followed in a hybrid contract. AAOIFI in its Shari'ah Standard No. (25), Para 4, stipulates that a hybrid contract:

(a) When combining contracts, it is important to adhere to Shari'ah principles. Hence, a hybrid contract cannot include cases that are explicitly prohibited, such as combining sale and lending within a single contract.
(b) It is crucial to emphasise that it should not be employed as a means to engage in prohibited practices like *bay' al-'inah* or *riba*

al-fadl, where two parties enter into an agreement as a deceptive method for committing *riba*.

(c) It should not be employed as a justification for engaging in *riba* (interest-based transactions). There is a potential for misuse by the two parties involved, such as when they enter into a lending contract that includes additional compensatory gains. For instance, they may stipulate in the contract that the borrower should provide accommodation in their house to the lender or grant them a gift. Another potential misuse of contracts' combining is imposing excessive repayment obligations on the borrower in terms of quantity or quality.

(d) It is crucial to ensure that combined contracts do not display any inconsistency or contradiction in terms of their underlying principles and actual objectives. Examples of contradictory contracts include situations where an asset is simultaneously gifted and sold/leased to someone, the combination of *mudarabah* with lending the *mudarabah* capital to the *mudarib*, merging currency exchange with *ju'alah*, combining *salam* with *ju'alah* for the same contract value, or blending leasing with selling (as seen in traditional hire-purchase agreements). Such contradictory combinations should be avoided to maintain compliance with Shari'ah principles in a hybrid contract.

The Shari'ah Advisory Council of Kuwait Finance House, in its meeting No. 23/2006 held on September 19, 2006, in Kuwait, justified four requirements to execute the *Ijarah* Rental Swap Product combined with the contract of unilateral binding promise on transaction of *musawamah* and *tawarruq* as hybrid products which can also be the base for other hybrid products in general where applicable (Dusuki, 2008). Those are:

(a) The contract agreement in a transaction must be genuine and not fictitious. This means that when a transaction occurs, there must be a real exchange where the seller genuinely desires to sell and the buyer genuinely intends to purchase the real subject matter. Otherwise, it resembles the concept of fictitious tawarruq, which has been utilised by numerous Islamic banks worldwide. In fact, based on collected data, only 2.7% of commodity murabahah and tawarruq transactions involve actual delivery to end users, while 97.3% are employed for derivative transactions by speculators.

(b) Every contract that is executed carries its own set of consequences. For instance, in a sale contract, the transfer of ownership of the asset from the seller to the buyer is a fundamental requirement that must be fulfilled after the sale transaction takes place.
(c) One contract to another has to be separated.
(d) The contract does not put any conditions in the transaction between the buyer and the seller.

9.4 *Shari'ah* Concessions in Combined Contracts

Although several restrictions exist in Shari'ah-compliant financial contracts; besides, Shari'ah offers concessions for those contracts where they are necessitated. AAOIFI Shari'ah Standard No. (25), Para 5 and its sub-paras exhibit the circumstances where concessions can be applied:

(a) Fundamentally, Shari'ah concessions provided to implicit and subsidiary contracts during the process of combining contracts cannot be granted to the same contracts when they are independently concluded. Implicit and subsidiary contracts refer to contractual commitments that are not explicitly stated in the original agreement or those that follow the initial commitments of the transaction. The decision regarding concessions in such cases should be based on established traditions, industry practices, and professional expertise and must receive approval from the Shari'ah Supervisory Board of the institution.
(b) Concessions offered to implicit and subsidiary contracts involve exemptions from the following prohibited actions: (I) *gharar* (uncertainty), which can impact financial contracts, may be disregarded in the case of implicit and subsidiary contracts; (II) *Jahalah* (ignorance), which can also impact financial contracts, may be disregarded specifically concerning the object of a subsidiary contract; (III) Sale-based *riba* and violations of currency exchange rules, such as the neglect of spot delivery in a contract that combines currency exchange with money transfer, can also be overlooked in the case of the subsidiary and implicit contracts; (IV) The practice of selling debt for another debt can be disregarded when it occurs within the context of a subsidiary contract. A relevant example is the purchase of shares (on credit) from a company that is already in debt; (V) In certain cases, subsidiary

and implicit contracts may be exempted from certain prerequisites that are essential for the validity of contracts, such as the requirements of offer and acceptance. This relief is granted when there is a genuine need or desire to accomplish a permissible interest.

9.5 Other Issues in the Contemporary Application of Hybrid Contact

One of the notable forms of modern financial transactions is represented by contractual arrangements that involve multiple contracts and commitments agreed upon in advance, to be executed in a specific manner and according to a predetermined sequence of stages. These arrangements are designed to fulfil a particular purpose or interest of the contracting parties. Examples of such arrangements include executing *Murabahah* on Order of Purchase, *Ijarah Muntahia Bittamleek*, or *Musharakah Mutanaqisah* Partnership (diminishing musharakah).

The pledges that are included within these combined contract sets are binding for the parties involved. These newly developed sets of combined contracts must adhere to the overarching principles of Shari'ah, ensuring compliance in terms of structure, rulings, requirements, and conditions. However, if any of the parties involved in combined contracts fail to fulfil their contractual obligations, the other party has the right to seek compensation for the actual harm suffered as a result.

Chapter Review Questions

1. A hybrid contract can be understood in Arabic as:
   a. *'Uqud al-murakkabah*
   b. Combination contracts
   c. *'Uqud al-ijarah*
   d. *'Uqud ghayr murakkabah*
2. A hybrid contract can be formed:
   a. By a single contract
   b. More than one contract
   c. Neither a nor b
   d. a & b
3. A hybrid contract requires:
   a. Only one contracting party
   b. More than two contracting parties

   c. No contracting party
   d. All above
4. What is the legal status of a hybrid contract?
   a. Unanimously permissible
   b. Unanimously Prohibited
   c. Scholars agree and disagree
   d. None of above
5. What is the preferred opinion on the permissibility of a hybrid contract?
   a. Impermissible
   b. Not specified
   c. Permissible if it meets Shari'ah requirements
   d. All above
6. Based on AAOIFI Shari'ah Standard, combining sale and *ijarah* within a single contract is:
   a. Permissible
   b. *Makruh*
   c. Obligatory
   d. Prohibited
7. How many requirements are justified by the Shari'ah Advisory Council of Kuwait Finance House to execute the *Ijarah* Rental Swap Products that combined with the contract of unilateral binding promise on *musawamah* and *tawarruq* as hybrid products?
   a. One
   b. Three
   c. Six
   d. Four
8. The pledges that are included within the combined contracts are:
   a. Binding
   b. Optional
   c. Not applicable
   d. a & b
9. If any of the parties involved in combined contracts fail to fulfil their contractual obligations, the other party has the right to seek compensation:
   a. True
   b. False
   c. Neutral
   d. All above

10. HPSM, MMP, BBA and IMD are:
    a. Hybrid contracts
    b. Classical contracts
    c. Prohibited contracts
    d. None of above

Answers

1. a
2. b
3. b
4. c
5. c
6. d
7. d
8. a
9. a
10. a

References

Al-Funaysan, S. (2000). Al-'ijar al-muntahi bi al-tamlik'. *Majallah al-Buhuth al-Fiqhiyyah al-Mu'asirah,* 48.

Al-Shawkani, M. I., & Ali. (1984). *Nayl al-Awtar Sharh Muntaqa al-Akhbar* (Vol. 3). Maktabah al-Kulliyyat al-Azhariyyah.

Dusuki, A. W. (2008). Banking for the poor: The role of Islamic banking in microfinance initiatives. *International Journal of Systems and Ethics, 24,* 49–66.

Hama, A. O. (2007). *Islamic Hire-Purchase Transaction.* International Islamic University Malaysia.

Hammad, N. (2005). *Al-Uqud al-Murakkabah fi al-Fiqh al-Islami,* 1st Edition. Damascus. Dar al Qalam.

Ibrahim, M. A. (1987). *Hukm Bay' bi al-Taqsit fi al-Shariah wa al-Qanun.* Maktabah al-Risalah al-HadItha. Jordan.

Khan, M. (1984). *The Translation of the Meaning of Sahih al-Bukhari,* Vol. 3. Kitab Bhavan. New Delhi.

Ibn Majah (2007). *Sunan Ibn Majah,* Vol. 2. Dar al-salam. Riyad.

Ibn Taymiyyah, Ahmad Ibn Abd al-Halim. (2011). *Al-Qawa'id al-Nuraniyyah al-Fiqhiyyah,*Vol. 2. Maktab al- Rashid. Riyad.

CHAPTER 10

Conclusion

Abstract In this concluding stage, this chapter consolidates the key findings from the preceding chapters of the study, offering readers a comprehensive overview of the entire study. Emphasising the significance of the findings, it puts forth substantial recommendations derived from the study's insights. These recommendations are designed to enhance the transparency of the application of HPSM in modern financial contexts in various jurisdictions, concerning its legality, religious adherence, and economic considerations. Indeed, the fundamental objective of this chapter is to underscore the importance of scrutinising HPSM with a focus on stakeholders' interests, all while maintaining the integrity of Shari'ah obligations.

Keywords HPSM · Hire purchase · Hybrid contract · Islamic hire purchase · Hire Purchase under Shirkah al-Milk

In the contemporary financial landscape, Islamic banks around the world employ various products and contracts for financing purposes, including hire purchase under *shirkah al-milk* (HPSM). This financing mode combines three distinct contracts: *shirkah*, ijarah, and sale, and is considered a hybrid contract due to its departure from traditional structures. Hybrid contracts, in general, have faced criticism from Shari'ah and legal experts

M. K. Hassan et al., *Hire Purchase Under Shirkah al-Milk (HPSM) in Islamic Banking and Finance*, https://doi.org/10.1007/978-3-031-50105-0_10

due to the absence of explicit Shari'ah texts specifically addressing these newly formed hybrid contracts. However, after conducting a comprehensive analysis, it has been determined that HPSM is a permissible mode of financing as it adheres to all Shari'ah requirements, essential elements, and necessary conditions of a valid Shari'ah contract.

Furthermore, the Shari'ah compliance of HPSM has been examined by highlighting the significant differences between conventional hire purchase and Islamic hire purchase. Conventional HPSM combines three contracts into one, which is prohibited by Shari'ah, whereas HPSM in Islamic banking and finance (IBF) is executed through three separate contracts sequentially. Conventional HPSM is based on loans and interest, whereas HPSM in IBF operates on the principles of financing and profit generation. Additionally, in conventional HPSM, the lessee is responsible for bearing all maintenance costs of the property, whereas, in HPSM in IBF, the lessor and lessee agree on the allocation of maintenance costs as per the terms of the agreement.

The book also provides an in-depth discussion on the Shari'ah issues surrounding gift (*hibah*) contracts with conditions. There is a difference of opinion among scholars regarding the validity of *hibah* contracts when conditions are attached. Some scholars, including certain Hanafis, Shafi'is, and Hanbalis, argue that *hibah* contracts with conditions are invalid. They contend that the transfer of ownership should occur immediately after the execution of the contract without any delay. In the case of a *hibah* contract, where ownership transfer depends on the completion of rent instalments for the leased asset, there is a possibility of uncertainty due to the delay in transferring ownership.

However, many other scholars hold the opinion that *hibah* contracts with conditions are valid. According to their perspective, the contract begins as a *hibah* and eventually transitions into a sale contract. Zufar, for instance, states that this *hibah* contract is essentially a sale contract from start to finish. Most Hanafi scholars consider it a hybrid contract, characterised as a *hibah* in form but a sale in essence. Therefore, they argue that the contract is valid as long as it fulfils accurate and known conditions. Furthermore, for Maliki scholars, this contract is primarily viewed as a sale contract but occasionally as a *hibah*. Based on the majority opinion of jurists, it can be concluded that *hibah* contracts with conditions are valid contracts.

The book also extensively examines the legal status of a promise (*wa'd*) and whether it carries binding obligations or not. The majority of scholars hold the view that a promise is not legally binding, but it carries religious significance. However, if a promise includes specific conditions, it becomes legally binding as well. On the other hand, some scholars argue that a promise is binding both legally and religiously, considering it a noble virtue. They believe that a promise should be enforceable in a court of law, particularly in modern economic activities.

Therefore, it is recommended to favour the opinion that a promise should be binding to fulfil both legally and religiously, aligning with the requirements of modern economic activities to protect the interests of all parties involved. This perspective is supported by evidence from the Qur'an and Sunnah, which emphasise the importance of fulfilling promises. By recognising the binding nature of promises, it ensures accountability and trustworthiness in business transactions and other aspects of life.

A contentious issue surrounding hire purchase transactions is the interpretation of three different hadiths that prohibit the combination of two contracts in one. Through an extensive investigation into the chain of narrations, sources, and essence of these hadiths, the majority of scholars have concluded that despite their varying wording, they convey the same meaning. However, the discussion regarding the prohibition of two contracts in one encompasses the prohibition of the simultaneous occurrence of two contracts within a single transaction.

Therefore, hire purchase under *shirkah al-milk* (HPSM) does not fall under the prohibition mentioned in these hadiths. HPSM does not involve the simultaneous combination of three or two contracts into one. Instead, each contract in HPSM is formed separately and sequentially, ensuring that the contracts of *shirkah*, ijarah, and sale occur individually, one after the other. Consequently, HPSM is not encompassed by the prohibition mentioned in these hadiths.

The term "hire purchase under *shirkah al-milk*" (HPSM) is often referred to as "*ijarah muntahiyyah bi al-tamlik*" in Arabic. However, it is important to note that using "*ijarah muntahiyyah bi al-tamlik*" as a direct translation for hire purchase under *shirkah al-milk* is not entirely accurate. This is because "*ijarah muntahiyyah bi al-tamlik*" specifically refers to a lease contract that ends with the transfer of ownership, and it does not encompass the full meaning of HPSM. In order to confine the precise meaning of HPSM, various alternative Arabic terminologies have been suggested, such as "hire purchase" (Ramli & Onn, 2007), "leasing ending with ownership" (Abdullah, 1988; Al-Shadhili, 2014; Al-Taskhiri,

2014; Ibrahim, 2014), "lease ending into ownership" (Abu Ghuddah, 1998), "*ijarah thumma al-bay'*" (Ramli & Onn, 2007), or "*ijarah wa al-iqna'*" (Abu Ghuddah, 1998), which are synonymous with the concept of HPSM. However, it is important to note that "*ijarah muntahiyyah bi al-tamlik*" does not encompass all the elements of HPSM. It only includes two components, namely, "*ijarah*" and "sale", whereas HPSM actually consists of three distinct elements: *shirkah*, *ijarah*, and sale. Therefore, the recommended Arabic terminology for HPSM could be "*ijarah muntahiyyah bi al-tamlik taht al- 'aqd al-shirkah*", which includes all the necessary components of HPSM. Hence, in our opinion, the accurate and comprehensive Arabic term for HPSM is to be "*ijarah muntahiyyah bi al-tamlik taht al- 'aqd al-shirkah*". Without including the phrase "*taht al- 'aqd al-shirkah*" with "*ijarah muntahiyyah bi al-tamlik*", the Arabic terminology used for HPSM may not fully deliver its intended meaning.

According to the general principle of insurance coverage or *takaful*, the cost of insurance should be borne by the bank or owner of the property rather than the customer or lessee (El-din & Abdullah, 2007). However, in practice, it is often observed that the client in an HPSM contract is required to pay for insurance coverage, including an additional amount for risk costs, especially in the case of IBBL.

In the HPSM contract, which begins with a *shirkah* contract and then transitions to *ijarah*, it is argued that if the lessee is responsible for paying the insurance coverage, they actually should only be liable for the portion of the property they own. They should not be obligated to pay for insurance covering the portion of the asset that they do not own. This is because the lessee retains the right to use and benefit from the bank's portion of the property under the lease agreement without assuming ownership. Therefore, based on this principle, it is the lessor or bank who should bear the cost of insurance coverage for their portion of the property. Additionally, the additional 10% risk mitigation cost should be divided proportionally based on the percentage of ownership of the property. Since the lessee is still considered a lessee and pays monthly rent for the bank's or lessor's portion, it is not reasonable for them to be responsible for insurance coverage of the owner's portion that they do not own. In short, the argument suggests that in HPSM contracts, the lessor or bank should bear the cost of insurance coverage for their portion of the property, and the additional 10% risk mitigation cost should also be divided proportionally based on the ownership percentage.

There is a diversity of opinions among Muslim investors regarding the payment of insurance contributions in a leased property. Some argue that the owner, rather than the lessee, should bear the cost of insurance (El-din & Abdullah, 2007). Alawi (1986) suggests that in the case of a total economic loss, the owner or bank must pay for the insurance, while in the case of a partial loss, the settlement is yet to be determined. Usmani holds the view that if a property is insured under a Shari'ah-compliant *takaful*, the expense should be borne by the lessor, not the lessee. However, it is worth noting that a legal opinion (*fatwa*) issued by the Kuwait Finance House states that it is permissible to hold the lessee responsible for insurance payments if the amount is known. This is because the insurance payment may serve as a substitute for the lease payment (El-din & Abdullah, 2007). Overall, there are differing perspectives on whether the owner or lessee should be accountable for insurance contributions in a leased property. While some argue for the owner's responsibility, others believe that the lessee can be held accountable, especially if the amount is known and the insurance payment can replace the lease payment.

In the context of Malaysia's hire-purchase practices, it is observed that the responsibility for insurance coverage is usually borne by the lessor or bank in the first year, with the cost being adjusted through rental payments. In subsequent years, the lessee is required to pay for the insurance coverage. This approach is widely supported by most Islamic jurists in Malaysia (El-din & Abdullah, 2007). However, there is another ruling endorsed by the Islamic Development Bank (IsDB) regarding insurance coverage. According to this ruling, the contribution for insurance can be shared between the lessor and lessee. For instance, the IsDB may assume responsibility for insurance coverage in cases of total damage, loss, and third-party liability exposure, while the lessee is responsible for insuring risks incidental to the use of the property, such as operational hazards, accidents, and negligence. This mechanism ensures a balanced distribution of responsibilities between the bank and the customer to cover both internal and external risks associated with the property's use (El-din & Abdullah, 2007). Eventually, it can be recommended that either the Malaysian practice of insurance contribution, in which the bank contributes for the first year and the lessee/client contributes for the following years, or the practice of the resolution of IsDB, in which the insurance contribution is shared between lessor or bank and the lessee can be applied for the insurance matter of HPSM in other jurisdictions.

In this case, the ruling of IsDB in insurance contribution can be preferred because of its offsetting nature. Hence, the IBFIs, where still their insurance policy is arguable, may observe the method of IsDB to attract potential customers to hire purchase-based products. Furthermore, since insurance coverage is a significant controversial issue in HPSM, further comprehensive research can be conducted in the future.

While the use of mortgages in Shari'ah-based contracts is considered permissible according to the Qur'an, Sunnah, and consensus (AAOIFI Shari'ah Standard No. [39]), it is worth noting that the mortgage policy, similar to insurance, can sometimes favour the bank over the client. In Islamic financial institutions, the practice involves holding the leased property as collateral or using another property with an equivalent value to secure the lease. However, in commercial activities, it is common for lessees to provide a security deposit to cover any potential future loss or misconduct related to the leased property. The determination of the security deposit amount varies across different jurisdictions of Islamic banking and finance. For instance, in Iran, the security deposit is typically around 20% of the property's cost price, which is considered part of the cost price during the leasing period. In Pakistan, clients are required to pay a security deposit ranging from a minimum of 20% to a maximum of 50% of the property value. In Malaysia, both Islamic and conventional hire purchase transactions typically require a 10% deposit. Additionally, another method practised in the Malaysian finance industry is to collect an equivalent amount of three months' rental for the leased property, which is deposited into an Islamic investment account. Considering the various approaches mentioned above, it is recommended to adopt any of these methods for the security deposit (*hamish jiddiyah*) purposes instead of mandating a full mortgage on the leased property or its equivalent value. This approach would alleviate the burden of mortgage arrangements, making it easier for clients to acquire property. Consequently, this would enhance the marketability of the HPSM contract and make it more attractive to customers.

In order to protect the financier's interests and ascertain the lessee's details, Islamic banking and financial institutions (IBFIs) may require the lessee to provide a guarantor, as practised in Malaysian hire-purchase agreements. While individual guarantors are commonly used, some financial institutions may accept guarantees from public companies, cooperatives, or trust organisations instead of individuals. The inclusion of guarantees in financing arrangements serves to enhance the creditworthiness of potential customers, enabling them to secure the necessary financing. Guarantors act as an additional security measure for the financier.

Although the concept of a guarantor is traditionally associated with the "*kafalah*" contract, it can also be applied as a separate contract within the framework of HPSM. A guarantee is a legal contract that obligates someone (the guarantor) to make payments on behalf of the principal debtor if the debtor fails to fulfil their payment obligations. In the event that the principal debtor defaults on their debt, the financier has the right to pursue legal action against the guarantor.

If IBFIs choose to include a guarantor as part of the security measures in HPSM contracts, it is advisable to conduct a comprehensive study on the eligibility criteria for guarantors, the standards for individual and corporate guarantors, and the rights and responsibilities of guarantors. This will help establish clear guidelines and ensure the effectiveness of the guarantor arrangement. Therefore, it is recommended that IBFIs consider incorporating the role of a guarantor as an additional security measure to safeguard their investments.

Ensuring compliance with Shari'ah principles is a fundamental aspect of IBF. The process of Shari'ah deliberation and interpretation plays a crucial role in maintaining this compliance. The harmonisation of Shari'ah interpretations is essential for the comprehensive and sustainable development of the IBF sector. It strengthens regulatory and supervisory oversight while cultivating a pool of competent Shari'ah advisers. The Shari'ah screening process serves as a key measure for approving products and services in the IBF industry. Several Shari'ah regulatory domestic, regional, and international institutions, such as AAOIFI, OIC-IIFA, IFSB, and Bank Negara Malaysia (BNM-Shari'ah Resolutions), are dedicated to developing Shari'ah standards and guidelines. These standards address the applicability and underlying issues of hire-purchase, and many IBFIs around the world adhere to them. However, there are still some IBFIs that have not yet adopted these Shari'ah standards in their operational processes. To minimize controversies surrounding hybrid products like HPSM and to instil confidence among stakeholders, it is recommended that these IBFIs align themselves with the Shari'ah standards set by regulatory bodies. By doing so, the controversy surrounding hybrid products can be mitigated, and HPSM, as one of these products, can be better understood and implemented.

In certain jurisdictions, it is common for HPSM clients to be required to obtain "all risk" insurance or insurance for the leased property from reputable and licensed Islamic insurance companies recognised by the bank. However, in the case of IBBL in Bangladesh, they recommend their clients consider "Shadaran Bima Corporation" as an alternative option for insurance coverage. It is crucial to understand that "Shadaran Bima Corporation" is a conventional insurance company rather than an Islamic one. As an Islamic bank, it is generally expected that IBBL would prioritise recommending clients to deal with Islamic financial institutions, including Islamic insurance companies, in order to ensure compliance with Shari'ah principles. This is because there are Islamic insurance companies available in the country that could provide the required insurance coverage. It would be advisable for IBBL to consider promoting and recommending Islamic insurance alternatives to their clients in line with their commitment to Islamic banking principles. This would not only align with Shari'ah requirements but also provide clients with options that are more in line with their religious beliefs.

In the book, there are a few other financing contracts, i.e. MMP, BBA, IMD, *ijarah*, and *musharakah sukuk*, that convey the same purpose or are similar to the HPSM in nature from many aspects are discussed. All of those contracts are investigated by scholars and addressed positively and negatively from the Shari'ah conformity. However, except for the BBA contract, the other contracts have been recommended to be applied in IBFS if they incorporate the public interests (*maslahah*) and benefits (*manfa'ah*) and do not contradict the explicit Shari'ah ruling(s). The BBA contract has been suggested to be altered by other contracts like MMP due to its major issues related to assuming *riba*.

In summary, it can be said that the study on Hire Purchase under *Shirkah al-Milk* (HPSM) has important policy implications. The research sheds light on the legal, religious, and economic aspects of HPSM, providing valuable insights for policymakers. Key findings emphasise the importance of adhering to Shari'ah principles while accommodating modern economic needs. Transparency, clear contractual terms, and consumer protection are crucial for ensuring fairness in HPSM transactions. Standardisation and harmonisation across Islamic financial institutions are necessary to enhance consistency and reliability. The establishment of a robust regulatory framework is essential for upholding the integrity and promoting financial inclusion. Overall, this study contributes to the development and refinement of HPSM as a responsible financing option within the realm of Islamic banking and finance.

References

Abdullah M. A. (1988). Al-ta'jir al-muntaha bi al-tamlik wa al-Suwar al-Mashru'iyyah fih. *Majallah Majma' al-Fiqh al-Islami, 4*(5).

Abu Ghuddah, Abd al-Sattar. (1998). *Ijarah*. al-Barakah Banking Group.

Alawi, L. (1986). Leasing an Islamic Financial Instrument. In M. El. Helwi (Ed.), *Islamic Banking and Finance* (pp. 120–127). Butterworths.

Al-Shadhili, H. A. (2014). Leasing Ending with Ownership. In *Leasing Ending with Ownership and Leasing Bond (al-Ijarah al-Muntahiyah bi al-Tamlik) Its Ruling and Contemporary Application* (pp. 21–81). Islamic Banking and Financial Institute Malaysia (IBFIM).

Al-Taskhiri, M. A. (2014). Leasing Ending with Ownership and Concept of Promise. In *Leasing Ending with Ownership and Leasing Bond (al-Ijarah al-Muntahiyah bi al-Tamlik) Its Ruling and Contemporary Application* (pp. 103–115). Islamic Banking and Financial Institute Malaysia (IBFIM).

El-din, S. I. T., & Abdullah, N. I. (2007). Issues of Implementing Islamic Hire Purchase in Dual Banking Systems: Malaysia's Experience. *Thunderbird International Business Review, 49*(2), 225–249.

Ibrahim, A. (2014). Leasing Ending with Ownership. In *Leasing Ending with Ownership and Leasing Bond (al-Ijarah al-Muntahiyah bi al-Tamlik) Its Ruling and Contemporary Application* (pp. 117–124). Islamic Banking and Financial Institute Malaysia (IBFIM).

Ramli, R., & Onn, H. (2007). *Islamic Hire-Purchase (Ijarah Thumma al-Bay'-AITAB): The Handbook* (1st ed.). Islamic Banking and Finance Institute Malaysia (IBFIM).

References

AAOIFI. (2017). *Shari'ah Standard*. Accounting and Auditing Organisation for Islamic Financial Institutions.

Abadi, Abu Abd al-Rahman. Sharf al-Haq. (2001). *Awn al-Ma'bud Sharh Sunan Abi Dawud* (Vol. 9). Dar 'Ihya al-Turath al-Arabi.

Accounting Education University. (n.d). *Accounting for Hire Purchase*. https://www.svtuition.org/2011/07/accounting-for-hire-purchase.html. Accessed 5 October 2023.

Abdullah, A. M. (2014). Leasing Ending with Ownership: Its Permissible Forms. In *Leasing Ending with Ownership and Leasing Bond (Ijarah al-Muntahiyah bi al-Tamlik wa Sukuk al-Ijarah) Its Ruling and Contemporary Application* (pp. 3–19). Islamic Banking and Financial Institute Malaysia (IBFIM).

Abdullah M. A. (1988). Al-ta'jir al-muntaha bi al-tamlik wa al-Suwar al-Mashru'iyyah fih. *Majallah Majma 'al-Fiqh al-Islami, 4*(5).

Abdullah, N. I. (2005). *Islamic Hire-Purchase in Malaysian Financial Institutions: A Comparative Analytical Book*. Loughborough University.

Abu Ghuddah, Abd al-Sattar. (1998). *Ijarah*. al-Barakah Banking Group.

Abu Ghuddah, Abd al-Sattar. (2007). Al-tatbiqat al-amaliyyah li al-ijarah al-mawsufah fi al- dhimmah. Paper presented *at the 28th al-Barakah Symposium on Islamic Economics*. Jeddah.

Abu Sulayman, Abd al-Wahab I. (1992). *Aqd al-Ijarah, Masdar min Masadir al-Tamwil al-Islamiyyah: Dirasah Fiqhiyyah Muqaranah*. Al-Bank al-Islami li al-Tanmiyyah.

Abu Yahya, M. (2003). *Al-Ijma Inda A'immah ahl Sunnah al-Arba'ah*. Maktabah al-Ubaikan.

M. Hassan et al., *Hire Purchase Under Shirkah al-Milk (HPSM) in Islamic Banking and Finance*,
https://doi.org/10.1007/978-3-031-50105-0

Ahmad, A. U. F. (2010). *Theory and Practice of Modern Islamic Finance: The Case Study from Australia*. Brown Walker Press.

Ahmad, A. U. F., Monawer, A. T. M., & Ayinde, L. (2020, June). *Takyif fiqhi* on the Permissibility of *ijarah mawsufah fi al-dhimmah*: A Critical Analysis. *International Journal of Islamic Thought, 17*.

Al-Amine, M. B. M. (2001). The Islamic Bond Market: Possibilities and Challenges. *International Journal of Islamic Financial Services, 3*(1).

Alawi, L. (1986). Leasing an Islamic Financial Instrument. In M. El. Helwi (Ed.), *Islamic Banking and Finance* (pp. 120–127). Butterworths.

Albani, M. Nasir al-Din. (1985). *Irwa al-Jalil fi Takhrij Ahadith Manar al-Sabil* (2nd ed., Vol. 5). Al-Maktabah al-Islami.

Al-Dasuqi, Mohammad Ibn Ahmad Ibn Arafa. (1996). *Hashiyyah al-Dasuqi ala al-Sharh al-Kabir* (Vol. 4). Dar al-Kutub al-'Ilmiyyah.

Al-Dusri, Ahmad Abd al-Latif. (2001). Al-bu'd al-tanmayi li al-ijarah. Paper presented at *Mu'tamar al-Mu'assasat al-Maliyyah al-Islamiyyah*, 5–6 May, Sheraton Hotel. Kuwait.

Al-Farisi, Ala al-Din. (1993). *Sahih Ibn Hibban bi Tartib Ibn Bilban* (2nd ed., Vol. 11). Mu'assasah al-Risslah.

Al-Funaysan, S. (2000). Al-'ijar al-muntahi bi al-tamlik. *Majallah al-Buhuth al-Fiqhiyyah al-Mu'asirah, 48*.

Ali, M. I., & Falahi, I. R. (2016). *Islamic Banking: Principles and Practices*. Marifa Academy.

Alish, M. A. (1958). *Fath al-Ali al-Malik fi al-Fatawa ala Madhhab Malik* (Vol. 1). Maktabah wa Matba'a Mustafa al-Babi al-Halbi wa Awladuhu.

Al-Kasani, A. B. Ibn Muhamad. (1998). *Bada'i' al Sana'i fi Tartib al-Shara'i'* (Vol. 4). Dar Ihya al-Turath al-Arabi.

Al-Kasani, A. B. Ibn Muhammad. (2005). *Bada'i al-Sana'i' fi al-Tartib al-Shara'i'* (Vol. 5). Dar al-Hadith.

Al-Kawamelah, N. A. K. (2008). *Musharakah Mutanaqisah and Its Contemporary Practice: Jordan Islamic Bank as an Example*. Dar al-Nafa'is.

Al-Musili, A. (n.d). *Al-'Ikhtiyar* (Vol. 2). Dar al-Arqam.

Al-Nasa'i, A. Ibn Shuayib. (1991). *Sunan al- Nasa'i al-Kubra* (Vol. 3). Dar al-Kutub al-'Ilmiyyah.

Al-Qaradaghi, A. M. (2000). Al ijarah al-muntahyyah bi al-tamlik. *Majalat al-Majma' al-Fiqh al-Islami, 1*(1).

Al-Qaradaghi, A. M. (2009). *Buhuth fi Fiqh al-Muamalat al-Maliyyah al-Mu'asarah* (1st ed.). Dar al-Basha'ir al- Islsmiyyah.

Al-Rajihi Bank. (n.d.). *The Resolution of the Shariah Board of Al-Rajihi Banking and Investment Corporation*. Al-Rajihi Bank.

Al-Sanhuri, A. Abd al-Rajjaq. (n.d.). *Al-Wasit fi al-Sharh al–Maudu'i* (Vol. 4). Dar al-Nahdah al-Arabiyyah.

Al-Sarakhsi, M. Ibn Ahmad. (2013). *Al-Mabsut* (Vol. 5). Dar al-Nawadir.

Al-Shadhili, H. A. (2014). Leasing Ending with Ownership. In *Leasing Ending with Ownership and Leasing Bond (al-Ijarah al-Muntahiyah bi al-Tamlik) Its Ruling and Contemporary Application* (pp. 21–81). Islamic Banking and Financial Institute Malaysia (IBFIM).

Al-Shawkani, M. Ibn Ali. (1984). *Nayl al-Awtar Sharh Muntaqa al-Akhbar* (Vol. 3). Maktabah al-Kulliyyat al-Azhariyyah.

Al-Sharbini, M. Ibn Muhammad al-Khatib. (1994). *Mughni al-Muhtaj* (Vol. 2). Matba'at al-Babi al-Halabi.

Al-Shiribini, M. Ibn Muhammad al-Khatib. (2000). *Mughni al-Muhtaj ila Ma'rifat Maani Alfaz al-Minhaj* (Vol. 3). Dar al-kutub al-'llmiyyah.

Al-Sundi, Nur al-Din. Abdul Hadi. (1998). *Sahih Al-Bukhari bi Hashiah al-Imam al- Sundi* (Vol. 2). Dar al-Kutub al-Ilmiyyah.

Al-Taskhiri, M. A. (2014). Leasing Ending with Ownership and Concept of Promise. In *Leasing Ending with Ownership and Leasing Bond (al-Ijarah al-Muntahiyah bi al-Tamlik) Its Ruling and Contemporary Application* (pp. 103–115). Islamic Banking and Financial Institute Malaysia (IBFIM).

Al-Zuhayli, W. (2002). *Al-Mumalat al-Maliyyah al-Muasarah: Buhuth wa Fatawa wa Hulul*. Dar al-Fikr.

Al-Zuhayli, W. (2003). *Financial Transactions in Islamic Jurisprudence* (M. A. El-Gamal, Trans.). Dar al-Fikr al-Mu'asir. Beirut.

Aqil, Jamal al-Din T. (1978). *Aqd al-Hibah bayna al-Fiqh al-Islami wa al-Qanun al-Muduni*. Dar al-Huda.

Arshad, N. C., & Ismail, A. G. (2010). Shariah Parameters for Musharakah Contract: A Comment. *International Journal of Business and Social Science, 1*(1), 145–162.

Asqalani, Ibn Hajr. (1999). *Fath al-Bar* (1st ed., Vol. 5). Dar al-Manar li al-Tab wa al-Nashr wa al-Tawji'.

Blossom. (2020). *Classifications of Sale Contract*. https://blossomfinance.com/posts/classifications-of-sale-contracts. Accessed 25 June 2023.

BNM. (2007). *Distinct Features of Islamic Financial Transactions: Perspective on Musharakah Mutanaqisah (Diminishing Partnership)*. Bank Negara Malaysia.

BNM. (2010). *Shariah Resolutions in Islamic Finance, Part 1* (2nd ed.). Bank Negara Malaysia.

BNM. (2013). *Bai''Inah (Shariah Requirements and Optional Practices) Exposure Draft BNM/RH/CP 028-2*. Bank Negara Malaysia.

Daruqutni, Abu al-Hasan D. (1966). *Sunan Aa-Daruqutni* (Vol. 3). Dar Al-Ma'rifah.

Daruqutni, Abu al-Hasan D. (2004). *Sunan al-Daruqutni* (Vol. 3). Mu'assasah al-Risslah.

De Lorenzo, Y. T. (2000). *A Compendium of Legal Opinions on the Operation of Islamic Banks: Ijarah, Sarf, and Riba*. Institute of Islamic Banking and Insurance.

Dieng, M. M. (2019). The Applicability of ijarah al-mawsufah fi al-dhimmah in Malaysia. *International Journal of Management and Applied Research, 6*(4), 196–207.

Doyan, Ibrahim Ibn M. Ibn Salim. (1989). *Manar al-Sabil* (7th ed., Vol. 1). al-Maktab al-Islami.

Dusuki, A. W. (2008). Banking for the Poor: The Role of Islamic Banking in Microfinance Initiatives. *International Journal of Systems and Ethics, 24*, 49–66.

Dusuqi, I. Abu al-Layil. (1994). *Al-Bay' bi al-Taqsit wa al-Buyu' al-Itimaniyah 'Ukhra*. Kuwait University Press.

El-din, S. I. T., & Abdullah, N. I. (2007). Issues of Implementing Islamic Hire Purchase in Dual Banking Systems: Malaysia's Experience. *Thunderbird International Business Review, 49*(2), 225–249.

El-Gamal, M. A. (2006). *Islamic Finance: Law, Economics, and Practice.* Cambridge University Press.

Fatma, A. (n.d). *Meaning of ijarah.* https://www.academia.edu/3583126/meaning_of_ijarah. Accessed 29 December 2022.

Fincyclopedia. (2021). *Forward ijarah.* https://fincyclopedia.net/islamic-finance/f/forward-ijarah. Accessed 6 July 2023.

Ganti, A. (2022). *What Is a sukuk? Sharia-Compliant Bond-Like Financial Instruments.* https://www.investopedia.com/terms/s/sukuk.asp. Accessed 6 July 2023.

Hakim, M. Ibn Abdullah. (1987). *Al-Mustadrak ala al-Sahihayn fi al-Hadith* (Vol. 2). Dar al-Fikr.

Hama, A. O. (2007). *Islamic Hire-Purchase Transaction.* International Islamic University Malaysia.

Hammad, N. (2005). *Al-Uqud al-Murakkabah fi al-Fiqh al-Islami* (1st ed.). Damascus.

Hasan A. A. H. (2007). *Sales and Contracts in Early Islamic Commercial Law.* Islamic Research Institute.

IBBL. (2022). *IBBL at a Glance.* http://www.islamibankbd.com/abtIBBL/abtIBBLAtaGlance.php. Accessed 19 December 2022.

IBBL (n.d.a). *Hire Purchase Under Shirkatul Meelk.* https://www.islamibankbd.com/prodServices/prodServHPUSM.php. Accessed 22 December 2022.

IBBL. (n.d.b). Islami Bank Bangladesh Limited: Manual of Investment Under Hire Purchase Under shirkah al-milk. In *Procedure for Investment Under Hire Purchase Under Shirkah al-Milk (Ijarah Muntahiyyah bi al-Tamlik) Mode of Investment*, Part 1. Islami Bank Bangladesh Limited, Dhaka.

IBBL. (n.d.c). Islami Bank Bangladesh Limited: Manual of Investment Under Hire Purchase Under shirkah al-m milk. In *Procedure for Investment Under Hire Purchase Under Shirkah Al-Milk Mode of Investment*, Part 2. Islami Bank Bangladesh Limited, Dhaka.

Ibn-Bayyah, A. al-Mahfuz. (2014). Leasing Ending with Ownership. In *Leasing Ending with Ownership and Leasing Bond (al-Ijarah al-Muntahiyah bi al-Tamlik) Its Ruling and Contemporary Application* (pp. 83–102). Islamic Banking and Financial Institute Malaysia (IBFIM).

Ibn Juzi, M. (n.d.). *Al-Qawanin al-Fiqhiyyah.* Dar al-Qalam.

Ibn Majah, I. (1957). *Sunan Ibn MAjah* (Vol. 2). Mustafa al-Babi al-Halabi.

Ibn Majah. (2007). *Sunan Ibn Majah* (Vol. 2). Dar al-salam. Riyad.

Ibn Majah (n.d.). *Sunan Ibu Majah* (Vol. 2). Dar al-Fikr.

Ibn Mandhur. (n.d.). *Lisan al-Arab* (Vol. 7). Dar al-'Ihya al-Turath al-Arabi.

Ibn Qudamah, Muwaffaq al-Din. (1994). *Al-Mughi* (Vol. 4). Dar al-Fikr.

Ibn Taymiyyah, Ahmad Ibn Abd al-Halim. (2011). *Al-Qawa'id al-Nuraniyyah al-Fiqhiyyah* (Vol. 2). Maktab al-Rashid.

Ibrahim, A. (2014). Leasing Ending with Ownership. In *Leasing Ending with Ownership and Leasing Bond (al-Ijarah al-Muntahiyah bi al-Tamlik) Its Ruling and Contemporary Application.* Islamic Banking and Financial Institute Malaysia (IBFIM) (pp. 117–124). Kuala Lumpur.

Ibrahim, M. A. (1987). *Hukm Bay' bi al-Taqsit fi al-Shariah wa al-Qanun.* Maktabah al-Risalah al-HadItha.

IIFA. (2021). *Resolutions and Recommendations of the International Islamic Fiqh Academy of Organization of Islamic Cooperation.* International Islamic Fiqh Academy.

Islamic Bankers Resource Centre. (n.d.). *Discussions on Islamic Banking.* https://islamicbankers.me/islamic-banking-islamic-contracts/credit-cards-ujrah/. Accessed 4 June 2023.

Kamali, M. H. (2007). A *Shariah* Analysis of Issues in Islamic Leasing. *J.KAU: Islamic Economics, 20*(1), 3–22.

Kenton, W. (2020). *What Is Musharakah? Meaning and How It Works in Finance.* https://www.investopedia.com/terms/m/musharakah.asp. Accessed 22 December 2022.

Kenton, W. (2022). *Hire Purchase Agreements: Definition, How They Work, pros and cons.* https://www.investopedia.com/terms/h/hire-purchase.asp. Accessed 29 January 2022.

Khafif. A. (n.d). *Ahkam al-Mu'amalat al-Shar'iyyah.* Bank al-Barakah.

Khan, M. A. (2013). *What Is Wrong with Islamic Economics? Analysing the Present State and Future Agenda.* Edward Elgar Publishing.

Khan, M. (1984). *The Translation of the Meaning of Sahih al-Bukhari* (Vol. 3). Kitab Bhavan.

Kharofah, Ala al-Din (1997). *Transactions in Islamic Law.* A.S Noordeen.

Kuwait Finance House. (2016). *Al-ta'jir ma'a al-mawa'idah bi al-tamalluk.* http://www.kfh.com/commercial/cars/Lease/index.asp. Accessed 27 June 2016.

Lahore, A. (2009). *The Concept of Musharakah.* https://www.scribd.com/doc/17223453/The-Concept-of-Musharakah. Accessed 29 December 2022.

Latman & Watkins LLP. (n.d). *The Sukuk Handbook: A Guide to Structuring Sukuk.* Latman & Watkins LLP.

Lewis, M. K., & Algaoud, L. M. (2001). *Islamic Banking.* Edward Elgar.

Mohamed, B. F., Abdi, S. M., Siad, S. A., & Adawe, F. N. (n.d.). *Tawarruq.* https://slideplayer.com/slide/17072900/. Accessed 12 July 2023.

Monawer, M. A. T., & Aziz, A. A. (2015). Dispute over the Legality of al-ijarah al-mawsufah fi al-dhimmah: A Survey of fiqhi Opinions. *ISRA International Journal of Islamic Finance, 7*(1), 49–74.

Moustafa, S. Q. (2001). *The Sale of Debt as Implemented by Islamic Financial Institutions in Malaysia.* International Islamic University Malaysia.

Muhammad, M. Z., & Chong, R. (2007). The Contract of bay'Al-Salam and Istisna'in Islamic Commercial Law: A Comparative Analysis. *Labuan e-Journal of Muamalat and Society (LJMS), 1*, 21–28.

Mubarakpuri, Abu Ala M. (2001). *Tuhfah al-Ahwazi Sharh Jami' al-Tirmizi* (Vol. 4). Dar al-Kutub al-'Ilmiyyah.

Mundhir, I., & Abu, B. M. (2003). *Al-Ijma'* (2nd ed.). Dar al-Alam al-Kutub.

Mydin Meera, A. K., & Abdul Razak, D. (2009). Home Financing Through the musharakah mutanaqisah Contracts: Some Practical Issues. *Journal of King Abdulaziz University: Islamic Economics, 22*(1).

Niazi, L. A. K. (1991). *Islamic Law of Contract.* Doyal Sing Trust Library.

Nizam, Al-Sheikh. (2000). *Al-Fatawa al-Hindiyyah* (Vol. 4). Dar al-Kutub al-'llmiyyah.

Osmani, N. M., & Abdullah, M. F. (2010). Musharakah mutanaqisah Home Financing: A Review of Literatures and Practices of Islamic Banks in Malaysia. *International Review of Business Research Papers, 6*(2), 272–282.

Qurtubi, M. Ibn Ahmad Ibn Rushd. (2001). *Bidayat al-Mujtahid wa Nihayat al-Muqtasid.* Dar al-Kutub al-'Ilmiyyah.

Rashid, S. N. M., Abd Rahman, M., Hadi, A., Yahya, N. C., & Md Rasid, N. F. (2020). Bai bithaman ajil (BBA) and musharakah mutanaqisah (MM): Comparative Analysis. *Advances in Business Research International Journal, 6*(2), 19–29.

Rohmatunnisa, D. (2008). *Design of Ijarah Sukuk.* University of Nottingham.

Ramli, R., & Onn, H. (2007). *Islamic Hire-Purchase (Ijarah Thumma al-Bay'-AITAB): The Handbook* (1st ed.). Islamic Banking and Finance Institute Malaysia (IBFIM).

Saad, N. M., & Razak, D. A. (2013). Towards an Application of Musharakah Mutanaqisah Principle in Islamic Microfinance. *International Journal of Business and Society, 14*(2), 221–234.

Saeed, A. (1996). *Islamic Banking and Interest: A Book of the Prohibition of Riba and Its Contemporary Interpretation.* In R. Peters, B. Weiss & B. J. Brill (Eds.). Studies in Islamic Law and Society.
Saleem, M. Y. (2003). *Islamic Commercial Law.* Wiley.
Samarqandi, M. (1984). *Tohfah al-Fuqaha* (2nd ed., Vol. 1). Dar al-Kutub al-'Ilmiyyah.
San'ani, Abd al-Razzaq Abu Bakar. (1983). *Musannaf Abd al-Razzqa* (Vol. 8). al-Maktabah al-Islami.
Sarakhsi, M. Ibn Ahmad. (2000). *Al-Mabsut* (Vol. 8). Dar al-Fikr.
Sarakhsi, M. Ibn Ahmad. (2013). *Al-Mabsut* (1st ed., Vol. 15). Dar al-Nawadir.
Shafi'i, M. Ibn Idris. (2000). *Kitab al-'Umm* (1st ed., Vol. 2). Dar Ihya al-Turath al-Arabi.
Slide Share. (2011). *Al-Ijarah.* http://www.slideshare.net/emkay84/isb540-ijarah. Accessed 22 December 2022.
Smolo, E. (2007). *A Theoretical Comparison Between al-Bay' Bithaman Ajil, Musharakah Mutanaqisah Partnership and Ijarah Sukuk* (Master's Dissertation). International Islamic University Malaysia, Kuala Lumpur.
Surah, M. Ibn 'Isha (1999). *Sunan al-Turmidhi* (Vol. 3). Dar al-Hadith.
Tamer, S. (2005). *The Islamic Financial System.* Peter Lang.
Usmani, M. T. (1998). *An Introduction to Islamic Finance.* https://tinyurl.com/9zfmsbcv. Accessed 28 December 2022.
Usmani, M. T. (2001). *An Introduction to Islamic Finance.* Brill.
Usmani, M. T. (2008). *An Introduction to Islamic Finance.* Idarah Isha'at-E-Diniyyat (P) Ltd.
Utsmani, S. M. (1998). *Al-Mu'amalat al-Maliyyah al-Mu'asarah fi al-Fiqh al-Islami* (2nd ed.). Dar al-Nafa'is.
Visser, H. (2009). *Islamic Finance: Principles and Practice.* Edward Elgar.
Zakariyyah, H. (2004). *Aqd al-Ijarah al-Muntahiyah bi al-Tamlik: Dirasah Muqaranah fa al-Fiq al-Islami wa al-Qanun al-Maiizi.* International Islamic University Malaysia.

Further Reading

Abd al-Rahman, Abd al-Qadir. (1993). *Al-Wasit fi Aqd al- Ijarah fi al- Fiqh Al-Islami.* Dar al-Nahdah al-Arabiyyah.
Abd al-Aziz Hasan, Z. M. (1996). Al-Ijarah bayna al-Fiqh al-Islama wa al-Tatbiq al-Muasarah fi al- *al- Muassasat al-Masrafiyyah wa al-Maliyyah al-Islamiyyah.* al-Ma'had al-AlamI lil-Fikr al-Islami.
Al-Abidin, Z. (2010). *Tatbiq al-Buyu' al-Mashru'ah fi al-Bunuk al-Islamiyyah fi Bangaladesh: Dirasah Fiqhiyyah Muqaranah.* Cairo University.

Al-Jassas, A. Ibn Muhammad. (1417H). *Mukhtasar Ikhtilaf al-Ulama,* Ubayd Ullah (Vol. 3, Nadhir Edn., 2nd ed.). Dar al Basha'ir al-Islamiyyah.

Arif al-Hajj, M. M. Y. (2003). *Aqd al-Ijarah al-Muntahiyah bi al-Tamlik min Tatbiqat al-Muasairah li aqd al-Ijarah fi al-Fiqh al-Islami.* The Naza National University.

Hamid, N. (2008). *Hire Purchase.* Gavel Publications.

Shathri, Abd al-Aziz. Saad bin Nasir. (2004). *Aqd al-Ijarah al-Muntahiyah bi al-Tamlik.* Dar Kunuz Ishbiliyyah lil-Nashr wa al-Tawzi.

Index

M. Hassan et al., *Hire Purchase Under Shirkah al-Milk (HPSM) in Islamic Banking and Finance*,
https://doi.org/10.1007/978-3-031-50105-0

GPSR Compliance

The European Union's (EU) General Product Safety Regulation (GPSR) is a set of rules that requires consumer products to be safe and our obligations to ensure this.

If you have any concerns about our products, you can contact us on ProductSafety@springernature.com

In case Publisher is established outside the EU, the EU authorized representative is:

Springer Nature Customer Service Center GmbH
Europaplatz 3
69115 Heidelberg, Germany

FSC
www.fsc.org
MIX
Papier | Fördert
gute Waldnutzung
FSC® C083411

Kolibri 360 GmbH
Ferdinand-Jühlke-Straße 7
99095 Erfurt, Deutschland
produktsicherheit@kolibri360.de